AF251833

JOSEPH CONRAD

JOSEPH CONRAD

Interviews and Recollections

Edited by

Martin Ray

University of Iowa Press Iowa City

UNIVERSITY OF IOWA PRESS
Iowa City 52242

International Standard Book Number 0–87745–290–3
Library of Congress Catalog Card Number 89–52160
First edition, 1990

Printed in Great Britain

Contents

PART VIII PEN PORTRAITS

PART IX CONRAD'S DEATH

Preface

The wide and diverse appeal of Joseph Conrad's personality is demonstrated in this volume of interviews and recollections by the sheer variety of people who were moved to record in print their meetings with him. Conrad here is seen through the eyes of his very English wife and sons and also in the words of some Polish compatriots.[1] He is remembered by shipmates and fellow writers, by closest friends and fleeting acquaintances, by Lawrence of Arabia and by a regular at his local pub.

Conrad always hated the popular image of himself as, in his own words, 'a sort of freak, an amazing bloody foreigner writing in English'. Certainly, as some of these recollections show, the first and lasting impression that he made on casual acquaintances is very much that of the exotic émigré, stumbling over the simplest words and pronouncing 'vowel' as 'wowvel'. Beneath the bizarre superficial oddities, however, lay an extraordinarily complex character, and it is one which Conrad seems to have been willing to display only to the very closest friends, most of whom were fellow writers and artists.

Perhaps the greatest testimony to the force of Conrad's personality is to note just how quickly the unemployed seaman of 1895 became the intimate friend of nearly all the leading writers of his day, such as H. G. Wells, Henry James, Cunninghame Graham, Arnold Bennett, Ford Madox Ford and John Galsworthy (whom he had met as a passenger on his ship). Much later, as his commercial success finally came, he grew to be a figure of some social curiosity, yet he always remained the ever elusive prey of the blue-stocking hostess, preferring the anonymity and seclusion of his Kentish home.

These sixty recollections present some of the many facets of this most enigmatic and brilliant writer: Conrad the adventurer and the recluse, the Polish gallant and the neurotic modernist, the Edwardian country gentleman and the penniless beggar.

NOTE

1. Many of the Polish documents concerning Conrad's early life are collected in Zdzisław Najder's *Conrad Under Familial Eyes* (Cambridge: Cambridge University Press, 1983).

Acknowledgements

Special gratitude is owed to Frances Arnold and Sarah Roberts-West of Macmillan for their invaluable editorial assistance.

The editor and publishers wish to thank the following who have kindly given permission for the use of copyright material:

John Calder (Publishers) Ltd, for the extract from *My Father: Joseph Conrad* by Borys Conrad.

Cambridge University Press, for the extract from *Joseph Conrad: Times Remembered* by John Conrad.

Daily Telegraph, for the letter from Fred Arnold.

J. M. Dent & Sons Ltd, for the extract from *Everyman Remembers* by Ernest Rhys.

Faber & Faber, for the extracts from *Ottoline: The Early Memoirs of Lady Ottoline Morrell*, edited by Robert Gathorne-Hardy; from *Joseph Conrad's Mind and Method: A Study of Personality in Art* by R. L. Mégroz; and from *Experiment in Autobiography: Discoveries and Conclusions of a Very Ordinary Brain (since 1866)*, by H. G. Wells.

Sir Rupert Hart-Davis, for the extracts from Hugh Walpole's diary, published in *Hugh Walpole: A Biography* by Rupert Hart-Davis.

David Higham Associates Ltd, for the extract from *Return to Yesterday* by Ford Madox Ford.

Little, Brown & Co., for the extract from *Experiment in Autobiography: Discoveries and Conclusions of a Very Ordinary Brain (since 1866)* by Herbert George Wells; copyright 1934 by Herbert George Wells; copyright © renewed by George Philip Wells and Francis Richard Wells.

Macdonald & Co (Publishers) Ltd, for the extract from *The Last Twelve Years of Joseph Conrad* by Richard Curle.

Oxford University Press, for the extract from *Review of English Studies*.

Sir John Rothenstein and Michael Rothenstein, for the extract from *Men and Memories: Recollections of William Rothenstein 1900–1922*.

Whilst every effort has been made to locate owners of copyright, in some cases this has been unsuccessful. The publishers apologise for any infringement of copyright or failure to acknowledge original sources and shall be glad to include any necessary corrections in subsequent printings.

A Note on the Text

In the extracts given, spelling errors in the original have been silently corrected, and English forms have replaced American spellings. Titles of books are printed consistently in italics, and those of short stories and essays within quotation marks.

Quotations from Conrad's works have been altered, where necessary, to conform with the text of the *Collected Edition of the Works of Joseph Conrad*, 21 vols (London: J. M. Dent, 1946–55).

Conrad's Life: A Chronology

1857 (3 Dec) Józef Teodor Konrad Nałęcz Korzeniowski born in the Ukraine, only child of Apollo and Ewa Korzeniowski.
1861 His father arrested for political conspiracy.
1862 His parents exiled to Russia. Conrad accompanies them.
1865 Conrad's mother dies of tuberculosis.
1869 Conrad's father dies in Kraków, following his return to Poland the previous year. His uncle, Tadeusz Bobrowski, becomes his guardian.
1874 Leaves for Marseilles, and later joins the French merchant navy.
1877 May have been involved in gun-running for the Spanish royalists.
1878 (Mar) Attempts suicide in Marseilles by shooting himself in chest, without serious injury. Uncle pays all his debts.
(Apr) Joins his first British ship, the *Mavis*, and hears his first words of English.
1879 Arrives in Sydney in the *Duke of Sutherland*.
1880 Qualifies as second mate in London.
1882 Arrives in Bangkok in the *Palestine*.
1884 Qualifies as first mate.
1886 Becomes a British citizen and obtains his master's certificate.
1887–8 Four trips to Borneo in the *Vidar*.
1888 His first and only command, in the *Otago*. Sails from Bangkok to Singapore, Sydney, Melbourne, Mauritius and Adelaide.
1889 Begins his first novel, *Almayer's Folly*, in London.
1890 Works in the Belgian Congo in the *Roi des Belges*.
1891–3 Two round trips from London to Australia as mate in the *Torrens*.
1893 Meets his future wife, Jessie George.
1894 His uncle and guardian dies. *Almayer's Folly* is completed and accepted by Fisher Unwin.
1895 *Almayer's Folly* published.
1896 Publication of *An Outcast of the Islands*. Meets H. G. Wells. Marries Jessie George.
1897 Meets Henry James, Stephen Crane and Cunninghame Graham. *The Nigger of the 'Narcissus'* published.

1898 Borys Conrad born. Conrads move into Pent Farm, near Aldington, Kent. Begins collaborating with Ford Madox Ford. *Tales of Unrest* published.
1899 J. B. Pinker becomes Conrad's literary agent; 'Heart of Darkness' serialised.
1900 *Lord Jim* published.
1901 *The Inheritors* (in collaboration with Ford) published.
1902 Publication of *Youth: A Narrative; and Two Other Stories.*
1903 Publication of *Typhoon and Other Stories* and *Romance* (with Ford).
1904 *Nostromo* published.
1905 Holiday in Capri.
1906 John Conrad born. *The Mirror of the Sea* published.
1907 The Conrads move to the Someries, Luton Hoo, Bedfordshire. Publication of *The Secret Agent.*
1908 *A Set of Six* published.
1909 The Conrads move to Aldington, Kent.
1910 Completion of *Under Western Eyes* followed by nervous breakdown. The Conrads move to Capel House, near Ashford, Kent.
1911 *Under Western Eyes* published.
1914 *Chance* published. The Conrads visit Poland.
1915 Publication of *Within the Tides* and *Victory.*
1917 *The Shadow-Line* published.
1919 The Conrads move to Oswalds in Bishopsbourne, near Canterbury. *The Arrow of Gold* published.
1920 Publication of *The Rescue.*
1921 Visit to Corsica. *Notes on Life and Letters* published.
1923 First visit to United States. *The Rover* published.
1924 Declines knighthood. (3 Aug) Dies of a heart attack at home. Buried in Canterbury.
1925 *Tales of Hearsay* and *Suspense* published.
1926 *Last Essays* published.
1928 *The Sisters* (unfinished novel) published.

Part I
Conrad's Family

Joseph Conrad as I Knew Him*

JESSIE CONRAD

My husband's books were to me as so many children, so to speak, and each in turn should have its place in these recollections. There is attached to one and all some tender remembrance and unforgotten episode. It was Conrad's unfailing custom to make me a present when each book was finished, and those presents varied in money value according to the state of our finances. Sometimes a promise was all that was possible – a promise to be redeemed later by some stroke of fortune or lucky find in some unexpected place.

Almayer's Folly was written before I knew him – written in many strange places, under changing conditions.[1] It survived only by the merest chance its many adventures, and got itself finished, or at least nearly finished, in the home of an early friend, Mr E. L. Sanderson – on his father's sermon paper.[2] Some chapters were written in shabby, sordid lodgings on the bank of the river Thames, in the little village of Greenhithe.[3] Conrad once showed the house to me when we were paying a visit to Borys, then a *Worcester* cadet.[4] Although that little place so close to the river was sordid in the extreme, there was a charm, even to me, in the view of the swiftly running water, in the group of dirty urchins clustered round the boats – poorly clad little mortals, who were as much at home in a boat as any old salt, and who could handle an oar as well.

This first book is the only one that bears on its fly-leaf my full maiden name, and I can recall my pride when it was presented to me quite early in our acquaintance.[5] A mutual friend introduced us early in November 1894.[6] I think my first feeling was one of surprise and awe. To me, ours was certainly a strange friendship. Not only because Conrad was the first foreigner I had ever known intimately, but he was also the first grown man I had met who appeared to take a particular interest in me.

Several months elapsed between our fourth and fifth meeting – months in which I heard little of the strange and courteous gentleman, the author of my inscribed copy of *Almayer's Folly*. In fact, the book

* From *Joseph Conrad as I Knew Him* (London: Heinemann, 1926) pp. 100–6.

was the one concrete fact left me to prove that our acquaintance had been no dream.

Our next meeting was not long before the next book, *The Outcast of the Islands* [*sic*], was finished;[7] but our friendship had by this time become much more intimate. We had reached the stage when he became a frequent visitor to my home. Even in those days I seemed to have influence over him – an interest for him perhaps I should rather have said – and my curiosity about this second venture appeared to please him . . . when I grew bold enough to show it. It was not long after this that he appeared one evening with a bulky package of manuscript from which he suggested I should read him some pages right away. That night was my first experience of his characteristic impatience; and after all these years, I can still feel as I felt that night, trembling with pleased interest, and with my mouth as dry as a cinder. He sat a few feet from me, his compelling eyes fastened on my face. I was even then conscious of something restless in him, of a sort of inward fire that robbed me of nearly all my powers of speech. I read on, stumbling over the corrections that interlined the closely typed pages. Sometimes he interrupted me, urging me to disregard this or that pencilled sentence: 'That is not going to stand – never mind it – start three lines lower – over leaf, over leaf.' After a time he gave a short, impatient laugh and said irritably, drawing the pages none too gently from my hands: 'Speak distinctly; if you're tired, say so; don't eat your words. You English are all alike, you make the same sound for every letter.'

These words and his gesture of exasperation almost reduced me to tears. He sat with his face buried in his hands for some few moments, and with a mighty effort I recovered myself somewhat. After that I frequently read his manuscript aloud to him, taking great pains to speak the words as he seemed to wish, and passing as sensible comments as I was capable of making. It must be remembered that I was strange to literature, and too anxious perhaps to appear at my ease. Then came the day when the book was finished and I received my first present to mark the event. A little ruby and pearl bracelet – a great treasure – now, alas! too small for me to wear.

This book was to have appeared in November 1895, but the stereo plates were burnt in a big printer's fire, and the publication was delayed till the year we were married. In fact, the book was born only a day or so before our wedding on 24 March 1896.[8]

It was in the early December 1895 that by medical advice he went to stay for a month in La Roseraie, Champel, to take a cure.[9] During these weeks of absence, his letters were frequent, and I saw that our friendship would soon undergo a change. When he returned, we picked up the threads of our life with perhaps a little restraint. Then came that never-to-be-forgotten day when we became engaged. Surely such a compact has been seldom entered upon in quite the same manner. We had spent a long morning in the National Picture Gallery; we had engaged ourselves, and afterwards we had had some lunch in a strange restaurant. Was it one of these events, or was it the combination of all three that produced such disastrous results? The question remained a matter of argument between us afterwards. Instead of following our plan of taking a long drive into the country, we each returned to our separate homes in haste.[10] Awful sensations had come over us both at the same moment. I caught sight of my own face passing a shop window, and a horrified glance at Conrad discovered on his the same expression of acute suffering. It needed little urging to persuade me to let him drive me home. We parted hurriedly at my door, and he hastily re-entered the hansom, which drove rapidly away, urged to even greater speed by a hand waved frantically through the trap in the roof.

I said no word at home. After a third day had passed without a word from him, I felt very humiliated. I was tortured by the thought that perhaps he had already repented of his offer. It was surely a strange proposal of marriage. He had begun by announcing that he had not very long to live and no intention of having children; but such as his life was (his shrug was very characteristic), he thought we might spend a few happy years together. At the end of the third day an invitation came for my mother and for me to lunch with him near Victoria Station. The interview he had with her must have been conducted on much the same lines, judging by her artless remark to me a little later, 'that she didn't quite see why he wished to get married'. But a climax was reached a day or so later when he demanded that we should be married in less than six weeks and go abroad.

Those weeks passed very quickly. My time was fully occupied with my preparations, and I was not a little sad, for I was to be the first of my family to leave home. My mother made no secret of her distress and dismay at the prospect of my leaving her. A few days before our wedding-day, he came and solemnly insisted that all my precious letters, those few letters he had written when he was staying in Geneva, should be burnt, and what was more, he himself superintended the sacrifice. Not one escaped.

NOTES

Jessie Emmeline Conrad, née George (1873–1936) was fifteen years younger than her husband Joseph Conrad. One of nine children, her father was a warehouseman and shopkeeper who died three years before her marriage in 1896. She was working as a typist when Conrad met her, and, although not well-educated or intelligent, she was to prove an undoubted source of domestic comfort and stability to Conrad throughout the many years of his often tortured writing life. In a letter to a friend, written just two weeks before the wedding, Conrad described her as 'a small, not at all striking-looking person (to tell the truth alas – rather plain!)'.

1. Conrad's first novel, *Almayer's Folly*, was begun in September 1889 in his lodgings in London, and was completed on 24 April 1894. Conrad took the manuscript with him during the last few years of his career at sea.

2. Edward Lancelot Sanderson met Conrad in March 1893 on board the *Torrens*, of which Conrad was chief officer. John Galsworthy, Sanderson's friend and fellow Harrovian, was also present on this occasion and he describes the event on pp. 62–3.

Sanderson helped his father run a preparatory school for boys at Elstree in Herts. In mid-April 1894, Conrad went to Elstree for ten days and began there the twelfth and final chapter of *Almayer's Folly*. His second novel, *An Outcast of the Islands*, was dedicated to Sanderson.

3. Greenhithe is three miles west of Gravesend, on the Thames. Conrad possibly lived there in about 1890.

4. For a note on Borys Conrad, their first child, see p. 13. Borys served in the *Worcester*, a Royal Navy training ship moored at Greenhithe, from 1911 to 1913.

5. The inscription is dated 2 April 1895. This was an advance copy of the novel, prior to its publication on 29 April. Although the inscription indicates a close relationship between the two, Conrad also gave a copy of *Almayer's Folly* to Emilie Briquel the next month (see note 9 below).

6. The mutual acquaintance was possibly G. F. W. Hope, who had known Conrad since 1880, when they had met in London. He was a sailor and director of a South African mining company. The Hopes claimed to have known Jessie since she was a child.

7. *An Outcast of the Islands* was begun in August 1894, completed on 16 September 1895 and published on 4 March 1896.

8. The stereo plates of the American edition were destroyed by fire in New York.

9. La Roseraie was a large pension in Champel-les-Bains, on the outskirts of Geneva. Conrad had first visited there in 1891 for hydrotherapy.

Contrary to Jessie's dating here, Conrad in fact set off for Geneva, his third visit, only two days after the publication of *Almayer's Folly* and arrived on 2 May 1895, returning to London on 3 June. While there, he courted Emilie Briquel, a twenty-year-old French girl.

10. Conrad was then living at 17 Gillingham Street, behind Victoria Station. These two rented, furnished rooms had been his London base since 1891.

Conrad's Wedding*

JESSIE CONRAD

The great day dawned without a cloud in the sky.[1]

Here, again, Joseph Conrad took refuge in the most matter-of-fact attitude. To begin with, he kept me waiting to be married just half an hour, and even when his two friends, Mr Hope and Mr Krieger,[2] did persuade him to make a move, he delayed still further in some futile argument with the cab-driver. I was feeling physically sick at this delay and rejoiced when the ceremony was over and we were on our way to a little café in Victoria, where we five lunched. My mother was the only one of my vast family in attendance, and I was touched to see her pitiful attempts to keep calm. Still, lunch over and Joseph Conrad having duly signed his will which his two friends witnessed, they departed. Mr Krieger had presented me with a beautiful bouquet of early roses, red and white, the Polish colours. These I had reluctantly to relinquish for my husband flatly refused to allow me to carry them to my home, where we were due for the purpose of cutting the wedding-cake and bidding my family farewell.

I have thought many times with amusement of the comic distress displayed by my husband on the day of our wedding when the whole of my many brothers and sisters raised their voices in loud lament when the time came for us to leave.

'Good Heavens, if I had known this would happen, I – well, I would never have married you,' he muttered, turning away with an expression of utter disgust.

We dined that night at Overtons, and then we walked the short distance to the bachelor rooms that Joseph Conrad had retained for our last night in town. First of all I tackled a huge heap of masculine garments that had somehow to be included in my trunks which had been sent there the day before. I managed very well on the whole and the trunks swallowed the last pair of socks without a strain. Surreptitiously I shook out a quantity of the telltale rice in the process.

This done, I seated myself at the table and took my share of the heap of correspondence that had to be disposed of before we could leave England. A great deal of it I found was nothing less than our two photographs and a curiously formal and grandiloquent

* From *Joseph Conrad and his Circle* (London: Jarrolds, 1935) pp. 19–21.

announcement of the day's proceedings. My awe increased and I felt shy and a little disconcerted. Still he gave me no time to think much of my personal feelings, but pushed the pile of envelopes towards me and called my attention to a list of addresses in his note-book. It was thirsty work licking the stamps, but at last this task was finished and the tearful landlady appeared with a welcome tray with tea.

After this my strange husband insisted upon going out to post the batch that night. He took no heed of my protest that it was then nearly two in the morning and they might well wait until a little later in the day. Just as he closed the street-door, the curtain-pole fell to the ground and our brilliantly lighted windows faced the street uncovered. An unkind stroke of fate – with the dawn yet some few hours distant.

The next morning, or rather, some seven hours later we were ready to start on the first stage of our big adventure.[3] My mother had elected to come to us for lunch and to see us off at Waterloo. I had received the strictest orders that there should be no tears or display of emotion on my part. I was rather concerned because I knew that this restraint would be a lasting reproach in the eyes of my parent. She stood at the door of the railway-carriage, and behind the back of my new husband I raised my handkerchief effectively to my eyes as the train steamed out of the station, then I turned to him dry-eyed and quite composed. This little deception may, I hope, be forgiven me.

One incident disturbed me greatly during that run to Southampton. We were passing through a long tunnel, there was no light in the carriage and we were sitting opposite each other in the most decorous fashion. Without the least warning there was a terrific detonation somewhere very close at hand and the carriage was momentarily filled by a blinding flash. I was startled and for a second a sickening fear held me dumb. It was then that I realised how great an adventure it was on which I had so lightheartedly embarked, and how little I really knew of the man I had married. Suppose he turned out to be a member of some secret society? The flash and explosion had seemed to be in the very compartment, and he had made no sound since. I held my breath as the train cleared the tunnel and the welcome daylight filled the carriage. He smiled across at me, evidently quite undisturbed. I was ashamed to tell him the reason of my sudden fright, but I suppose my face betrayed me. I explained as best I could. 'Silly little donkey, it was only a fog signal they were using as a warning to the men at work on the line.'

My relief was almost painful, but I decided not to give a complete explanation. Instinct somehow showed me that I might be misunderstood. He might think I distrusted him, and anyhow, my feeling was too indefinite, too unreal for me to give it expression – least of all to him.

NOTES

1. The wedding of Jessie George and Joseph Conrad took place on 24 March 1896 at St George Register Office in Hanover Square, London. Conrad had proposed in early February. Although both were Roman Catholic, it was a civil ceremony. Jessie had just had her twenty-third birthday in the previous month, and Conrad was thirty-eight. He gave his name as Joseph Conrad Korzeniowski, his profession as Master Mariner and his father's occupation as Landowner.

2. Adolf P. Krieger, who, with G. F. W. Hope, was one of Conrad's two close friends in England at this time. They had met in 1880. An American of German parentage, he worked for a firm of shipping agents. Krieger and Conrad were estranged in 1897, probably as a result of Conrad's financial debt to him. *Tales of Unrest* (1898) was dedicated to him, 'for the sake of old days'. Conrad's friendship with Hope, a sailor, also began in 1880. The third witness to the wedding was Jane George, Jessie's mother.

3. The couple departed on honeymoon for Brittany, where they stayed until (probably) late September before returning to England.

My Father: Joseph Conrad*

BORYS CONRAD

The next picture from those now distant days, is of the period immediately preceding my brother's arrival into the world.[1] This major event took place in Uncle Jack's London flat, which he had put at the disposal of my parents for the occasion, and our arrival at 14 Addison Road was marked by an incident which remains very clearly in my memory.

The flat was equipped with electric light, a method of illumination of which my parents, having always lived in the depths of the country,[2] had had little experience. It must have been late when we took possession, or perhaps the day was dull and foggy; anyway the lights were switched on immediately and provided illumination of unaccustomed brilliance for a period of about ten minutes: then they went out abruptly and left us groping around in darkness. My Father, having indulged in his usual mild expletive of 'damn and blast' and used up the few remaining matches in his possession, announced his intention to sally forth and buy candles – and matches. My Mother,

* From *My Father: Joseph Conrad* (London: Calder & Boyars, 1970) pp. 50–2, 92–3, 95–8.

in her calm and unruffled manner, said she had not noticed any shops in the immediate vicinity and suggested that the telephone she had seen as we entered the hall should be made use of in order to solve our dilemma.

The telephone was even more unfamiliar to my parents than the electric light and they both regarded this method of communication with the utmost suspicion. My Mother was, in fact, frightened of the instrument whereas my Father, although in no way intimidated by it, considered it necessary to hold it at arm's length and bellow at it. On this occasion much explanatory shouting at the mouthpiece eventually produced an official from the electricity company. This individual quickly realised the cause of our predicament and asked my Father for a shilling. His indignation at the man's apparent impertinence in asking for a gratuity and moreover, without having done anything to merit it, was quite alarming and it was some time after the man had inserted the coin in the meter and thus restored our light, before he calmed down sufficiently to have the mysteries of shilling slot-meters explained to him.

* * *

When we arrived in Cracow we went back to the hotel. The friendly manager had, by now, gone off to face whatever the fates had in store for him on the battlefield and his place had been taken by a much older man. There were a number of army officers billeted in the hotel and we found it very different from when we first stayed there.

My Father went at once to see the Military Commandant and was told that the necessary travel permit would be sent to us at the hotel the next day. Several of our Polish friends came to see us during the course of the evening, and we heard from them that there was a lot of cholera among the troops. Upon hearing this my Father decided that we should carry our own water supply on the journey to Vienna and asked one of his friends to secure water bottles for us. In due course he returned with four army-type water bottles – I suspect they were later found to be missing from one of the military stores in the city – which my Father had filled with boiled water under his own supervision. My young brother carried one strapped on his back like a haversack. Meantime Mother arranged with the manager for some food to be packed for us, so that, when the travel-permit was delivered, as promised, in the morning, we were ready to go to the station and await the train – in fact we waited nearly all day – and when it did arrive it proved to be full of sick and wounded troops; among the former we heard there were some cases of cholera. One of the Commandant's Aides was at the station to supervise our departure, and he had one compartment cleared of troops for us. We spent two days and nights in that train before it eventually crawled into Vienna.[3] It stopped innumerable times on the way and on several occasions some of the sick or wounded were removed on stretchers. My Father had obviously acted very wisely in arranging for us to carry our own supplies of food and water. We had practically no sleep during the journey and were thankful to get to a hotel and rest. It must have been a great ordeal for Mother but she remained outwardly calm and placid as always.

The next morning she went into action and announced her determination to search every railway station and goods yard in Vienna for our lost luggage. My Father remonstrated with her in vain – she could be as stubborn as a mule at times – and finally he flung up his arms and stamped out of the room, pausing for a moment before slamming the door to tell me: 'Go with your Mother, Boy, and take care of her.'

* * *

When we got back to the hotel my Father expressed no surprise at our success, and merely remarked that he 'hoped his suits were not completely ruined'.[4]

During the days that followed I accompanied him to the American Embassy and he was able to see the Ambassador – Mr Penfield[5] who was most helpful and did, I believe, arrange for some news about us to be sent to the US from whence it was eventually passed on to England. What was more important is that through his influence, we eventually secured a permit to leave the country and cross into Italy. However, this took some time and during the period of waiting we were able to see something of Vienna, although we had to be far more circumspect in our movements than we had been in Cracow where we were among Polish people who regarded my Father as a fellow-countryman and took pride in his reputation as an English writer. However, the Austrians treated us very well and put no irksome restrictions upon our movements. We all went for one or two drives about the city and once even caught a glimpse of the old Emperor, Franz Josef,[6] passing in his carriage with a cavalry escort.

My Father and I went about together a lot as usual, and one day as we wandered through the streets, he suggested we should patronise a shooting gallery which seemed to be attracting a lot of customers. When we got inside, however, we were shocked at finding that this was no ordinary shooting gallery; it appeared to be a sort of War propaganda entertainment. Instead of conventional targets there were cinema screens on which was being shown a film of kilted Scottish infantry charging with fixed bayonets, and the marksmen had to fire at the figures as they ran across the screens. When a hit was made the film stopped and the marksman was invited to choose a prize from the trays of junk displayed. My Father paused and uttered a startled exclamation when he saw what we had walked into, and then gripped my arm and urged me forward saying: 'We have to go through with it, Boy, to retract now would draw too much attention, but take care you don't hit any of those fellows.' This admonition was accompanied by one of his most virulent glares. When our turn came he purchased the minimum amount of ammunition – five rounds each – and we took the rifles handed to us. I took a deep breath, hoped for a lot of luck, and concentrated on missing those running figures. My relief at seeing them still running after firing my last shot was abruptly dissipated by my Father who handed me his five cartridges growling: 'You had better use these as well.' I realised that this action on his part was no gesture of paternal affection – he just felt he dare not fire them himself – so I took another deep breath, and, I am thankful to say, succeeded in 'missing' five more times. He would have been terribly distressed if I had hit one of those running figures.

As the days passed, it became clear that he was feeling the strain of waiting and hoping for a permit to leave the country, and Mother, although as always she gave no outward sign of anxiety, told me that she feared an attack of gout was imminent. I had also been expecting something of the sort, and we were greatly relieved when at last a message came asking my Father to call at the US Embassy. Although I went with him, I was not actually present during his interview with the Ambassador. All I know is that a document was provided which was to enable us to travel to Udine, on the Italian Frontier.[7]

Before setting out on this stage of the journey which, although long and tedious, was without incident, our water bottles had been refilled and a supply of food packed for us by the hotel. So far as I remember it was early morning when the train eventually reached the frontier and my Father at once alighted and went to present his papers at the Austrian frontier post, taking me with him. We found that the Austrian troops had been withdrawn from duty and replaced by Germans.[8] This, as we heard later, had been done on direct orders from the Kaiser's headquarters with the object of tightening up the restrictions against people trying to leave the country. A Prussian non-commissioned officer took our papers and, after a casual glance, handed them back with a contemptuous gesture which clearly indicated that he considered them unacceptable.

My Father had always insisted that he could only speak a few words of German; however, in this emergency, it seemed to me that he spoke at considerable length and with great fluency, but the only effect this had on the Prussian was to cause him to lose his temper and start shouting at us.

My Father eventually shrugged his shoulders and turned away with a gesture of despair, saying 'It's "no go" Boy.' Then he stopped abruptly, put his hand into the breast pocket of his coat and pulled out our British Passport which he opened at the page bearing the German visa that had been necessary to enable us to travel through Germany on the outward journey. He turned back and thrust it under the Prussian's nose. The result was remarkable – the fellow examined the visa and then clicked his heels smartly and assumed an expression which might conceivably be described as friendly as he handed the passport back to my Father and waved us to our compartment. When discussing his action later we concluded that he must have accepted the visa solely because it was written in German, and overlooked the fact that it was in a British Passport. We were very lucky – far more so than we realised at the time, because after we got back to England, we heard through US diplomatic channels, that soon after we left Vienna, orders came from Berlin to detain Joseph Conrad and his family.[9]

NOTES

Alfred Borys Leo Conrad (1898–1978) was the elder of Conrad's two sons. He was gassed and shell-shocked in Flanders in October 1918, and married secretly in 1923, without telling his father. The birth of his son, Philip, in January 1924 reconciled Borys and Conrad shortly before the latter's death in the following August. Borys's name was chosen to indicate his Anglo-Saxon and Slavonic parentage.

The two extracts from Borys's book describe, firstly, the birth of his younger brother, and then Conrad's return to Poland in 1914, when he undertook his first visit there since 1893, and his first visit to Cracow, his boyhood home, for forty years. He set off with his invalid wife and two sons on 25 July, travelling by train via Harwich and Hamburg. He was returning to Poland at the invitation of his friends, the Retingers, intending to spend six weeks there.

War broke out between Austria–Hungary and Serbia on 28 July, the day of their arrival in Cracow. Three days later, general mobilisation was declared, and all civilian transport was about to be suspended. The Conrads moved on 2 August from Cracow to Zakopane, a distance of 65 miles, to stay with Conrad's cousin. On 4 August, Great Britain and Germany were at war. Conrad, as a British subject, was liable to be interned by the Austrian authorities, but he had been protected so far by his Polish name. The Conrads left Zakopane on 7 October, having received permission to travel to Vienna. At this point, Borys's second extract begins.

1. John Galsworthy (see note on p. 63) is the 'Uncle Jack' who lent the Conrads his London house during Jessie's pregnancy. They moved there from Kent on 10 July 1906 and stayed nearly two months. Their second child, John

Alexander, was born on 2 August and named in honour of Galsworthy.

2. Since 1898 they had been living mainly at the Pent, a farmhouse near Aldington, Kent.

3. The train journey from Cracow to Vienna took 26 hours, five times longer than usual, and the Conrads arrived on 10 October.

4. Jessie Conrad, now a citizen of a hostile country, found in the goods depot of Vienna's railway station two trunks which had been lost ten weeks earlier on the way from Berlin to Cracow.

5. Frederick C. Penfield, to whom Conrad later dedicated *The Rescue* (1920).

6. Franz Josef I (1830–1916), emperor of Austria since 1848.

7. The whole family left Vienna on 18 October, after a stay of eight days, heading for Milan. They reached neutral Italy on 20 October.

8. Zdzisław Najder finds this incredible, since Austria–Hungary was a sovereign state and would not have permitted such an incursion by German guards (*Joseph Conrad: A Chronicle* (Cambridge: Cambridge University Press, 1983) p. 403, note).

9. On 25 October they sailed from Genoa in a Dutch steamer to London, arriving 3 November.

Joseph Conrad: Times Remembered*

JOHN CONRAD

There is one day I shall never forget in the late summer when I was playing on the lawn outside the open window of the drawing-room where my father worked. I was quietly rigging a ship in preparation for an official launching which JC had promised to perform later in the day. Suddenly I heard a 'quarter-deck' shout followed by far from subdued imprecations. Without waiting to see if I was the culprit I bolted for my hideout in the loft of the middle shed that stood beside the drive. I scrambled up the ladder closely followed by one of my pet cats, also suffering from fright, and there we stayed listening. There seemed to be much coming and going in the house and it was getting on towards lunchtime before I heard my name being called. I reluctantly left my refuge and went into the house to make myself tidy for, no matter what I had been doing, I had to be clean and tidy before I sat

* From *Joseph Conrad: Times Remembered* (Cambridge: Cambridge University Press, 1981) pp. 33–7.

down to a meal. Everyone seemed rather subdued and even the gardener had no friendly word for me but went about his work muttering. Lunchtime came and I went to my place and sat down to wait, rather surprised that JC's chair was piled up with cushions. Presently he came in walking between two sticks and looking annoyed. I kept my eyes down waiting for the storm which I felt must break at any moment. He saw the cushions on his chair then looked at me but there was no smile on his face as he said, 'Well, what mischief have you been up to, you young scamp?' I denied having been up to any mischief and then my mother came in and asked JC how the sting felt. Seeing my look of surprise JC explained how he had sat on a wasp which had not respected him in the least and then went on to tell me that I should never assume responsibility for the action of others however small they might be. He tried to keep a straight face as he looked at me but I started to laugh and he joined me as he took the cushions and threw them into the corner of the room, remarking that he did not want all that 'damned fuss' just because of a wasp sting. My mother was really put out for JC had in fact made a lot of fuss before, calling for 'bluebag', onion and anything else that might alleviate the discomfort of the sting.

The orchard at Capel was a favourite place for wasps to build their nests and every summer there were quite a number of colonies. We would be at supper in the evening of a hot day with all the windows and doors open, when we would hear footsteps followed by a knock on the back door. Someone would answer it and we'd hear the deep voice of Mr Knight, who farmed the land round Capel House, saying: 'Would you tell the "maister" I be goin' t' take the "wopsies" nests. 'e might like t' come.'

JC always liked to accept these invitations and would call out, 'I'll be with you in a minute, presently.' He would ask me to fetch his cap and stick and we would go with Mr Knight to the orchard. During the day the old man would have marked the little holes of the entrances to the nests with twigs so that we did not have to search for them in the fading light. To 'take' the nest Mr Knight produced a length of gas pipe about three quarters of an inch bore and eighteen inches long with a cap on one end, with a small touch hole. This was filled with gunpowder and a length of fuse stuck into the touch hole. The open end of the pipe was pushed down into the nest and the fuse lit while everyone stood well away to one side and waited for the dull 'bumph' as the pipe was blown about four feet from the hole. Mr Knight then dug up the nest just to make 'sairtin' that all the occupants had been exterminated. It was a very efficient way of dealing with wasps and I do not remember anyone ever being stung on these expeditions.

One morning JC called me into the drawing-room after breakfast.

This was an unusual and vaguely worrying occurrence though I could not remember having done anything for which to be reprimanded so I tidied myself, pulled my jersey down, my stockings up and cautiously approached his desk. He was not writing but took no notice of me while he continued to fold a strip of paper into a kind of 'plat'. He put it on the blotter and pressed it down with his thumb nail before pushing it towards me. 'Do you know what that is?'

I knew better than to say a piece of paper so I was silent for a while and then said, 'A thing to put in a book to show where you are?'

He laughed saying, 'Yes, You could use it for that but it is called a sennit. If you were shipwrecked in the tropics you would collect wide grasses and after making a number of sennits you would fix them together to make a hat. Take it when you go and try to make one like it.'

Then, inviting me to sit on his knee he said, 'Now listen. Monsieur Gide[1] is coming to lunch. I want you to be tidy, hands clean, hair brushed and waiting with me to receive him. He is a Frenchman so you will say "Bon jour, Monsieur. Comment allez-vous?" Now say that after me.' So for some minutes I repeated these words after JC though they did not mean anything to me. After a while JC asked me what was the matter.

'I don't know what the words mean.' You may well think this did not matter, but it mattered a great deal to me and other people because JC had the gift of making people do their best. He explained at some length, and after a few more repetitions by me I was allowed to go. What a long morning that was because as soon as I started doing something there was 'Mind you don't get dirty', or 'Leave the cat alone or you'll get covered in hairs.' Oh dear, everything was taboo so I went and sat on the window-seat in the dining-room to wait. After a while I saw the taxi turn into the drive and jumped up to go and tell my father and in doing so butted him amidships as I had not heard him come and stand behind me. Monsieur Gide was a little surprised at JC's rather breathless greeting but I was forgiven as I did remember what to say.

After lunch, during which I was ticked off for giggling at the funny noises JC and Gide were making at one another, I escaped to the den to play with my toys. Later in the afternoon I was very busy building something and was so intent on what I was doing that I did not notice them come into the room and remained so absorbed that they were on the point of leaving before I realised I was being spoken to – something about meccano. JC had shown me an advertisement some days before so I knew what it was. Gide was speaking to me but I didn't understand so JC explained that he was going to send me a box of meccano. I needed no coaxing to say 'Merci, monsieur' and spent the rest of the day in a happy dream about all the things I was going to build. It seemed an awfully long time before the set arrived – I was told later that I got quite annoyed with the postman for not bringing it.

I remember that JC was almost as excited as I was when it did arrive and we undid the parcel on the dining-room table. He spent most of the first evening helping me to build a simple model. He tried to put some of the parts together but his gouty fingers did not make it easy for him to handle the tiny nuts and bolts. I soon began to get the hang of things with his help and he would place an 'order' for a trolley or a cart and I would dash off and start building it without paying enough attention to the picture in the instruction book. I would get things a bit mixed up and JC would come and help me sort them out. As time went on I got better and his help was not so frequently needed. He encouraged me and whenever he went up to London he brought back an accessory set, going by taxi to Mr Lorberg's shop in Kensington High Street, before catching the train home.

I remember the first time he came home with an accessory set for me, as it caused a rift in the lute. He entered the house with a flat rectangular parcel under his arm, patted me on the head and kissed my mother as he usually did. He said something to her which I didn't catch and then in reply to something she said turned away from her saying, 'Well, I'm sorry Jess, I did not get anything for you. I'll make it right.'

A day or so later after he had been to Ashford I noticed my mother had on a new brooch and later on he gave me my first accessory set of meccano. After that he always gave my mother some trinket or piece of jewellery before giving me whatever he had got for me. He was most particular about getting the right accessory set so that my meccano set got progressively more complete. I think that Mr Lorberg must have kept a list of the sets that JC bought, so that he was able to hand him the right one as none was duplicated and each additional set enabled me to build larger and more intricate models. As soon as I had finished one I took it into JC's room and, if it was a model of a crane, I had to hold it down on the desk while JC operated it to lift a book from the floor. After the first time when the book fell from the hook he showed me how to make slings for lifting various objects and how to 'cord' a barrel to lift it 'upright' or horizontally. If he took a liking to a particular model it was just too bad because he wanted it left in his room so that he could have a good look at it. Still, it was very rarely that he kept it for more than an evening.

As I became more proficient at building models some form of power was often needed so JC bought me various steam engines which between us we managed to adapt to drive the models. I use the word 'we' because he had a knack of spotting weakness in the design or arrangement of machinery and very often made suggestions for its improvement. His knowledge of steam engines was very extensive and he spent a long time operating the throttle valve and adjusting the timing while he explained how it worked and also improved its performance. If he went up to London after one of these sessions held in an atmosphere of steam, hot oil and metal, I could be pretty certain that he would return with an engine having even more refinements than the one I had. As my collection increased he insisted that I should be given a 'kitchen' table so that the spilt oil and water did not have to be constantly mopped up. This table was placed in the den and the various engines were screwed to it but I doubt if my mother was ever consulted about it or about the smell and noise in which she was expected to type my father's manuscripts. There were many occasions when I was told to put on my hat and coat and get out for a breath of fresh air, and to 'Open the windows before you go to blow the room clear.' The breath of fresh air usually meant climbing a tree or playing by the moat so it was no real hardship.

NOTES

John Conrad (1906–82) was Conrad's younger son. His birth is described by his brother Borys on p. 9. He trained as an architect and practised professionally until a few years before his death. Like Borys, he took an active interest in preserving his father's literary reputation.

The extract recalls memories from the period 1910–14, when the Conrads were living at Capel House, near Ashford in Kent.

1. André Gide (1869–1951), the French novelist, had first visited Conrad at Capel House in July 1911, and they remained good friends.

Part II
Conrad at Home

A Visit to Joseph Conrad*

JAMES HUNEKER

Once, in his peculiarly amiable manner, George Bernard Shaw reproached me with being a hero-worshipper of the sort who, finding his idol not precisely as he had pictured him, would paganlike tweak his nose.

Possibly G.B.S. fancied that I did not think him a fine figure of a man, yet there was some truth in his words; the words of a man who is also a hero-worshipper, his bright, particular deity, himself.

I couldn't help recalling Mr Shaw and his humorous criticism when a few weeks ago I received a summons from Joseph Conrad in London. I say 'summons' advisedly, as no royal 'command' would have so stirred my imagination as did his. Joseph Conrad, the mirror of the sea, a master of English prose though writing in a foreign language – as Flaubert wrote French – large, sonorous, fluid, picture-evoking prose; Conrad, the only man in England today who belongs to the immortal company of Meredith, Hardy and Henry James; as microscopic in his analysis as Paul Bourget, as exotic as Pierre Loti,[1] without the egoism of that essentially feminine soul; withal a Slav, even when he most seems an Englishman; and the weaver of magic variations on the most tremendous of all themes, the sea.

I was summoned, as I say, to his country home in Kent, and in the most cordial fashion. I really had not expected a typhoon blast in the form of an invitation, nevertheless for the author of *The Nigger of the 'Narcissus'* I had looked for something more Homeric, more epical, something like this: 'What ho! luff to and run your miserable little writing yawl into my harbour, and don't be too slow about it, blast your buttons!' But I had forgotten that I was visiting Joseph Conrad and not the merry Mr Jacobs.[2]

It's best to begin at the beginning, isn't it? Interviews are usually abominable, alike to both interviewer and interviewed, and I believe the reading public is not less bored. So when I awoke the fateful Saturday and found dear old London in the black embrace of fog, my heart wasn't any too cheerful. Charing Cross Station was hard by, but the greater part of a half hour was consumed in getting there. What a

* 'A Visit to Joseph Conrad, the Mirror of the Sea', *New York Times* [Magazine], 17 November 1912, p. 4.

morning! The sun was shining overhead, but you couldn't see it; only a dirty vapour that choked and depressed one surrounded you. The native here, who has been in New York, dilates with pride upon the superiority of London climate over our poor, monotonous sunshine and Italian blue skies; on a morning like the one I can't describe – for it was indescribable – the feeling that the English tourist is a subtle humorist is not to be denied. But behold! ten minutes outside of London and I found myself gazing upon a serene autumn landscape, only a hint of haze on the hills to remind me that I had escaped from the city of smoke-eaters and of dreadful night.

The train, with true British phlegm, had left the station only ten minutes late – a record performance, I have been told – and pursued its winding way at a leisurely gait. The general view recalled certain parts of Connecticut. The sky was warm, low and homelike. Men golfed. Men shot. Cows munched grass, and at intervals we read the American liver-pill advertisements pinned to the landscape. Kent is charming. Kent is hospitable. But it took two hours to reach a little station called Hamstreet, after changing at Ashford. Slow but sure is the motto of the railway service of this land. My spirits had risen as the day waxed, but only to be depressed when a motor car met me and I learned that it belonged to Mr Conrad. Again Mr Shaw's admonition came to my mind. If it had been a flying machine or a steam launch I wouldn't have been more surprised. But a motor car and Joseph Conrad couldn't be made to modulate in my mind, all of which proves the folly of preconceived portraits. I had seen photographs of Mr Conrad, bearded, mature, with commanding eyes, a master mariner as well as a master psychologist. Would he resemble his pictures? Of course not, and I prepared for the worst. I was delightfully disappointed. At the door of what he calls his 'farmhouse' I was met by a man of the world, neither sailor nor novelist, just a simple-mannered gentleman whose welcome was sincere, whose glance was slightly veiled, far-away at times, whose ways were Polish, French, anything but bluff, or English or 'literary'.

He is not so tall as he seems. He is very restless. He paces an imaginary quarter-deck and occasionally peers through the little windows of his quaint house as if searching the weather. A caged sea-lion, I thought. His shrug and play of hands are Gallic, or Polish, as you please, and his eyes, shining or clouded, are not of our race, they are Slavic; even the slightly muffled voice is Slavic. One of the most beautiful languages is the Polish – the French of the Slav tongues, as it has been called. When Mr Conrad speaks English, which he does with rapidity and clearness of enunciation, you can hear, rather overhear, the foreign cadence, the soft slurring of sibilants so characteristic of Polish speech. In a word, he is more foreign looking than I had expected. He speaks French with fluency and purity, and he often lapsed into it during our conversation. Like many another big man, he asked more questions than he answered mine. I underwent the same experience with Walt Whitman at Camden,[3] who was an adept in the gentle art of pumping visitors. In the case of Joseph Conrad his curiosity is prompted by his boundless sympathy for all things human. He is, as you must have surmised by his writings, the most human and lovable of men. He takes an interest in everything except bad art, which moves him to a vibrating indignation, and he is extremely sympathetic when speaking of the work of his contemporaries. What a lesson for the critic with the barbed-wire method would be the remarks of Conrad upon art and artists! Naturally, he has his gods, his half-gods and his major detestations. The Bible and Flaubert were his companions throughout the many years he voyaged in strange, southern seas. From the Bible he absorbed his racy, idiomatic and diapasonic English; from the supple, shining prose of the great French writer he learned the art of writing sentences, their comely shape and vigorous rhythmic gait, their colour, perfume; the passionate music of words and their hateful power. He also studied other masters. He is an admirer of Poe, Hawthorne, Walt Whitman and Henry James among American writers. The late Stephen Crane was an intimate of his.

Henry James once wrote of the difficult approach to the mind and art of Ivan Turgenev for his French colleagues. His Gallic side, a side frequently shown by Russians, they appreciated, and his German culture, above all the vast and mysterious reservoir of his Slavic temperament, was for them non-existent. So close a friend as Flaubert was unresponsive to what was greatest in Turgenev. Here I can't help thinking of Conrad. No prophet has been more envied out of his own country. His fellow-artists, Thomas Hardy, Henry James, Kipling, Wells, Galsworthy, Arthur Symons – and how many others? – are his warmest admirers. His critics are sometimes extravagant in their praise of his art, yet I haven't thus far read a criticism that gives me a sense of finality. They miss his Slavic side, or are repelled by it. Irony is the one unforgivable offence in a country where is read Hall Caine and Marie Corelli.[4] Mr Shaw, himself, found this out early in the game and uses a bludgeon, and that is why he is called subtle when he is drawing blood with the blunt edge of his razor. Joseph Conrad is not ironical. It is an illuminating model for the elect, but it has not endeared him to certain of his critics. They take him solemnly when his pages are most suffused with tragic [*sic*], as in the case of *The Secret Agent*.

It's a new kind of detective story, said the critics, and judged the book as they would one by the author of *Arsène Lupin* or Conan Doyle or by the ingenious Mr Oppenheim.[5] And what critical havoc was wrought at the appearance of *Under Western Eyes*, which might have been by Turgenev, in so far as its verbal artistry is concerned, and planned by Dostoevsky because of its revelation of mystic power, yet is unlike any book by either of these Russian writers. In vain the critics searched for the symphonic motive of the sea. We don't like Conrad on dry land, said they, and they recalled his *Heart of Darkness* – forgetting that its marvellous art does not deal with the sea, but the soul; they recalled *Lord Jim*, 'Typhoon', and they recalled 'The End of the Tether' and Captain Whalley half blind on the deck of the *Sofala*. They forgot that it is first and last the human soul which concerns Conrad, whether that soul spills itself to him in the jungle or in the forecastle, or among the beachcombers of a South Sea island, or at St Petersburg or Geneva. Give an author the name of a specialist, and you will hang him – critically speaking – when you discover his versatility. Conrad is pre-eminently versatile, and in the back garden of his culture, in the enormous storehouse of his experiences, is somewhere flitting, an uneasy shadow at times, at others a very ogre that threatens, his Slavic temperament. As with Turgenev, its possession has led to numerous critical misapprehensions.

I told him that in the choice of a certain theme he had been anticipated by Shakespeare, Balzac and Turgenev, and his curiosity was veritably charming. King Lear, Père Goriot and Turgenev's tale 'A Lear of the Steppes'[6] are in the same key as 'The End of the Tether' (the last story in the volume entitled *Youth*). He was pleased at the comparison, and then confessed that the love of a father for his son or daughter was very attractive to him as an artist. Fault has been found with him because he has not, like the popular novelist, made woman the central motive of his books. But if you will recall his finished portraits, his fugitive sketches, his little etchings of women you may be surprised at their number and variety in the work of one who has been called a novelist for men. His treatment of woman is always reverent, more reverent, in fact, than is the case with so many ladies who attack their sex without gloves. Full-length pictures of society women, or of morbid, complicated creatures he has not given us; nor will he ever. His women are wives, not nervous cats or hysterical geese; mothers, daughters and young lovers, too, presented in their relation with other humans, and never as mere automatons of passion or intrigue. The life of Joseph Conrad has been too close to the soil for him not to have heard the humming of the human heart and its overtones. The elemental things are his chief concern, not the doings of dolls. He is not a propagandist. He tries to prove nothing. He is the artist pure and simple. Look at his newly published tales assembled under the head of *'Twixt Land and Sea*, and mark the conjunction of poet and realist in such a tale as 'A Smile of Fortune', or the grim power of 'Freya of the Seven Isles'. Yes, a poet writing prose – not hybrid poetic prose, mind you – one whose vision is romantic, yet one who never leaves the rim of the mundane in pursuit of the inane ideal. (I mean false idealism, of course.) He would not be Polish and a man of genius if the Polish *Żal*[7] were not in his gaze, in his words, in his writings; that half desire, half melancholy, half yearning, half sorrow, a divine discontent, and withal not to be put into a phrase, except the magical musical phrase of his fellow-Sarmatian, Frédéric Chopin.

To Joseph Conrad has come fame, if not fortune (the English still prefer their favourite mixture of molasses and brimstone in fiction). Yet I doubt if his work has brought him happiness. He has followed the ancient injunction of looking into his own heart and writing – he the most objective of artists, with the clairvoyance of the seer; nevertheless these gifts, this wonderful success has not made him happy. His true happiness lies nearer the core of his nature – his love for his family. For those young writers, incipient Maupassants and Nietzsches, this very human trait of Conrad's may seem banal. Anyone can love his wife and children, and art is a jealous mistress, we are told by the pale youths who wearily look down from their Ivory Tower upon a stupid world. It is true, but not every one can write like Joseph Conrad and also be a loving father and husband. There is no paradox in this. It is just because he is so human in his sympathies that Conrad is so masterful a writer. He can sound the strings of pity and humour and terror. But if you speak of him as a 'literary' man he waves an emphatic negative. He admires literary virtuosity, but does not practice it. He admires Anatole France, but his own art is exactly the reverse of that velvety sophist. He takes pride in his profession, but is free from vanity or self-seeking; indeed, he is far from being a practical man. This worries him more than it worries his friends, and the fact that he is not a well man is another thorn in the flesh. Rheumatism, or rheumatic gout, tortures him for months at a time. A fitful worker at his best, his illness keeps him away from his desk; thereat much wrath and many regrets. However, the optimistic spirit of the man shines clearly through his occasional lapses into pessimism. '*Noch ist Polen nicht verloren*',[8] might be his motto.

In his *Reminiscences* you will find a veracious account of the author, of his early passion for the sea, of his first tale, *Almayer's Folly*, and how he came to write it; of his grand-uncle Nicholas – a portrait as massive and vital as a Holbein; of his youthful experiences with the pilots of Marseilles (one old chap recalled Napoleon as '"a little fat fellow in a three-cornered hat, buttoned up in a long straight coat, with a big pale face, inclined on one shoulder, looking something like a priest. His hands were clasped behind his back. . . . It appears that this was the Emperor"'.[9] Heine in his *Reisebilder* painted no better picture[10]) and the description of an omnibus that might have been penned by Flaubert.

Conrad is only one of his names – his family belonged to the Polish nobility. But the magnetism of the waters drew him to ships, and then by sheer accident he became a writer. How? He could not tell me. He was a toiler of the sea and with pen. These matters are incommensurable. He had the genius for narration, and his life gave him rich material. 'Imagination, not invention, is the supreme master of art as of life', he has written.[11] Imagination is the supreme element in the art of Conrad.

He astonished me later in the afternoon by suddenly transforming himself into an Englishman. He sported a monocle, his expression was almost haughty as he drove me in his car over the smooth Kentish roads. The Slav had disappeared. He spoke no more of his art, but dwelt on his gout – poor man's gout, he smilingly called it. We might have gone as far as the home of Arthur Symons – who is quite recovered from his recent nervous breakdown[12] – but the clock forbade this pleasure, and soon I was standing on the platform of Ashford station, and not too soon did I arrive at Charing Cross – the train this time was only a half hour late – and welcomed by the blackest and most sinister of London fogs. After all, I said, he writes only to recall his memorable past; the little blundering book clerk in the rue de Rivoli was not far wrong when he asked me if I wished a copy of *Conrad in Quest of His Youth*.[13] All imaginative and unimaginative men and women seek for their youth; it is the eternal mirage. And in this he is one with all of us, Joseph Conrad, mirror of the sea and of the human heart.

NOTES

James Gibbons Huneker (1860–1921), American author and critic, began corresponding with Conrad in 1909. The visit which Huneker records here occurred at Capel House on 12 October 1912. Huneker was the first American man of letters, apart from Stephen Crane, to establish a correspondence with Conrad.

1. Paul Bourget (1852–1935), French critic; Pierre Loti (1850–1923), French naval officer and author of exotic fiction.
2. William Wymark Jacobs (1863–1943), author of popular maritime tales.
3. Walt Whitman (1819–92) spent the last years of his life at Camden, New Jersey.
4. Marie Corelli (1855–1924), popular novelist. For a note on Hall Caine, see p. 112.
5. Arsène Lupin was the hero of the thrillers and detective stories written by Maurice Leblanc (1864–1941). For a note on Oppenheim, see p. 48.
6. Honoré de Balzac's *Le Père Goriot* (1834–5); Ivan Turgenev's 'A Lear of the Steppes' (1870).
7. *Żal* means 'grief' or 'sorrow'.

8. A proverb implying that 'Where there's life, there's hope', while Poland is not yet lost.

9. Joseph Conrad, *A Personal Record* (London: J.M. Dent, 1946) p. 132. This book was originally called 'Some Reminiscences'.

10. Heinrich Heine's four-volume *Reisebilder* (1826–1831) contains a famous account of Napoleon.

11. Conrad, *A Personal Record*, p. 25.

12. Arthur William Symons (1865–1945), poet, translator and critic. His health broke down in 1908, and he spent two years in mental hospitals. He lived at Wittersham, Kent.

13. Leonard Merrick, *Conrad in Quest of his Youth: An Extravagance of Temperament* (London: Grant Richards, 1903).

'He has never met "civilised" women'*

LADY OTTOLINE MORRELL

The next really interesting event was my visit to Joseph Conrad at Ashford in Kent. At this time Henry James came to see us fairly often, and as I knew that Conrad was a friend of his I timidly said that I should very much like to see him, as I much admired his writings. Henry James held up his hands in horror, and was so perturbed that he paced up and down the grey drawing-room. I remember best some of his exclamations and expostulations: 'But, dear lady . . . but dear lady . . . He has lived his life at sea – dear lady, he has never met "civilised" women. Yes, he is interesting, but he would not understand you. His wife, she is a good cook. She is a Catholic as he is, but . . . No, dear lady, he has lived a rough life, and is not used to talk to –', an upward movement of the arms had to describe who – and it was, of course, myself. This was not encouraging, but it was not the sort of discouragement that would turn me aside from what I had so set my heart upon. I think Henry James must have written to Conrad to prepare him for the visit of the lady that Henry James thought so grand, for I received a letter of welcome and went down to Ashford, reading that wonderful book of his reminiscences[1] in the train, or rather

* From *Ottoline: The Early Memoirs of Lady Ottoline Morrell*, ed. Robert Gathorne-Hardy (London: Faber & Faber, 1963) pp. 240–5.

trying to keep my attention fixed on it, for I was so excited and nervous that it was difficult.

When I had told Desmond MacCarthy[2] of my projected visit, he had given me elaborate meandering advice – especially was I to wear a smart and rather elaborate dress, as he was sure anyone like Conrad who saw few ladies from London would appreciate the note of fantasy in his guest. This was not difficult for me to supply, for my trouble was always to appear conventional and discreet. Conrad's eldest son, John,[3] met me in a motor, and I found Conrad himself standing at the door of the house ready to receive me. How different from the picture Henry James had evoked, for Conrad's appearance was really that of a Polish nobleman. His manner was perfect, almost too elaborate; so nervous and sympathetic that every fibre of him seemed electric, which gave him the air of a highly-polished and well-bred man.

He talked English with a strong accent, as if he tasted his words in his mouth before pronouncing them; but he talked extremely well, though he had always the talk and manner of a foreigner. It seemed difficult to believe that this charming gentleman with high square shoulders, which he shrugged now and again so lightly, and the unmistakably foreign look, had been a captain in the English Merchant Service, and was, too, such a master of English prose. He was dressed very carefully in a blue double-breasted jacket. He talked on apparently with great freedom about his life – more ease and freedom indeed than an Englishman would have allowed himself. He spoke of the horrors of the Congo, from the moral and physical shock of which he said he had never recovered, the impression had been so deep that he felt he would never lose it – but that out of this experience had come *The Heart of Darkness* and *The Outpost of Duty* [*sic*], which he wrote on his honeymoon in Brittany, as he also did *The Idiots*;[4] but of this story he obviously didn't think very highly – it was too much derived from Guy de Maupassant. I wondered what his wife thought of these strange and haunting companions of their honeymoon! But she seemed a nice and good-looking fat creature, an excellent cook, as Henry James said, and was indeed a good and reposeful mattress for this hypersensitive, nerve-wrecked man, who did not ask from his wife high intelligence, only an assuagement of life's vibrations.

He complained with a great deal of movement and manner that writing was a most painful effort, and that he did not feel the need of expression, but obviously he would never have made the first attempt if he had not felt the gnawing and discomfort of the creator. As I sat there I could hardly believe that I was really talking to the man whose work had haunted me for years, and about whom I had thought and wondered with such intensity. He made me feel so natural and very much myself, that I was almost afraid of losing the thrill and wonder of being there, although I was vibrating with intense excitement inside; and even now, as I write this, I feel almost the same excitement, the same thrill of having been in the presence of one of the most remarkable men I have known. His eyes under their pent-house lids revealed the suffering and the intensity of his experiences; when he spoke of his work, there came over them a sort of misty, sensuous, dreamy look, but they seemed to hold deep down the ghosts of old adventures and experiences – once or twice there was something in them one almost suspected of being wicked. I was amused some years later when I was talking to a dear old Canterbury canon's wife – the mother of Mrs Inge[5] – who had known Conrad and who was obviously fascinated by him, to hear her say, 'But I am afraid he might drag me down to Hell and I don't want to go there.' To which I laughingly replied, 'I would willingly go with Conrad.' But then I believe whatever strange wickedness would tempt this super-subtle Pole, he would be held in restraint by an equally delicate sense of honour.

He talked with great admiration of Henry James. I, unfortunately, said that sometimes Henry James's very exaggerated and perfunctory and rather false worldly humour annoyed me. This Conrad, I felt, did not like, and I was sorry I had said such a stupid thing, which was so open to misunderstanding.

Yes, it was a tangled, tortured and very complex soul that looked out through those mysterious eyes, sensitive and understanding – one who had gone down in his imagination and experience into the hell which others had contrived to make of their lives. He had never sat on the bank and watched coldly; that one could see at once, for he was so obviously battered by the journeys he had taken through the souls of the men whom he had known. The sea with its calm, its storms, to him was but a mirror of the restless motion of the souls of men. His prose that has such a magic and vibrating beauty seems the outcome of these mysterious experiences upon an instrument so sensitively tuned.

In his talk he led me along many paths of his life, but I felt that he did not wish to explore the jungle of emotions that lay dense on either side, and that his apparent frankness had a great reserve. This may perhaps be characteristic of Poles as it is of the Irish. I find in an article of an unknown writer in a review of Conrad's letters, this sentence, which I have kept by me:

> In *A Personal Record* the public were taken into the Park but were kept to the broad paths, no intimacies there. We were eluded still by the impalpable suggestion of huge conflicts of good and evil, of beauty and ugliness, in which the things of good report in a faithful world were trampled under the hoofs of infamy and ignorance.[6]

I myself thought the central mystery consisted of the bruised ideals of a sensitive idealist combined with the courage of a man of action who was also an artist, that he had to face truth at all costs.

A short time after this first visit I took Bertie Russell down to see him.[7] It was, indeed, he that had recommended me to read Conrad's books. They understood each other immediately and even as they walked together in Conrad's garden had a moment of intense intimacy, some spell caught them and made them look deep down into each other's eyes. Such things happen rarely, it was obviously the recognition that both these souls belonged to the kingdom of the sufferers, and the passionate and the unreconcilable.

He told Bertie Russell that he found it difficult to talk to his boys or to young people, as he disliked being insincere, and at the same time he shrank from burdening them with his own experience and knowledge of life.

I visited him again once or twice, but as he was very patriotic I did not dare go during the war, as I felt sure he would disapprove of my views,[8] but in 1923 while Philip and I were staying with Bernard Holland[9] not far from Conrad's new home in Kent we all went over to see him (he had not met Philip before). It was a perfectly happy day. We found him in a pleasant country house on the edge of a park, an old-fashioned house with large, low rooms, which he had furnished with great distinction and with something of the air, it seemed to me, of a Polish château. It was the sort of garden that you might find described, with its view over the rather monotonous landscape of the Park, in a Henry James novel, and Conrad with his polished air was, you might have supposed, very well set there. But the view was too narrow for his taste. He missed, as he said, one thing: 'It has no horizon.'

As we sat round a large table at tea he talked with even more freedom, and I felt easier than before. He sat by me and he told me of his early love of England and the sea, and his longing to get upon an English ship. His first sight of the sea had been at Venice.[10] He was then a boy travelling with a tutor and he described to us in his swift way some of the emotion that he felt. But it was later at Marseilles that his life at sea began.[11] The Carlists were then a power in the Mediterranean, which made the life more exciting; and looking down with a smile, he murmured – with what strange memories in him, which also flitted across his face – 'It was here that I sowed my wild oats.' When at last he got taken upon an English ship and came to England, he did not know anything of the language, and it was in a little inn at Lowestoft,[12] frequented by sailors, at which he stayed between his voyages, that he puzzled out in the articles of *The Standard* – the only English literature to be found there – his first lessons in

English. Frequently in his talk this love of England and the English would recur. He specially liked simple young men who went into the Army and the Navy; clear, true and direct; he delighted in their fairness of mind. They were the people, he said, with whom he got on most easily – 'Not the learned or the intellectuals'. It was the simple adventurous Englishman that he liked, but as a rule Conrad's talk was gay and witty. He liked to surprise you by some slight, swift sentence. I remember how, when we happened to talk of poetry and I was urging him to read T. S. Eliot's poetry, he professed that he never read it – 'Oh, I'm not caught by poetry,' he said, 'not I.' He also spoke again of the Congo. Knowing that he had met Casement[13] there I asked about him. All that I now remember of what he said was that he met him emerging from one of the densest and most perilous jungles in a white linen jacket and white tennis shoes, and for arms and protection a walking-stick and a native boy. As he described it I felt that in spite of disapproving of what Casement did in the war he bowed before such quixotic and aristocratic behaviour and nonchalant courage.

And again when he was describing his adventures in Poland where he and his wife and children, after many years of voluntary exile, had gone to show his ancestral home to his boys, the war was declared the day of their arrival, and it was with great difficulty that they were able to return to England – 'Oh, it was a circus, a perfect circus,' he kept saying, 'with my wife and two boys there.'[14]

When we first arrived Conrad brought up a little chair and sat down to talk to me about all this, but his wife at once came and sat on my other side and showed me page by page of a little book of snapshots of this journey – dull, ill-focused, conventional little photographs – and it was only with the greatest difficulty that I made myself polite to her. But I knew he was very exacting that she should be treated with proper respect.

After tea we walked in the garden, on brick-paved paths, roses and flowers of all sorts around us. I had remembered Desmond's advice of old, and had put on a very lovely blue Persian jacket, over a lavender silk dress. Mrs Conrad and I walked on ahead, while he and Philip followed. It was a lovely early autumn evening, with a mellow sunset light. On turning back from our slow pacing (Mrs Conrad was lame), I saw the two men looking at us, and I knew that Conrad had been pleased with the touch of fantasy that I had been able to add to his garden. I asked Philip afterwards and found that Conrad had said, 'How beautiful your wife looks in her colours against the green.' Philip said, 'Yes, that coat came from Persia.'

Before leaving he took me into his own little room where he worked – small and simple, books round the walls, a photograph of his youngest boy with himself stuck up against the books. He found a book that had lately been privately printed – *The Ship's Mate* – which he wished to give me. He sat down at the large writing-table and with a fat pen wrote my name and his own in a book. As I stood opposite him he looked up, and I caught with my eyes one of his surprising and exciting glances – it was one that I had not seen before. I received it and carried it with me, precious and unforgettable. But one can only remember such things, not write of them. How may a stranger to these imperial looks know them from eyes of other mortals?

NOTES

Lady Ottoline Violet Anne Morrell (1873–1938) was the leader and patroness of a bohemian and intellectual circle which included Bertrand Russell, D. H. Lawrence (who portrayed her as Hermione in *Women in Love*), W. B. Yeats, T. S. Eliot, Augustus John and Virginia Woolf. Lord David Cecil wrote of her that 'she was a character of Elizabethan extravagance and force, at once mystical and possessive, quixotic and tempestuous; . . . her own personality was, in its way, a considerable work of art, expressing alike in her conversation, her dress, and the decoration of her houses, a fantastic, individual, and creative imagination'. In 1902 she married Philip Morrell, Liberal MP (1906–18). Lady Ottoline's first visit to Conrad occurred in early August 1913.

1. Joseph Conrad, *Some Reminiscences* (London: Eveleigh Nash, 1912), later issued as *A Personal Record*.
2. For details of Desmond MacCarthy, see p. 35.
3. Borys Conrad, the elder son, was fifteen years of age at this time.
4. Conrad wrote three short stories ('The Idiots', 'The Lagoon' and 'An Outpost of Progress') during his six-month honeymoon in Brittany, 1896.
5. Mary Catharine Inge, daughter of H. M. Spooner, Archdeacon of Maidstone, niece of W. A. Spooner, wife of W. R. Inge, Dean of St Paul's Cathedral.
6. Unidentified review.
7. Bertrand Russell (1872–1970), the philosopher. He and Lady Ottoline were lovers at this time. The visit occurred in the September following Lady Ottoline's first visit.
8. Lady Ottoline and her husband were pacifists, and they made their home a refuge for conscientious objectors during the First World War.
9. Bernard Henry Holland (1856–1926), barrister and man of letters, lived in Canterbury. This visit occurred in autumn 1923, at Conrad's home, Oswalds, in Bishopsbourne, Kent.
10. Conrad claimed to have seen the sea for the first time from the Lido in Venice in the summer of 1873, during a visit to Switzerland and Italy undertaken for the sake of his health.
11. For details of Marseilles and the Carlists, see p. 180.
12. Conrad arrived at Lowestoft in the *Mavis*, setting foot on English soil for the first time on 10 June 1878.

13. Roger David Casement (1864–1916) travelled widely in Africa as a young man, and later served as British Consul in Mozambique, Angola and the Congo Free State. In 1903 he produced a damning report on the atrocities in the Congo. He was knighted in 1911 for his services to the Crown.

Conrad met Casement in June 1890 during his trip to the Congo, where Casement was supervising the building of a railway. They shared a room for some days and made several expeditions into the nearby villages in search of native porters. Conrad noted in his diary at the time that he had 'Made the acquaintance of Mr Roger Casement, which I should consider as a great pleasure under any circumstances and now it becomes a positive piece of luck. Thinks, speaks well, most intelligent and very sympathetic.'

Born in Dublin of Protestant parents, he became an extreme Irish nationalist, and during the war he sought the aid of Germany in his pursuit of Irish independence. After landing in Ireland from a German submarine in 1916, he was arrested, convicted of high treason and executed.

14. Conrad's visit to Poland in 1914 is described on pp. 11–13.

'Reserves of caustic severity'*

DESMOND MACCARTHY

Did I know him? No; I only saw him once. I lunched with him and spent the afternoon one spring day four years ago. The orchards of Kent were in blossom, the poles of its hopfields bare when the train took me down to Canterbury. It was a drive of some miles from there to his new home,[1] a large, airy, Georgian rectory, a few strides from its church – one of those short, heavy-towered little country churches which lie like great grey dogs about the fields and among the trees of England. His face was already familiar to me, though he was among the least photographed, least paragraphed of celebrities, for, once seen, his photograph was not easy to forget. The length of his head from chin to crown struck me, and this was accentuated by a pointed greyish beard, which a backward carriage of his head on high shoulders projected forwards. Black eyebrows, hooked nose, hunched shoulders gave him a more hawk-like look than even his photograph had suggested. His eyes were very bright and dark when he opened them wide, but, unless lit and expanded by enthusiasm or indignation, they remained half-hidden, and as though filmed in a kind of abstruse

* From 'Literary Causerie: To a Distant Friend (VIII)', *Empire Review*, vol. XL (Sept. 1924) pp. 291–9.

slumberous meditation. Very quiet in voice and gesture, somewhat elaborate in courtesies, his manner was easy without being reassuring. He had the kind of manners which improve fifty per cent those of a visitor, whoever he or she may be. He was very much the *foreign* gentleman. He evidently expected others not only to respect his dignity (that went without saying) but their own. I surmised that, like his own people, the Poles, and like the Irish, he might be lavish in compliment, but that anyone would be a fool who did not divine that his delicious generous praise might hide reserves of caustic severity. Following the sea had not left a trace of bluffness in his manner. His talk was that of a man who cares for what is delicate, extreme and honourable in human nature – and for the art of prose. Intellectually, he seemed something of a Quietist; he did not enjoy provoking discussion. He praised, I remember, Henry James, and admiration in that direction might have been anticipated. For though the worlds of the two novelists were so different, their literary methods were not unlike, and again and again 'the point of honour' provided both with subjects; they had the same kind of devotion to their calling. His scorn, which in his seafaring days would have withered a slack-twisted officer whose heart was not in his ship, was ready now to strike the counterpart of such a character in the world of letters. Clearly, in life and literature *noblesse oblige* was Conrad's motto, and I doubt if he would have been able to decide which of the two, life or literature, subjected men to the more stringent tests. It was evidently a necessary passport to his literary esteem to be able to write a fine sentence.

Though it would be absurd on the strength of an hour or two of desultory conversation, part of which was in French (a French lady was present), to pronounce upon his literary preferences; still I did get an impression that originality of mind in an author counted for little with him if unaccompanied by an aesthetic sense. Perhaps, however, this is really a deduction (and a fairly safe one) from his own writing, which shows so strong a love of the sentence engraved as with a ring. He would have understood Henry James's pathetic cry, 'I have sweated blood to give an amusing surface to my style!' I expect Conrad 'sweated blood', too, in the same endeavour, so laudable, so often, too, a waste of pains! – and on the top of that he was impelled as well to attempt himself an intenser vividness in description. Try, just try, describing something so that the inattentive reader must see it and the attentive one can never forget he has seen it. You will find it an exhausting task – especially if you are also determined your sentences shall run sonorously and gracefully. The easiest half of his life was that he spent at sea, hard though that was.

I remember thinking it characteristic that he should have expressed disgust at an eminent author, remarkable for gay candour, because on his first visit he had described how his father had taken to drink. This appeared to have shocked Conrad both as a sign of insensibility in his visitor and as a breach of good manners, their relations not warranting such confidences. More obviously characteristic, too, was his remark when, after lunch, he hobbled with me up a paddock avenue of elms. He stopped – the spring wind was fluttering the daffodils at their roots and roaring in their budding tops – lifted his face, and said: 'I walk here for the sake of that sound; it reminds me of the sea.' This peaceful nook in Kent did not seem his natural home; nor in the neat, white, quiet rooms did I perceive the impress of his peculiar personality – a sailor's tidiness, cleanliness, perhaps; nothing more.

NOTES

Sir Desmond MacCarthy (1877–1952), literary and dramatic critic. At the time of his visit to Conrad in the spring of 1920, MacCarthy was literary editor of the *New Statesman*, and he later became senior literary critic on *The Sunday Times*, writing weekly articles for the paper from 1928 until his death. A friend of the Bloomsbury group, he gained wider recognition through his journalism and broadcasting. One of the best conversationalists of his day, he described himself as a hero-worshipper in temperament, except when he was writing. He was knighted in 1951.

1. The Conrads had moved to Oswalds, Bishopsbourne, Kent, in October 1919.

Joseph Conrad at Home in England*

S. KARRAKIS

A five minute ride on the switch-off of the main line from Canterbury brought me to the trundling little town in which rests Oswalds, his estate. Visitors are few. And strangers can learn nothing about him from the globular station agent or from the twin spinster sister postmistresses, who, with their centenarian mother, monopolise the

* From 'Joseph Conrad at Home in England', *Poland*, vol. v (April 1924) pp. 225–8, 247–8.

local shopping marts. Sighting a man across the field I called to him. He knew there were two boys, one at work in London, the younger playing at farming and he pointed to a hillock behind which he went on to say was the farm. No, he couldn't say anything about their father. 'He's a writing man', was the sum of his knowledge. No, he had not read his writings. No one I approached in the village had read his writings, and I thought of the prophet who remained a stranger to those about him. On a bulletin board on the rear wall of the church I saw his name among others listed for parish duty of a sort, the sun had bleached the writing into invisibility almost.

My pilgrimage that afternoon was for information about him. All I had learned was negligible for my purposes. To get at the man was quite impossible through his neighbours. From the Falstaff Hotel in Canterbury I dispatched a special messenger on bicycle with a note requesting an interview. The answer was an invitation for three o'clock the following day. I was to stay for tea, too.

That day, seeing the man in the doorway, I said to myself, 'That's the man.'

He came into the room to his wife's side and raised a pleasant countenance, genial though disturbed, with that beard pointed ahead of him, and attempted an unpained salutation.

'How do you do!'

'I am here as you see, sir.'

He looked quizzically at me: I was not an unpleasant face to look at, and if the tenor of my note belied my appearance, I think the novelty delighted him, as many things I said did.

'I am sitting for an etching,' he referred with his hand, crooking the fingers, to indicate the place outside.

'Can we talk freely before the artist?' I was anxious to waste no time!

I did not know then why he received me so coldly. Showing me the way he allowed me to precede him, but caught up with me before I reached the path and said, 'I had the letter from Captain Bone. We are great friends. I do not see him often.' Then it was I noticed a certain hesitancy in his speech, not to eliminate the foreign accent which is not too pronounced, but as if selecting his words, conserving their use in conversation, as he is wont to elaborate their use in his writings. The artist was introduced and I was asked to comment on the sketch in the rough line. I begged off saying it was too early both in the sketch and our acquaintance for fair comment – perhaps later. At that point his wife came into this portico and rested on a *chaise-longue*. He took up his pose again in the high-backed straight chair and showed the artist three-quarters of his face. It was in that attitude that I had my opportunity to study those features.

The high cheek bones and hollows beneath them were covered with a transparent skin underneath which a fine network of veins blushed and blanched, the perfect barometer of his emotions and thoughts. All through our conversation I used that network of veins as guide, for pained as he was with my visit he was quick to irritation with what I came to urge from him. I write 'urge' advisedly because he had already written me, in no uncertain words he would not countenance what I had done without having beforehand advised him of my intention.

The greater part of three hours he posed in that chair except for interruptions to see how the half-finished sketch would look behind a frame or to ask me if I preferred to take a turn about the estate with his secretary who had but a few minutes before returned from a motor trip in his car. He was at perfect ease despite the necessity to hold the same position for the artist and to answer my talk. When I began to relate how it was that I 'dared' (the word had been his) to dramatise his novel *Under Western Eyes*, his interest in what I had to say changed. . . .

'I have come across the sea with no other purpose than to present my dramatisation to you in person.' I waited to hear him speak.

'It is my story,' he claimed indignantly.

'I have no wish to claim them as my own. I met them, as people meet, through your story. They attached themselves to me, clung to me, bound themselves to me. They wanted a medium for re-creation. They came to me for rebirth in dramatic form.'

'But you have used my words and my plot and my story. I don't grudge you the originality of your conception. I won't have you taking the words of my book. I laboured over those words until no other would fit the thought. It is as if the story and characters and the words were one, inseparable, indivisible.' . . .

'You have come on a hopeless mission,' he blanched as he thrust his characters back into the printed page there to be two-dimensional forevermore. . . .

Thus my play was never done on the stage. The characters come to me now and then and urge me to open negotiations with him again. I say no, for to have sat under his gaze for three hours and to have wielded words and arguments and logic and rights with him exhausted me for many days to come. There was something diabolical about him which did not make you fear him, yet sapped your vitality as if you had been on a spree – this time a mental spree.

Pole, with a long line of literary and astute lineage behind him, the summation of his people's genius a part of his own genius, he left his homeland, the soil itself, for two score years at sea. They were battering years, years rumbled and roved, years chuck full of hellish escapes and devilish intrusions into hopeless wastes of water and men, black and white and yellow, and years crowded with festering experiences which luckily did not corrupt him but, mellowing in his memory, served as the wells into which he dipped his pen and wrote. It was a curious process which settled the ugliness of those experiences into the bottom of the wells of memory, and what he brought forth shone more effulgently. And as his genius urged him to take up a career on the sea so it led him to return to the soil and to write.

I learned at tea, served in the dining room, what manner of woman his wife was. The table was plain but wholesome, with all of the baked foods home-made under her personal supervision. He displayed an unusual interest in the foods we Americans eat. Chop Suey symbolised for him the American way of oddly enough caricaturing a strange nation and then feeding upon the caricatured concoction with every evidence of relishing it. He thought us a purposeful country, whatever that finite purpose being still a matter of conjecture, but inquisitive enough to leave no undiscovered foot of soil. The Mississippi basin was to him a fascinating stretch of topography with unlimited possibilities. Somehow, the conversation returned to foods again – conversations often run in cycles – and a remark I made indicated to him the range of my experiences.

'You have never been hungry.' And I wondered what pangs of hunger made his assertion so poignant. Perhaps part of the thought was his recollection of his grand-uncle, Mr Nicholas B., who 'remains for me the unfortunate and miserable (but heroic) being who once upon a time had eaten a dog.'[1]

At another pause in the table talk he passed me the buttered bread. I said he must one day come to America. In all those years at sea he had never shipped to an American port. He answered he should like the trip but did not suppose he would ever make it. Of course he has since been to New York.[2]

He seldom goes to the theatre in England. While he was collecting material for *The Rover*, he spent some days in Paris,[3] and in the evenings saw several plays there. But his wife was a regular patron of the playhouse in Folkestone. He said he wished to write for the theatre one day.[4] Perhaps he would dramatise his novels.

The tea was over. We trailed into the drawing-room where the artist had placed the finished etching behind a glass and in a frame, and hung it modestly on the wall. It was a fine likeness and now we were all willing to express our delight to the artist. He was pleased. In the garden we picked some wall pears. They were to be packed for the artist and myself to be delivered to us when we should leave.

I stood alongside of my host and for the first time I realised how tall he must have been as a youth. Again I broached the purpose of my visit and with a decisive 'I will not allow it' I knew he must be determined for ever. He did, however, appreciate my insistence for his consent and suggested that I might get some ray of hope from his literary agent, Mr Pinker.[5] I accepted the cue. And for the rest of the afternoon we talked lightly about literature, politics, history; but never again mentioned the dramatisation.

So the visit to Joseph Conrad ended and in his motor, the artist and I were run to the station at East Canterbury, from which point we took the train for London.

NOTES

S. Karrakis, a Russo-American writer and journalist, visited Conrad in August 1921. David Bone (see p. 167) had earlier written to Conrad about Karrakis, who had dramatised *Under Western Eyes* as a stage play and had sailed from America on Bone's ship to submit it to Conrad for his approval. On receiving Bone's letter, Mrs Conrad later told him, Conrad 'continued brushing his hair fiercely for at least ten minutes'. Conrad wrote to Bone after meeting Karrakis and told him that 'I am very sorry that Mr K. should have taken this trouble. Of all my novels this, especially, is the one I do not want anybody to touch. If there is ever any adaptation it will be done by myself.'

1. Joseph Conrad, *A Personal Record* (London: J. M. Dent, 1946) p. 32. For a note on Nicholas B., see p. 53.
2. Conrad went to the United States in 1923.
3. Possibly this refers to Conrad's three-day stay in Marseilles in January 1921, during the writing of *Suspense*.
4. Conrad had in fact completed his dramatisation of *The Secret Agent* the previous year.
5. Karrakis did submit the play to J. B. Pinker, Conrad's agent, but to no avail.

We Visit Joseph Conrad*

HAMLIN GARLAND

We found Conrad's home to be a suburban cottage on the edge of a park in Bishopsbourne some six or eight miles to the eastward.[1] It was a quaint and shapeless structure, one that had just grown from an old cottage into a modern two-storey house. In front of it is a hedge and a

* From *My Friendly Contemporaries: A Literary Log* (New York: Macmillan, 1932) pp. 490–5.

circular lawn, and its doorway is most hospitable. It has no outlook, however – its seat is in a valley – and I could not associate Conrad, the sea rover, with it. It is a quiet, secluded village.[2]

As for Conrad, I had in mind a rather tall, austere, reserved man, one whose words were few and chosen with care – and when he came bustling out to meet us, I was amazed. He is short, broad-shouldered and grey-haired. His body radiates energy. His arms fly about like flails. His face was alight with welcome and his words came mumbling, tumbling out. He was altogether continental. He gesticulated like a Polish Jew, but his speech was filled with cockney accents. He said 'trine' for train and 'grite' for great. He was as gallant as a Frenchman as he greeted my daughter. He was swift, unresting and confused, yet sincerely cordial.

His volubility and his Polish accent, joined with his cockney pronunciation of words, made him utterly incredible. For a time I could only gaze and listen, struggling to readjust my concepts of him. To complete my confusion he fumbled in his vest pocket and produced a single English eyeglass which he nervously screwed into one eye.

He seemed moved by our visit. 'It is good of you to come all this way to see me. I have written for years with the thought in my mind, "What will Hamlin Garland think of my books?" but I had given up all hope of seeing you.'

This remark amazed me. I had never known that he was even aware of my existence. I replied, 'I have read you for more than twenty years – ever since Stephen Crane[3] wrote advising me to read *The Nigger of the "Narcissus"*. I particularly enjoyed *Nostromo*.' This pleased him, but he confessed that he knew very little of South America. 'I wrote it from material acquired elsewhere.'

Speaking of his house, he said, 'I have been here only three years, but I have lived in or near Bishopsbourne for thirty years. I am a Kentishman.' As he said this, he expressed himself as an Oriental and not as a Nordic. He made it plain that he, too, is a solitary. 'I know few of my fellow authors. I meet few people of any kind. I seldom go to London; the truth is, I am afraid to go – my doctor warns me that my heart is weak. My wife, poor thing, must needs go along.' This was in reference to her wounded knee which made it necessary for her to sit with her leg outstretched upon a chair. She is a large, fair woman, kindly and watchful. She is the mother of two sons, but Joseph is her unceasing care. She is wholly English, but has no pronounced accent of any kind.

Conrad talked freely, volubly of his early experiences. He told of going to sea as a common sailor, of being promoted to third officer, of winning command of a merchant ship at the age of twenty-eight.[4] 'I went round the world in these capacities. I traded in Burma, India, and the Congo. I was one of the first to know the Congo. I sailed up the great rivers of the Orient. There's where I got my material for *Almayer's Folly* and *Lord Jim*. I began to write while still a sailor. I began *Almayer's Folly* with no thought of its being published. I knew nothing of book publishing. I wrote part of it in a lodging in London and I carried the manuscript with me. I worked on it from time to time on several voyages, but had no hope of its getting into print, till one day in London as I was passing Fisher Unwin's publishing house I saw displayed several small-size volumes. "By Jove," I said, "my book would go into that set." I sent the manuscript to them. Three months went by. Not a word! Then one day a letter came, a typewritten letter, the first I had ever seen. It was from the publishers offering to take the book.'[5]

After a moment's pause he said with a touch of retrospective emotion, 'The writing of that story gave me more pleasure and satisfaction than anything I have done since. It was a novel experience. I took pleasure in every line; now, I am tired of writing. I groan and creak and swear as I crowd myself to the task.'

To lighten the momentary gloom, I asked, 'Aren't you coming to America?'

He shook his head rather sadly. 'No, I am afraid to go. I am not well enough to stand the strain.'[6] In answer to my statement, 'You have a loyal friend in Doubleday,'[7] he replied sharply, 'He is a good business man. I do not believe in mixing sentiment with business. Doubleday would not publish my books if he did not expect to make money. Publishers do not permit friendship to come into the making of contracts.'

Returning to *The Nigger of the 'Narcissus'*, he said, 'America would not buy a book about niggers, so my publishers changed the title to *Children of the Sea*. I accepted the change. I was in no situation to object. I had no success with any book till I sold a serial to *Hearst's Magazine*.[8] My friends were shocked, but I had no scruples; I was spoiling the Egyptians. Since then I have lived comfortably, but not, as you see, lavishly.'

He took us out to see his gardens. 'I have a tree that was a well-grown sapling when Queen Elizabeth visited Canterbury. I go every day to make my devotions to him.'

It was in truth a noble monument to England's past. As we stood looking at it he said, 'See how he clutches the earth. His roots are like the claws of a colossal lion. I bought this place to please my wife. She loves trees and flowers.'

I said, 'It seems a singular home for an old sea rover.'

This he admitted. 'Yes, but it is the only home I shall ever have. My powers are failing – I am fully aware of that. I save myself in every possible way, for I have two or three more books to write. I need the money. One of my sons is still at school and my poor wife is a cripple. She must be provided for. These are the reasons why I seldom leave my house. Nevertheless I am coming to London to see your family.'

I understood his feeling. He no longer writes with an exultant sense of power. Like all his contemporaries, he is a machine running down. He acknowledged a sense of weakness, of apprehension. 'I feel worked out,' he said, and he is. The world already has the best of him. In explanation of his spoken English, he said, 'While I converse, as you see, without hesitation, I am not, even now, absolutely sure of my English. My writing is based on the dictionary.' To this I replied, 'That is what gives it distinction and charm. It is entirely free from worn-out forms.'

As he grew more confidential, he confessed that he took no joy in his lovely home. 'It has no outlook, no horizon. It is a hole – for me. My wife loves it and so – I stay. It is no place for a seafaring man. I can see nothing but fields and a wall of woods.'

I spoke of Kipling's valley farm and he retorted, 'Yes, he is in a similar hole.'[9] He shrugged his shoulders in a continental gesture. 'However, I live and write. In imagination I am still on the sea.'

Like others of us he is going on with fixed purpose, grinding out copy in a last desperate spurt. He calls his trouble 'gout', but one does not die of gout. His fear of sudden death is due to some organic weakness of his heart.

To hear this rugged old sea dog who had weathered a thousand storms confess that he dared not spend a night away from his home was pitiful. 'I have a horror of falling sick in a hotel,' he confessed. There was little of the triumphant novelist about him. He seemed an anxious, hard-working professional man, a man who must keep going no matter how he suffers. This may be a pose, but if so it was most convincing. As Hewlett[10] said, 'I am a burned-out volcano,' so Conrad was confessing to a similar failure of creative energy. He indicated that he had had several seizures. 'I have lost confidence in the old machine,' he said.

In several ways he was unmistakably continental. He continually interrupted me, piling his own observations upon the back of mine. It was not precisely discourteous nor was it egoistic; it was in the habit of his race. By contrast with Kipling, Barrie, Galsworthy, Shaw (for Shaw can listen patiently) he was essentially European.

NOTES

Hamlin Garland (1860–1940), novelist and chronicler of the Middle Border, was born in Wisconsin and grew up in Iowa. He was best known for his stories which give a realistic and sombre portrayal of frontier life with its unrewarding toil and ceaseless struggle for survival. He met Conrad for the first time when he visited him at Oswalds in August 1922, accompanied by his daughter, Isabel.

1. East of Canterbury.
2. Oswalds was nearly a century old when the Conrads moved there in October 1919. The largest house that Conrad ever lived in, it was set in a hollow surrounded by woods, and the only distant view was of a cemetery.
3. For a note on Crane, see p. 188.
4. Conrad first sailed as third mate in the *Loch Etive*, on a round trip from Tilbury to Sydney, August 1880–April 1881. His first command was the *Otago* in 1888, when he was thirty years of age.
5. The writing and publication of *Almayer's Folly* are explained on pp. 74–6.
6. Conrad in fact did visit America the following year.
7. Frank N. Doubleday, publisher.
8. This puzzling remark is perhaps a reference to the serialisation in 1912 of *Chance* in the New York *Herald* (Magazine Section), owned by Harper's.
9. Rudyard Kipling lived at Bateman's, Burwash, Sussex.
10. Maurice Henry Hewlett (1861–1923), author and critic.

Conrad, the Man*

GRACE WILLARD

The world knew him as Joseph Conrad, author of many imaginative, beautifully written books more or less about the sea. To the rest of us he was simply 'J.C.', or 'Conrad', most brilliant and stimulating of companions, rarest of friends. Stephen Crane called him 'Joseph'. No one else ever did. Conrad didn't like 'Joseph'; but he liked Crane. It was all right.[1]

Less than a fortnight ago 'J.C.' sat in the drawing-room of his English country house,[2] smoking cigarettes (rather, abstractedly lighting them), sipping black coffee, talking, and with equal grace listening.

It was a charming room, with an Aubusson carpet, Second Empire furniture, a large mural painting, Adam period, of the fabled father presenting his sons with the bundle of faggots, and a grand piano.

* *New York Evening Post Literary Review* (9 Aug. 1924) p. 952.

Conrad liked these things. He liked green; he liked the music of Chopin.[3] There was always the chance that some one – Mr John Powell, possibly M. Paderewski[4] – would come down and play for him. French windows brought into the room the beauty of late twilight in an old park with cattle in the distance and elms.

Conrad was in the vein that night. He illuminated French poetry; a new star had just sent him his initial blaze of verse. But Paul Valéry was the first poet in France; everywhere else, for that matter.[5] *Un vrai.* He admiringly dissected Chesterton, who 'for once and with great difficulty had succeeded in being dull' in a recent essay.[6] With nicety he placed Mr Aldous Huxley as a poet.[7]

Speaking of Huxley reminded an English novelist who was present of a meeting with Sir Edward (now Earl) Grey at the Savoy Hotel. Sir Edward had said that he liked Mr Phillips Oppenheim's stories because he always brought the Savoy into them.[8] Oppenheim, in turn, reminded Conrad of America and his trip there. He had intended if ever he crossed the Atlantic, he said, to see the Mississippi River and the Kentucky mountains; to look at them, then to come back home. Instead he saw only New York, Boston and Concord. But Concord, he thought, might compensate one for missing our best river and our bluest hills. And then he described 'the most terrifying experience of his life'.

'It was the night I had promised to read from *The Rescue* in a New York ballroom filled with people. A ballroom like the nave of a cathedral. I was horribly frightened. I thought I was going to faint.'[9]

He threw back his head and laughed at the memory of a dear old gentleman who listened deferentially, with his hand at his ear. Conrad was paralysed (his own word) by such grave concentration and by the presence of many beautiful ladies. But gradually his stage fright left him; he ended by greatly enjoying himself. Everybody was so kind. For a shy man, Conrad thought America, in general, an ideal spot. No one ever stared. We were a tactful people.

And now the twilight has shortened; and for those who used to go down to the old cathedral town, drawn by the magic of 'J.C.'s' brilliant, eager talk, for the Canterbury pilgrims there is an unexpected emptiness in life.

For Joseph Conrad had [as in dedication, he said of his California friend, Miss Tobin[10]] a genius for friendship. A man of extreme reserve and of a certain old world formality, yet to his friends, once the bond was established, he gave himself generously and simply. He had a way in friendship, as in other affairs, of doing things *en prince*. His time, his interest, his house and purse, too, if need be, were yielded to those whom he liked, believed in and whom he felt that he might help. There was a spilt wine lavishness, in Galsworthy's phrase, about the man's nature. One feels this in his books. Young writers, young artists in all fields, regarded him with immense admiration, and from all directions came their homage. He liked youth, too; and how often has he not helped them to success by his kindliness, by the charm and wisdom of his counsel? For some reason he did not quite fancy being called '*Cher Maître*'. For exuberant novices the phrase had a fatal attraction.

His friends came to him almost wholly through his writing. His dislike of towns, crowds, strange people, his shyness, his dread of being fatigued and bored, made of him a recluse all his English life. London drawing rooms saw him rarely. But the man's extraordinary interest for people, the mystery his personality excited, brought the world to him whenever he would let it come. He sought seclusion always, and had it, on sea and land. But he was at heart immensely fond of congenial society and when it came to him on his own terms he revelled in it. Moreover, he had all the ancient Polish spirit of hospitality. Conrad's house, down among the hop vines of Kent – he liked Kentish people and was faithful to the county through three moves – became a Mecca for bookish travellers from America and the Continent, and the week-end rendezvous of a small, exclusive coterie of literary London. Everybody 'wanted to meet Conrad'. His post was full of social pleas. Obviously he could not receive all, nor anything like all; but it will be remembered that, rivalling his welcome in perfection, was the courteousness of his infinite regret.

One could not speak of delightful days with Conrad without paying tribute to the writer's remarkable wife. It was she who contributed the magic oil necessary to running happily the household of a genius. To her, too, was due much of Conrad's success, as he has been heard to say again and again. It was Mrs Conrad who from the first recognised that a Conrad MS was something distinctly worth saving, worth selling. Her unflagging courage, serenity and devotion, her many-sided helpfulness – this was a most touching thing. Conrad had a finely attuned sense of domestic life. One must perceive this from the delicacy and restraint with which he wrote of his father and mother in *A Personal Record*. His comradeship with his own boys was especially close.

Sunday luncheon at Oswalds (Papa Ibsen, as Conrad always called him, is evoked by the name of the Georgian manor house where Conrad spent the last seven years of his life)[11] was often the occasion for such a cosmopolitan coming together as 'J.C.' liked. An eminent London editor, perhaps; an American Ambassador, a Swedish prima donna, a Polish statesman, a sculptor *quelconque*, a painter, and always a writer, potential and promising, or arrived and analytical, might be found in this week-end group. Simple, unembarrassed, gay, Conrad was mine host *par excellence*.

The author's reserve, with him a sacred thing, was the most serious barrier between him and the indiscriminate world that loves a lion.

People did not always grasp quickly enough that Conrad disliked intensely to be asked about his work, to discuss his method of writing, or to be pinned down as to which was his favourite among his books. Innocent ones were apt to rush headlong into this pitfall. He might reveal things about himself, his novels and his craft to a few chosen intimates. But he was not expansive to others. He did not have a trace of the *salon* habit of talking about himself. He had less professional vanity, I think, than any great writer who ever lived. He had so little, indeed, that he did not especially demand that a person should have read Conrad or should like him enthusiastically to be *persona grata* with him. His theory that nothing one read was of any value unless one read for sheer love and rapture has its happy side.

But it was not in the green drawing-room; it was in the study that the unforgettable hours with his friends were passed. In the study (*The Arrow of Gold* was the great book written here;[12] for this Conrad had a curious affection; there was in it so much of himself when young), a room literally walled with books, his own polyglot favourites and the autographed firsts of the many writers who were his friends – in the study Conrad became most completely 'J.C.'. He had a way of dropping into French as soon as the study door was closed. Conrad, in form, talked wonderfully here, oblivious to time. It was a quaint affectation of Conrad's to disclaim, not without a slight contempt, being a 'literary' or a 'cultured' person. But his knowledge of books was, of course, immense; he had extraordinary freshness of impression and a memory like the morning. Not fruitlessly had he for years, 'a perfectly obscure person', as he described himself, spent his shore leave in libraries and made of his ship cabin a little *bibliothèque nationale*.[13] Talk ran far into the night then, fortified by relays of Russian tea and biscuits – and everything else. Conrad, a sybarite himself, liked everybody near him to have just what he wished.

During the last year white nights in the study became rarer. 'J.C.' seemed a weary, at times almost a vanquished, man. His old gaiety flashed less often. His wonderful laugh rang but seldom. He liked to call himself 'an old crock' – and to be contradicted. Writing, never with him a glib and easy art, became a burden.

Paradoxically, Conrad was an indoor man. No one ever saw him take any exercise. Did he pace the ship in the old days as sailors are thought to do? He never walked in the garden. It was a lovely garden, too; old, square, with much ancient box and plums ripening on rose-brick walls. I doubt if he cared for 'nature'. He disliked flowers in the house. The human comedy, observed as an analyst, interested him; the drama of souls. And that was almost all.

If he went abroad he motored. Sometimes in the old days he drove the car himself. It was an experience not without a thrill of peril for others. But Conrad enjoyed it. He drove fast, rather fantastically, but with complete joy. Now and then he would shout strange things in Polish to deliberate hens or silly Kentish sheep. Simple things amused him.

And less than a fortnight ago he was in his old, charming humour. 'Twenty-four Conrads,' some one said, glancing along a bookshelf with an evocative fleet of names. 'I must make it a round twenty-five,' said 'J.C.', 'and then –'

He did not finish the sentence. His eyes, with a sudden sombreness, sought the twilight spaces of the old park with cattle in the distance and elms, and rested there.

NOTES

Grace Willard was an old friend of the Conrads. She helped to furnish and decorate their homes (apparently her professional occupation). Borys Conrad remembered her and her daughter Catherine thus: 'It was during our tenancy of Spring Grove [1919] that an American lady and her daughter became frequent visitors. I have no knowledge of the circumstances under which they came to be included among our circle of friends and I think the first contact must have been made when I was in hospital or, possibly, still in France [1918]. Mrs Grace Willard – she was a widow – and her daughter Catherine, then about seventeen were very charming, but I have never been able to understand why they were upon such intimate terms with my parents. Catherine always called her mother 'Mama Grace' and it was not long before she was so addressed by all of us. . . . Mama Grace seemed to occupy most of her time in searching out various pieces of antique furniture, also old silver and cut glass, most of which she succeeded in selling to J.C. – he had a strain of the collector in him – and I am pretty certain that Mama Grace's income depended to a considerable extent upon these transactions' (*My Father: Joseph Conrad* (London: Calder & Boyars, 1970) pp. 138–9).

1. See p. 188 for details of Crane.

2. Oswalds, Bishopsbourne, near Canterbury, was Conrad's home for the last five years of his life.

3. Frédéric Chopin (1810–49) was a fellow Pole.

4. John Powell (1882–1963) was an American pianist and composer. Conrad met him in 1913, and during one visit Powell played Chopin for hours. Ignace Jan Paderewski (1860–1941) was a Polish pianist and composer who became Prime Minister of Poland in 1919. Conrad met him in America in 1923 and admired him enormously.

5. Paul Valéry (1871–1945).

6. G. K. Chesterton (1874–1936), novelist and critic. The recent dull essay may be *The End of the Roman Road*, published in March 1924.

7. Aldous Huxley (1894–1963) published four volumes of poetry between 1916 and 1920.

8. Edward Phillips Oppenheim (1866–1946) was a prolific and popular writer of thrillers.
9. On 10 May 1923, during a visit to New York, Conrad gave a reading from *Victory* (not *The Rescue*) before two hundred invited guests.
10. Agnes Tobin, a minor American poet, met Conrad in 1911, and his dedication to her in *Under Western Eyes* records her 'genius for friendship'.
11. Oswald Alving is a character in Ibsen's *Ghosts*.
12. *The Arrow of Gold* was in fact written while Conrad was living at Capel House.
13. 'National Library'.

More about Conrad*

GRACE WILLARD

Many who read 'Conrad, the Man' in the *Literary Review* of 9 August [1924] have asked for further reminiscences. It is an honour to share with others memories of this strangely fascinating genius whose friendship left one so rich in memories.

My first impression of Conrad is coloured by a brilliant January day with snow all over the fields of Kent. He greeted me in a little room with an open fire, and we sipped mulled claret and talked about *The Golden Bowl*, which had just come out[1] (Henry James was one of his earliest English loves), and Miss Ellen Glasgow, and Dostoevsky.[2]

'How can Western minds hope to understand Dostoevsky,' he said, a little scornfully; 'he reverences things which they hold in contempt and treats with contempt much that they reverence.'

We talked of Marseilles, his favourite among the ports of the world. The most dashing hours of his youth had been spent there. They called him *L'ami* at Marseilles in 1880.[3]

L'ami he remained, in the finest sense. It was Conrad's humanity, so profoundly expressed in his books, that made knowing him a great adventure. He understood life, how baffling it could be, its power to bruise or to break. He never lost sight of the inexorableness of temperament, nor of the ironic fact that fate, intransigent, tracks us from the cradle to the grave, do what we may. And he brought to his contact with human beings struggling against these forces an imagination and a passion for justice of the highest nobility. People often have not failed when the world judges them failures. Conrad's

* *New York Evening Post Literary Review* (30 Aug. 1924) p. 9.

books are full of these contradictions, and they were also among his friends. The malice of circumstance, and its victims, peculiarly haunted him.

'Winnie Verloc' (*The Secret Agent*), overcome by her terrible destiny through agencies wholly outside her own placid life, was, I think, almost his favourite among his own women characters. Rita, in *The Arrow of Gold*, came first, perhaps – there were autobiographical reasons for this[4] – but 'Winnie' is more poignantly flesh and blood.

Happily for the magic of his sympathy, Conrad wore no disconcerting halo. As Marlow said of Lord Jim, 'he was one of us'.[5] By nature extremely impatient, he suffered fools with effort. To many faults more than a little kind, he could not forgive intellectual sins. Pretentiousness met in him a foe without quarter. His admiration for Russian literature was compelled (the word is just; Conrad remained a Pole at heart) by the intellectual honesty of Russian writers.

He carried his dislike of pose and pretence so far that it determined his enthusiasms and fixed his attitude toward the world in general. Individuality he sought as a man hunting for precious gems. And when he found it he bound its possessor to him with something stronger than those hoops of brass which Horace mentions.[6]

'I like the man from *there*,' said J.C. He emphasised the 'there'. He had just parted with a quaint type from Georgia who had delighted him by the way he brought to Conrad's door the speech, the atmosphere, the very hum of the bees around the corn in the far-off, little country village where he lived, and where 'he had developed a point of view', Conrad added, delightfully. (The unlikeliest persons, often not literary in the least, read Conrad and found some way of telling him how much they liked his people. There was the Virginia farmer who sent him a barrel of Albermarle pippins every year; and every year or so Conrad would send him a book, generously inscribed: 'Art for apples is not a bad exchange.')

'A point of view.' Whatever else one had, or lacked, this touch was necessary to comradeship with Conrad. It was the Needle's Eye to his esteem. I can see now a little drawing-room with a group of people, more or less distinguished, and Conrad, silent, rather forbidding, among them. Suddenly he vanished. He was found later sitting in a window-seat in another room in animated conversation with a young man of painful shyness and no distinction whatever.

J.C. explained that he had been obliged to run away because of the petrifying gaze of a lady, a poetess of the hour. 'She sat looking at me like a pythoness.' As for his companion of the window-seat, he was enchanted with him. 'He has a point of view.' And the young man went away radiant – and poised. That was what Conrad's mind did to yours.

Once we drove over to Rye to see Henry James. (When Conrad came to own a Daimler, motoring delighted him. He liked comfort and things done quickly.) Afterwards, strolling out on one of the ancient ports J.C. fell into prolonged talk with an old sailor. He came back to the car flushed and excited. (He was always so when things pleased him.) '*Quel type*!' he cried; 'mate once on a sailing ship. He has been everywhere. In Malay, too.' He laughed. 'He got hold of a point of view out there. It was very funny.' I never learned what a Malay point of view was; but I felt more strongly than ever that a point of view of sorts one must have – even if he sailed the Seven Seas to get it.

Toward the work of other writers Conrad was cordial, with reservations. 'Derivative' literature he dismissed with indifference. A book, a writer so branded by him simply did not count. Pastiche in art annoyed him. Moreover he held with great tenacity that the individual quality in work entitled each to his own, unconfused place, higher or lower, but his own. He had an enormous admiration for Anatole France; yet an ominous look came into his eyes when he saw himself in print called 'the English Anatole France'.[7]

His respect for the imprint of originality made him impatient of changes in his own work when he knew that his instinct had been right. *The Nigger of the 'Narcissus'* (he had a great weakness for the *Nigger*. . . . 'One can't write a book like that twice', he said) was, he realised, a matchless title. In the first American edition it was changed to *Children of the Sea*. Though he recognised the reason for the change he suffered.[8]

He had the passion for liberty of the highly intellectual Pole. This gave him a definitely pronounced prejudice against certain popular tendencies to control. He viewed with mistrust, for example, the levelling march of village improvement societies in England. He could not believe that people would be any happier if coaxed from the plough or the 'pub', and taught Morris dances – and the benefits of stone ginger beer. And as for the people he cherished personal liberty as the breath of life, for the artist he insisted upon – with a vigour that had a stinging, salt spray tang in it – the most unfettered development, the most completely individual forging of his material.

Artistic cliques, 'precious' colonies, all organised influences of 'culture' were anathema to J.C. The message an artist has to deliver must be polished in secret; outside influences only crush distinctiveness, that fine flower. The ideal is not new (Flaubert, among others, advised ascetic lives that in art men might be violent) but Conrad upheld it with peculiar rigour.

I recall, *apropos*, a very young actress, the daughter of one of Conrad's friends,[9] in whose talent he believed. The girl was to play Lady Macbeth in London. Conrad, throwing himself into the affair as he would, sat up until three o'clock one night going over the scenes with her. Later it was proposed that the young actress place herself in the hands of a celebrated older actress to acquire technique. Conrad's scorn for this plan vibrates yet.

'What folly!' he exclaimed; 'you are not going to play the violin nor to sing Marguérite.[10] All that you have to offer is something within yourself, something that is yours alone. How do you know that Mme X. will not change this into something that isn't you? Something false, imitative, worthless. *Non, ma chérie*, from within must come your success – if it is to come. Keep away from the theatre. Study life – and yourself.'

The theory is interesting as Joseph Conrad's attitude towards the *feu sacré* (when found); screening from deflecting winds its faintest spark. His own life justified this doctrine of detachment. To him fame had come, as Victor Haldin wrote of Razumov in *Under Western Eyes*, in an existence 'unstained, lofty, and solitary'.[11]

He did not care for the play. 'I have too much imagination to sit through a modern comedy,' he said. The film he thought milk for very young children. A young novelist, of whom Conrad was very fond, said, mischieviously provocative, after hearing Conrad dispose of the cinema as '*bête*', 'The stupider it is the better I like it.' Conrad could be teased. He took nothing calmly.

Flashes of the man's gaiety and humour illuminate memories that he would not wish to be sad. At dinner one night in early July the talk ran on the Franco-Prussian War and the writers of that period. The salad came; with it Conrad dropped into French: '*Des tres belles contes ont été écrit à ce moment là*,' he went on; '*mais on ne les lit plus. Par exemple*, Sac au Dos *de Huysmans* –'[12]. He broke off suddenly and addressed himself to John the butler: '*Ecoutez, mon cher, on ne comprend pas la préparation du concombre à la cuisine*.'[13] John, pale, stooping, solicitous, looked alarmed, and Conrad recovered himself: 'The cucumber, *mon cher*, must be cut very thin, then soaked in salt water.' With a charming smile, 'Tell them, will you? *Very* thin.'

Somone remembered that at Hilaire Belloc's,[14] down in Sussex, the cucumber led the *hors d'oeuvres*, being brought in whole on a platter by itself and carved with great gusto by M. Belloc. Each person received a solidly generous segment. '*Ah, tout le monde ne sait pas ménager le concombre*,' said Conrad. '*Il faut y mettre de la subtilité*.'[15]

Without a trace of sentimentality in his nature Conrad had great tenderness and sentiment in matters relating to his own domestic life. Always on his desk stood a pair of red lacquer vases. 'My mother kept her crayons in them,' he explained. In an old-fashioned album in the drawing-room were pictures of his mother, who died, young and lovely, in Siberia, where she had followed his father in exile. Also pictures of

'Uncle Nicholas B.',[16] and of his many beautiful and aristocratic Polish cousins, and of Conrad himself as a very small boy, taken always with a fierce whip. He adored whips, and Uncle Nicholas B. bought him marvellous ones.

There is another picture of Conrad which will linger in my mind longest of all. It was during the dark days of the war and for a torturing interval Conrad had had no news whatever of his son at the front.[17] I had been at Capel House (the famous farm of earlier days), and was going back to London. Hunting up Conrad to say goodbye I saw him in his boy's room looking at the books, boyish books, taking one down and turning over the leaves, taking down another – as if it comforted him just to touch them. His hands trembled, his face was haggard with suspense and grief.

I left without speaking to him. All the way to the station I saw only the anguish in his eyes. A queer mist blurred my own. But it had begun to rain again; and I thought of how much harder that would make it for the men in Flanders.

NOTES

1. The first American edition of James's *The Golden Bowl* (New York: Charles Scribner's Sons) was published in November 1904, thus dating this first meeting in January 1905. (The first British edition (London: Methuen) was not until February 1905.)
2. Ellen Glasgow (1874–1945), American novelist.
3. Conrad spent some time in Marseilles between 1874 and 1878. *L'ami* means 'friend'.
4. Conrad's claims about the autobiographical nature of *The Arrow of Gold* (such as the love affair with 'Rita' and the duel) are now met with much scepticism.
5. Joseph Conrad, *Lord Jim* (London: J. M. Dent, 1946) p. 43.
6. In *Odes, Book I*, Ode III, Horace wrote:

   illi robur et aes triplex
   circa pectus erat, qui fragilem truci
   commisit pelago ratem
   primus, . . .

   (Oak and triple bronze must have girt the breast of him who first committed his frail bark to the angry sea.)

7. Anatole France (1844–1924), French novelist.
8. Dodd, Mead & Co., the publishers of *The Children of the Sea* (1897), had feared that the American public would not wish to buy the book with its original title.

9. Possibly the author's daughter, Catherine Willard, of whom Conrad was very fond.

10. The soprano in Gounod's *Faust.*

11. Joseph Conrad, *Under Western Eyes* (London: J. M. Dent, 1947) p. 135.

12. 'Very fine tales were written then, but they are no longer read. For example, *Sac au Dos* by Huysmans'. The French novelist, Joris Karl Huysmans (1848–1907), published *Sac au Dos* in 1880.

13. 'Listen, my dear, they do not understand the preparation of cucumber in the kitchen'.

14. Hilaire Belloc (1870–1953), poet and essayist.

15. 'Not everybody knows how to be sparing with cucumber . . . It has to be set with subtlety'.

16. Conrad's great-uncle Nicholas (Mikołaj) Bobrowski (1792–1864), of whom Conrad says in *A Personal Record* (London: J. M. Dent, 1946) that 'I knew, at a very early age, that my grand-uncle Nicholas B. was a knight of the Legion of Honour and that he had also the Polish Cross for valour, *Virtuti Militari.* [Yet] Mr Nicholas B. remains for me the unfortunate and miserable (but heroic) being who once upon a time had eaten a dog' (p. 32) to avoid starvation during Napoleon's retreat from Moscow.

17. Possibly this occurred in early January 1917, when Borys had been serving at Armentières. See C. T. Watts (ed.), *Joseph Conrad's Letters to R. B. Cunninghame Graham* (Cambridge: Cambridge University Press, 1969) p. 185.

Part III

Conrad and the Sea

Conrad: Two Biographical Episodes*

DOUGLAS HAMER

In 1929 or 1930 I lodged, while doing vacation research at the British Museum, with a family which had known Conrad from 1885 to 1894–5. My principal informant, Captain Arthur Burroughs, later of Elder Dempsters, made his first voyage as an apprentice, at the age of 15, in the full-rigged ship *Tilkhurst*[1] (Messrs W. R. Price of Austin Friars), Captain Blake[2] in command. Burroughs joined the ship at Penarth Docks, 2 June 1885, and the ship sailed on 10 June with a cargo of coal for Singapore.[3]

On going aboard, Burroughs, then a sickly boy sent to sea for his health, was asked by the ship's carpenter what *he* had come to sea for. To the reply, 'To be a sailor', the carpenter retorted that he would find a wooden box. This remark was overheard by Conrad, the second officer, who, with 'his courtesy and foreign manners', was also a contrast to the first mate, a gruff, foreboding man, to whose watch Burroughs was assigned. Conrad rounded on the carpenter.

There were no incidents on the voyage out, but on the voyage from Singapore to Calcutta in ballast a man went crazy and walked overboard.[4] Next day the men caught a shark which had been following the ship. Inside it they found the man's buttons. At Calcutta a cargo of jute was taken aboard for the voyage back to Dundee.[5] The round trip occupied thirteen months, and after his return Conrad took his master's certificate, but was never master of a ship.[6] Captain Blake died shortly after the return home. Conrad was described by Captain Burroughs as a good sailor, bearded, kind-hearted and with strong nerves. As second mate he was concerned with seamanship, not navigation.

Conrad was exceptionally kind to the young apprentice, who responded by taking Conrad home to see his widowed mother, whom I met on several occasions. She was then close on 86, the widow of a Lieutenant Burroughs who was one of the eight officers who stormed the Kashmir Gate, Delhi, during the Mutiny.[7] At the time she can only have been about thirteen, and so did not marry him until later.

* *Review of English Studies*, vol. XVIII (1967) pp. 54–6.

The daughters I met also remembered Conrad taking them on his knee.

Conrad frequently visited Mrs Burroughs down to 1894–5: he took a great liking to her. At her house he met a girl named Ida Knight, daughter of the Commissioner of Port Darwin, and for her he conceived considerable affection. She was then seventeen, but at about the same time Mrs Burroughs's youngest sister, Annette, twenty years her junior, also conceived a fondness for Conrad.[8] After a time the two girls quarrelled about Conrad, and did not speak to each other for several months. In consequence of Annette's jealousy Conrad ceased to go to the house, certainly for a time. He apparently still wanted to maintain the friendship with Mrs Burroughs, because some little time after the family moved from West Kensington a bearded man, whom they identified as Conrad, called at the house, and was distressed to find it empty.

Captain Burroughs took his master's ticket in 1894, and called on Conrad, receiving congratulations and 'what he would do for him', was patted on the back enthusiastically and reprimanded for going into steam. On the *Tilkhurst* Conrad had spent all his spare time writing, and Burroughs was not surprised when Contrad wished to present him with a signed copy of *Almayer's Folly* (1895) which, to his later regret, he declined. Mrs Burroughs continued to take an interest in Conrad's doings, and made a collection of cuttings about him, which she showed me, but she and Conrad never met again.

The above notes are taken from notes which I made at the time I met Mrs Burroughs and her family. The note on Contrad's 'strong nerves' contrasts with the report of John Sampson, Liverpool University Librarian, who, asked what Conrad was like (they had met a few months before Conrad died), replied: 'An old, querulous man, complaining of his digestion.'

NOTES

1. Conrad had joined the *Tilkhurst* as second officer in Hull on 24 April 1885, at £5 a month. This 1527-ton clipper was the largest sailing ship in which Conrad served. He sailed initially from Hull to Cardiff, where Burroughs joined the ship. During his five-day stay ashore (31 May–5 June), Conrad met Spiridion Kliszczewski and his family (see p. 88).

2. Edwin John Blake, aged forty-seven, the son of a Plymouth doctor. In *The Mirror of the Sea* (London: J. M. Dent 1946) Conrad recalled him as 'short, stout, dignified, perhaps a little pompous, he was a man of a singularly well-informed mind, the least sailor-like in outward aspect, but certainly one of the best seamen whom it has been my good luck to serve under' (p. 9). The

atmosphere in the ship must have been especially congenial, since only one member of the crew signed off at Singapore. On board the *Tilkhurst* was a fifty-four-year-old Irish illiterate, able seaman Daniel Sullivan, whom Conrad was to portray as the admirable Singleton in *The Nigger of the 'Narcissus'*.

3. The *Tilkhurst* reached Singapore on 22 September 1885, and left for Calcutta on 19 October.

4. One of the ship's crew, William Cumming, had received a blow on the head during a brawl ashore in Singapore on the day before departure. The crew took turns watching over him, since his behaviour was erratic, but he eluded them and jumped overboard, nine days out from Singapore.

5. The *Tilkhurst* arrived in Calcutta on 21 November 1885 and left for Dundee on 8 January 1886, reaching there on 17 June. Conrad signed off the ship on that day.

6. Conrad achieved his master's certificate on 10 November 1886 at the second attempt. He was later to command the *Otago* in 1888–9.

7. The Indian Mutiny occurred in 1857.

8. This incident apparently occurred in the middle of 1895, when Annette Burroughs was about thirty years of age.

Memories of Joseph Conrad*

T. ARCHIBALD DUKES

Sir, Your review of a volume of Conrad's letters had a personal interest for me. For when he was first mate of almost the last passenger sailing ship I was its medical officer.[1] I enjoyed playing chess with him more than with anyone else on board. We sat next to each other at meals. Many times have I heard him say, when the waiter asked him what he would have: 'Oh, wot you got.' And he repeated that phrase long after I tried to improve his English.

This was after he astonished me one day by asking me to correct the English of some of his writings.

'Your writings?' said I.

'Yes,' he replied, 'then I can get more money in port.'

I thought, 'Perhaps that is why he so often might be seen alone for hours thinking.'

He took corrections without question. One MS had already been corrected. I said it had been well done into good English; but suggested improvements. He seemed puzzled. I tried to explain the differences of

* *Spectator*, vol. CXLI (20 Oct. 1928) p. 526.

meaning in various wordings and class phraseology. But he left me doubting if he cared for the subtle distinctions expressed by English; and supposing that he preferred those words which *sounded* best.

He was curiously unemotional about important matters, very little moved by right and wrong. When the subject was raised he expressed no indignation at his expulsion from his country.[2] He only shrugged his shoulders. When assured that revolutions are followed by counter-revolutions, and that then Poland would welcome him back again he only shook his head. Yet I believe that his father did thus return.

However, he would show much emotion about unimportant matters of taste. And he was a sharp observer, without any apparent prying or gazing. Generally I beat him at chess. Once, through an oversight, I lost my queen to him, and then said with a smile: 'That gives you the game. Now let us start another.'

'Oh, no, no, no,' said Conrad, clutching the board.

'Well, then,' said I, 'this counts as a win for you. Will you give me back my last move, and see if you can win again.'

'No. No.' Conrad was determined to finish that game; and he took thought over each move, as long as in a more serious situation. He was a slow player, so I foresaw and followed each move as soon as his fingers left the board. Having mated me, he refused to play with me again for several days, being offended, I suppose, because I did not appear to take so much trouble over a hopeless game.

He seldom spoke much, even about his strange experience as a sailor and a refugee over much of the earth. I praised Old England for welcoming the refugees and outcasts from other lands, though I did not then expect that he would ever be honoured as a good English writer.

NOTES

1. Probably the *Torrens*, in which Conrad sailed as mate between Britain and Australia, 1891–3.
2. Conrad's decision to leave Poland was voluntary.

'He hated passengers'*

'BEN GUNN'

I knew Joseph Conrad fairly well, and sailed with him.

I have a notion that he hoped, at one time, to make a living as a black-and-white artist. He carried a supply of Indian ink and paper, and made a lot of drawings. I may have had a sea-urchin's ideas of art, but they seemed to me to be first-rate drawings. Anyhow, he could turn out a pretty wench, with a fine leg on her.

He was like every sailor I ever met in the old days, terribly anxious when at sea to get the voyage done and be clear of the ship. Ashore, no doubt, he had periods of longing to be afloat again.

He hated passengers. A great many of the old wind-jammer officers were like that. I was in the *Torrens* with him. She was a fine composite, full-rigged ship that could sail like a witch. In the London papers she used to advertise 'A health and pleasure voyage. Stewardess carried; also a cow'. The passengers were 90 per cent consumptives. The ship had no artificial heating, and in colder latitudes her cabins were damp and chill as a well. 'Way down in the tropic calms the same cabins were Hell-holes. No wonder the poor health- and pleasure-seekers died in a hurry! We had many a passenger's funeral and Conrad always looked happy.

He was a capital ship's officer, capable and courageous, but inclined to dream a little. One fine Sunday morning, when the passengers were below at church service, there happened to be a vessel coming towards us sailing a course that was likely to take her across our bows. The way the wind was it was our duty to keep clear of her. Conrad carried on, and when the Old Man[1] came on deck it looked very much as if the ships would come into collision. The skipper hated Conrad, and in front of a crowd of passengers made a great powwow of averting the disaster. Conrad was a gentleman, and the cold disdain he showed the captain was a caution. The Old Man was red as a turkey-cock, and spluttered all over the poop, but without saying a word Conrad had the best of the argument.

I have never seen an officer held in more respect or better liked by the crew than Conrad was. Sailors and boys all swore by him.

* From Christopher Morley, *Internal Revenue* (New York: Doubleday, Doran, 1933) pp. 192–3.

And yet – and yet I have never read a book he wrote!

NOTES

This article, by the unidentified 'Ben Gun' [*sic*], was first published in the Sydney *Bulletin* in 1927 and is reprinted by Morley. Conrad sailed in the *Torrens* as chief officer from November 1891 to July 1893, making two round trips from Britain to Australia. The *Torrens* was a passenger clipper of 1334 tons, and was one of the most famous sailing ships of her day, renowned for her quick voyages. On the second of Conrad's two trips to Adelaide, in the final quarter of 1892, a certain William Henry Jacques, a consumptive Cambridge student travelling for his health, became the first reader of the unfinished manuscript of *Almayer's Folly*. On the following return leg from Australia, John Galsworthy was a passenger (see p. 63).

1. The recently appointed Captain of the *Torrens* was W. H. Cope, whom John Galsworthy described, in a letter written aboard the ship, as 'a man of about 50, with grizzled hair, whiskers and moustache, a bluff – not too bluff – manner, almost devoid of accent, and a good seaman'.

Reminiscences of Conrad*

JOHN GALSWORTHY

It was in March 1893 that I first met Conrad on board the English sailing ship *Torrens* in Adelaide Harbour. He was superintending the stowage of cargo. Very dark he looked in the burning sunlight – tanned, with a peaked brown beard, almost black hair, and dark brown eyes over which the lids were deeply folded. He was thin, not tall, his arms very long, his shoulders broad, his head set rather forward. He spoke to me with a strong foreign accent. He seemed to me strange on an English ship. For fifty-six days I sailed in his company.

The chief mate bears the main burden of a sailing ship. All the first night he was fighting a fire in the hold. None of us seventeen passengers knew of it till long after. It was he who had most truck with the tail of that hurricane off the Leeuwin,[1] and later with another storm. He was a good seaman, watchful of the weather, quick in handling the ship; considerate with the apprentices – we had a long, unhappy Belgian

* From *Castles in Spain* (London: Heinemann, 1927) pp. 74–6.

youth among them, who took unhandily to the sea and dreaded going aloft; Conrad compassionately spared him all he could. With the crew he was popular; they were individuals to him, not a mere gang; and long after he would talk of this or that among them, especially of old Andy the sailmaker: 'I likéd that old fellow, you know.' He was friendly with the young second mate, a cheerful, capable young seaman, very English; and respectful, if faintly ironic, with his whiskered, stout old English captain.[2] I, supposed to be studying navigation for the Admiralty Bar, would every day work out the position of the ship with the captain. On one side of the saloon table we would sit and check our observations with those of Conrad, who from the other side of the table would look at us a little quizzically. For Conrad had commanded ships, and his subordinate position on the *Torrens* was only due to the fact that he was then still convalescent from the Congo experience which had nearly killed him.[3] Many evening watches in fine weather we spent on the poop. Ever the great teller of a tale, he had already nearly twenty years of tales to tell. Tales of ships and storms, of Polish revolution, of his youthful Carlist gun-running[4] adventure, of the Malay seas, and the Congo; and of men and men: all to a listener who had the insatiability of a twenty-five-year-old.

NOTES

John Galsworthy (1867–1933), novelist and playwright. After education at Harrow and Oxford, he was called to the bar in 1890 and took up marine law. Galsworthy began to write in 1897, and his first novel appeared in the following year. In 1906, he achieved a double success with his first play, *The Silver Box*, and the first of his Forsyte novels, *The Man of Property*. He was awarded the Nobel Prize for literature in 1932.

John Galsworthy and Edward Sanderson were returning from Australia and New Zealand in the *Torrens* when they met Conrad, the first mate. The ship left Adelaide on 23 March 1896, and Conrad was making his second and final return voyage from England in her. The twenty-five-year-old Galsworthy was not even thinking of becoming a writer at this stage, although he had literary interests, and one of the unfulfilled purposes of his journey had been to visit Robert Louis Stevenson on Samoa. Galsworthy left the *Torrens* at Cape Town in May, but Sanderson continued the voyage. Both men, who must have been among Conrad's first English acquaintances on shore, became his lifelong friends.

For a note on Edward Sanderson, see p. 6.

1. Cape Leeuwin, Western Australia.
2. W. H. Cope. See p. 62.
3. In his essay, 'The *Torrens*: a Personal Tribute', Conrad explains that 'I was then recovering slowly from a bad breakdown, after a most unpleasant

and persistent tropical disease which I had caught in Africa while commanding a steamer on the River Congo. . . . I confessed to him [the Captain of the *Torrens*] my doubts of my fitness for the post, from the point of view of health. But he said that moping ashore never did any one any good, and was very encouraging' (*Last Essays*, p. 27). Conrad had previously commanded the *Otago* in 1888–9.

4. See p. 180.

Conrad and Crippen*

ARCHIBALD MARSHALL

It was Conrad who made the deepest impression upon me. His magnificent head, surely one of the handsomest that was ever set on a pair of shoulders, if you are to take into account what a face reflects of the spirit that enlightens it, his dignity, austerity, kindness of heart, even his irritabilities, made him an unforgettable figure. I had no personal experience of those irritabilities, but used to hear enough about them, and they all seemed part of him, for nobody ever took his work as a writer more to heart than he did, and it was because he almost agonised over it that little outside impingements upon his brain annoyed him, like midge bites.

Some few years later, when I had come home from Australia, and was in the *Daily Mail* office, I went into the room where the books were dealt with, and saw a parcel of them, including a translation of one by Anatole France, which had been sent to Conrad for review, and had come back without being reviewed.

He had been persuaded to write about books occasionally for the *Daily Mail*,[1] and would, of course, have given of his heart's blood to the work, as he gave it to everything he wrote. It would have been setting a razor to cut a grindstone in any case, and perhaps it was as well for his sake that it came to an end when it did.

On the Saturday before Cowes week the news came through of the arrest of Crippen, the murderer, on his arrival in Canada.[2] Marlowe[3] had chartered a small yacht and called in at the office on his way to Southampton to join her. He found Kennedy Jones[4] there, excited by the news. More cablegrams were coming through, and one of them contained a list of the books Crippen had read on his voyage across.

* From *Out and About: Random Reminiscences* (London: John Murray, 1933) pp. 143–5.

Presently K.J. said, 'That list of books – there might be something in that. I wonder if anybody could be got to write an article about Crippen's sea library.' One of them thought of trying Conrad. Their practice was always to try everything, and he could only say no. The telegram was sent and Marlowe left for his yacht. Conrad might light his pipe with it, or he might reply declining the proposal. Or their luck might be in, and they would get an interesting article.

What happened was that poor dear Conrad exploded in epistolary fury[5] at being asked to do such a thing and severed his connection with our journal.

NOTES

Archibald Marshall (1866–1934) was well known as a novelist and contributor to *Punch*. At the time which he describes in the above reminiscence, he was editor of the *Daily Mail*'s Literary Supplement. He had also been a special correspondent for that paper in Australia, returning to Britain in 1910. He was an amateur in music and painting, and wrote some thirty novels.

Conrad used to meet Marshall occasionally at the Tuesday literary luncheons of the Mont-Blanc restaurant in Soho, London, and Marshall has been describing, immediately prior to the beginning of this extract, some of their fellow diners – Edward Garnett, Edward Thomas, John Galsworthy, Ford Madox Ford and W. H. Hudson.

1. Conrad wrote eleven articles for the *Daily Mail* between 1904 and 1924, three of them in 1910.
2. 'Dr' H. H. Crippen was arrested on board the *Montrose* on 31 July 1910, sailing from England to Canada. He had been sought for the previous three weeks concerning the murder of his wife earlier in the year, and he was executed in November 1910.
3. Thomas Marlowe (1868–1935), editor of the *Daily Mail* between 1899 and 1926.
4. Kennedy Jones (1865–1921), joint founder of the *Daily Mail* and Member of Parliament for the Hornsey division of Middlesex from 1916 till his death.
5. Borys Conrad and his mother give a slightly different account of Conrad's response: see respectively Borys Conrad, *My Father: Joseph Conrad* (London: Calder & Boyars, 1970) pp. 65–6, and Jessie Conrad, *Joseph Conrad and his Circle* (London: Jarrolds, 1935) p. 159.

A First Meeting with Joseph Conrad*

PERRITON MAXWELL

Joseph Conrad lies deep under the sod and yet the letter staring at me as I write is almost warm from his hands. It is dated 23 June [1924], Oswalds, Bishopsbourne, Kent, and it deals with an hypothetical question I put to 'the most romantic figure in English literature' concerning probable present-day conditions had America remained under the political domination of Great Britain.

This is the last of a number of letters I exchanged with the truly great novelist who, in his later years, became more and more interested in world affairs and in men and things generally quite apart from letters. His unfailing courtesy manifested itself in his merest notes to me and, as an editor, I think I must at times have tested his patience sorely with my importunings for 'copy'. His innate, wholly unaffected modesty shows itself in every line of this last communication sent across the Atlantic but a few weeks ago. That his reading and understanding embraced a range so wide as that of European, British and Colonial politics will, I suspect, be a matter of news even to his intimates.

I first met Joseph Conrad under circumstances bordering on drama and tinged with quaint humour. I was editor of *Nash's Magazine* in London, and on the night of 16 April 1912 had remained late at my desk in my office at 69 Fleet Street. This office was on the third floor of the building. The office staff had long since gone home. The elevator was stopped, the place was wrapped in silence and gloom. Outside there was a heavy fog and a good deal of it had crept into the room where I wrestled with a too verbose manuscript that had to be ready for the printer's hand next day. My office door stood wide, and as I wielded the blue pencil under the solitary glow of a shaded electric globe I suddenly became aware of another presence. Peering into the yellow darkness I beheld the quaintest figure I had seen since David Warfield's yiddish characterisation in *The Auctioneer.*[1] Under a pot derby with a narrow brim there gazed at me with eyes that penetrated and

* *New York Herald and New York Tribune* [Magazine – Fiction – Books], 24 Aug. 1924, p. 1.

yet were dreamy, an undersized man in an overcoat that fell far below his knees. Then he spoke:

'I am looking for the editor of *Nash's*. The lift was not working, so I walked up.'

His tones were unmistakably Slavic. His slight gesture, the right hand raised, palm uppermost, were identical with that of the conventional stage Hebrew.

'I am the editor,' I told him. 'What can I do for you?'

He removed his ridiculous headgear. 'I hope you will pardon my intrusion, but I have something on my mind which I think may be important and which I wish to write about. My name is Joseph Conrad.'

'Astonishing' is a weak word to use in attempting a description of my dominant emotion at that moment. I turned on a switch, flooded the room with light and invited the author to sit down. In twenty-four years of editorial experience I am sure there never was an hour so filled with interest, with the revelation of how much the outward man can belie the inner genius, as during the talk we had upon the theme then uppermost in the world's news and the minds of all mankind – the sinking of the *Titanic*.[2]

Conrad was full of the subject. He could not keep his chair. He strode the room as he must have strode the bridge of his ship when a typhoon was brewing. He gesticulated, he shrugged. His eyes became beacons of high-powered intelligence. His voice rumbled like a railroad train, but his words came clearer, precise, with that nicety of enunciation which characterises the expression of those who learn their English academically.[3] He grew angry over the first, foolish reports that the officers of the *Titanic* were in some measure responsible for the colossal liner's sinking.

'Don't people know that when a great ship sinks from a wide leakage there is always an explosion, that her decks are blown off, that her boilers usually break adrift with thundering noises? I don't believe the *Titanic* ran into a huge visible iceberg, or that the look-out men were not at their posts, or that her officers were below enjoying themselves. The ship probably had her bottom scraped clean off by a submerged piece of ice. Deity itself could not have made her float under such conditions.'

The facts, it must be remembered, were not then known. We only knew in London that the greatest passenger ship in the world ran afoul of some giant obstacle, presumably an iceberg, and had gone to the bottom, sucking down with her a considerable proportion of the 2000 souls (many of them famous, most of them wealthy) who were aboard. Conrad scoffed at the idea of an unsinkable ship of 45 000 tons, at the blind trust of men in material and appliances. He was shrewd in his surmises of what had happened, sure of the heroism of the *Titanic*'s officers and men, scornful of the ship's water-tight doors in the bulkhead which, it had been complacently declared, would keep the enormous craft afloat despite everything that might go wrong in her internal mechanism or her hull. As he wrote later: 'The famous closing apparatus on the bridge, paraded as a device of greater safety, with its attachments of warning bells, coloured lights, and all these pretty-pretties, was, in the case of this ship, little better than a technical farce.'[4]

You can readily believe that some of Joseph Conrad's hardly restrained emotion over this 'most miserable, most fatuous disaster',[5] was communicated to me, that I visioned the story of the *Titanic*'s sinking penned at white heat by this master seaman, with an unequalled gift for words and the effect his *tour de force* would have upon all lovers of the literature that is born of great historic events.

I explained to Conrad that my work was editing a monthly magazine, that at best I could not print his article in less than thirty days, but that I would cable at once to the New York newspaper with which my magazine was associated,[6] and that unquestionably it would commission the article, which he could then write and I could cable back.

Accordingly, I cabled Conrad's unique offer to the New York managing editor (since dead)[7] who, after a lapse of four hours, returned the curt message: 'Do not want Conrad story.' While waiting for this reply the author and I ate a hearty English supper at the famous Cheshire Cheese tavern directly opposite my office in Fleet Street. During the meal Conrad told me many memorable things about his life, his ships, his difficulties in selecting good crews in the early days, and how much he delighted in his 'farmhouse' down in Kent[8] and his quiet but productive life as a 'landlubber'.

The New York editor's refusal of his work and how to break the news of it to Conrad called for all the finesse and diplomacy I possessed. He went back to his hotel that night believing, I am afraid, that I had not made perfectly plain to my newspaper colleague across the sea what was being offered him. I did not show Conrad my long message in which I had made very clear indeed how big and compelling a feature his article would be in any newspaper at such a time and on such a theme.

When I saw Joseph Conrad a few months later he had developed something of the dandy. His beard was cropped close, the pot hat had given place to a more rakish 'bowler' and his coat had a note of Regent Street in its snugness and contours. He had written his article on the loss of the *Titanic* and it had appeared in the *English Review*. It was a leisurely, forceful, biting piece of work, and it now forms a chapter in his *Notes on Life and Letters*.[9]

Of his last letter to me (and one of his last to any one) I must make a brief comment. That he had become a thorough Briton in thought as well as in deed is indicated by his urgency in making clear that 'the Canadian government is not subservient to the English Parliament' and that 'the rule of the British monarch is not theoretical, it is symbolical'. I do not think a more loyal Englishman ever lived than Teodor Josef Konrad Karzeniowski,[10] the Pole, after he had taken the oath of allegiance to the British Crown as Joseph Conrad.

The more tender side of the man is strongly revealed in one of his letters to me, in which he discsusses the Christmas spirit and the Santa Claus myth. He says in part:

> I have been a stranger to Santa Claus all my life. You'll understand how the Polish children did not need a Germanic fairy saint to give them the sense of sanctity and joy attached to the day of Nativity in the hearts of Roman Catholics. But I have no feelings against him personally, and if American children want him – why should not they have him? What's the objection? . . . I want liberty for American men, women, children, for Santa Claus and for myself. 'Give me liberty – or give me death!' . . . With my love and Xmas wishes to all free Americans, believe me, faithfully yours (but still violently protesting as the curtain falls).

NOTES

Perriton Maxwell (1868–1947), editor, author and artist, was born in New York. His working life was spent in journalism, and he was editor of *Nash's Magazine* from 1910 to 1913, living at the Waldorf Hotel, London, during his period abroad. Before the meeting with Conrad which he describes, Maxwell had on several occasions written to him unsuccessfully to request an option on forthcoming work.

This article was originally published three weeks after Conrad's death.

1. In fact, Warfield starred in Aurhur and Klein's *The Auctioneer* in Washington in 1915.
2. The *Titanic* had sunk only a few hours earlier, on the night of 14–15 April 1912.
3. Conrad did not, of course, learn English in this way. See, for example, p. 208.
4. Joseph Conrad, *Notes on Life and Letters* (London: J. M. Dent, 1949) p. 230.
5. Ibid., p. 227.
6. The New York *American.*
7. Caleb Marsh Van Hamm (1861–1919) was managing editor of the *American*, 1910–19.

8. Capel House, Ashford.

9. Conrad wrote two articles about the disaster, 'Some Reflections, Seamanlike and Otherwise, on the Loss of the *Titanic*', *English Review*, 11 (May 1912) pp. 304–15, and 'Some Aspects of the Admirable Inquiry', *English Review*, 11 (July 1912) pp. 581–95. Both are reprinted in Conrad, *Notes on Life and Letters* (London: J. M. Dent, 1949) pp. 213–48, with slightly different titles.

10. Conrad's full name was Józef Teodor Nałęcz Konrad Korzeniowski.

Part IV
Conrad in the Nineties

An Unknown Episode of Conrad's Life*

ANDREW DE TERNANT

Sir, All the recent biographers of Joseph Conrad have overlooked the fact that he was employed for about two months as a translator of Slavonic languages during the early 'nineties[1] by a Translating Agency, a few doors away from Mudie's Library, New Oxford Street, WC. I remember Conrad calling one day at the office of the long since defunct *St Stephen's Review*,[2] in the Adelphi, and informing the assistant editor, the late Mr Edgar Lee,[3] that he had ceased calling for work at the Agency. Sometimes, Conrad said, his remuneration did not exceed ninepence per week. This was owing to the fact that most of the Slavonic firms doing business with English customers wrote in French or German. Conrad brought with him at the same time some translations of Polish short stories, which Mr Lee promised he would read. Mr Lee, however, afterwards told me that he was compelled to return the Polish tales to Conrad, because all of them were much too revolutionary for a Conservative weekly journal like the *St Stephen's Review*.[4]

NOTES

1. The exact date is not known, although Zdzisław Najder suggests 1891 (see *Joseph Conrad: A Chronicle* (Cambridge: Cambridge University Press, 1983) p. 149).
2. This journal ceased publication in 1892.
3. Edgar Lee (1851–1908) was, according to *Who's Who*, acting editor of *St Stephen's Review* between 1883 and 1890. If this is correct, then Conrad possibly undertook his translating work in 1889 (despite de Ternant's reference to the early 1890s). Conrad was not in London for two complete months in 1890.
4. Possibly these 'revolutionary' stories were early works by Stefan Żeromski (1864–1925), one of the foremost writers of the period.

* *New Statesman*, vol. xxxi (28 July 1928) p. 511.

Impressions and Beginnings*

EDWARD GARNETT

I first met Joseph Conrad in November 1894, some months after I, as Mr Fisher Unwin's reader, had written one of my hasty reports and had advised the acceptance of *Almayer's Folly*. My friend Mr W. H. Chesson, whose duty it was to take charge of the manuscripts, tells me that he called my particular attention to the manuscript.[1] My wife recollects that I showed her the manuscript, told her it was the work of a foreigner and asked her opinion of his style. What particularly captivated me was the figure of Babalatchi, the aged one-eyed statesman and the night scene at the river's edge between Mrs Almayer and her daughter. The strangeness of the tropical atmosphere, and the poetic realism of this romantic narrative excited my curiosity about the author, who I fancied might have Eastern blood in his veins. I was told however that he was a Pole, and this increased my interest since my Nihilist friends, Stepniak and Volkhovsky,[2] had always subtly decried the Poles when one sympathised with their position as 'under dog'.

Since I spent the greater part of every week in the country I rarely made the acquaintance of authors whose manuscripts I had read. But on this occasion Mr Fisher Unwin arranged a meeting between Conrad and me at the National Liberal Club. On the last Christmas before his death, Conrad described to Mrs Gertrude Bone[3] his recollection of this first meeting, and I quote from the account she has sent me.

> 'The first time I saw Edward,' Conrad went on, 'I dared not open my mouth. I had gone to meet him to hear what he thought of *Almayer's Folly*. I saw a young man enter the room. "That cannot be Edward so young as that," I thought. He began to talk. Oh yes! It was Edward. I had no longer doubt. But I was too frightened to speak. But this is what I want to tell you, how he made me go on writing. If he had said to me, "Why not go on writing?" I should have been paralyzed. I could not have done it. But he said to me, "You have written one book. It is very good. Why not *write another*?" Do you see what a difference that made? Another? Yes, I would do that. I *could* do that. Many others I could not. Another I could. That

* 'Joseph Conrad. I: Impressions and Beginnings', *Century Magazine*, vol. cxv (Feb. 1928) pp. 385–92.

is how Edward made me go on writing. That is what made me an author.'[4]

My other memory is of seeing a dark-haired man, short but extremely graceful in his nervous gestures, with brilliant eyes, now narrowed and penetrating, now soft and warm, with a manner alert yet caressing, whose speech was ingratiating, guarded and brusque turn by turn. I had never seen before a man so masculinely keen yet so femininely sensitive. The conversation between our host and Conrad for some time was halting and jerky. Mr Unwin's efforts to interest his guest in some political personages and in literary figures such as John Oliver Hobbes and S. R. Crockett[5] were as successful as an attempt to thread an eyeless needle. Conrad, extremely polite, grew nervously brusque in his responses and kept shifting his feet one over the other, so that I became fascinated in watching the flash of his pointed patent-leather shoes. The climax came unexpectedly when in answer to Mr Unwin's casual but significant reference to 'your next book', Conrad threw himself back on the lounge and in a tone that put a clear cold space between himself and his hearers, said, 'I don't expect to write again. It is likely that I shall soon be going to sea'.

A silence fell. With one sharp snick he had cut the rope between us and we were left holding the loose end. I felt disappointed and cheated. Mr Unwin expressed some deprecatory ambiguities and then, after turning his falconlike glance down the long smoking-room, apologised for having to greet some friends in a far corner.

Directly he had left Conrad and me alone speech came to me in a rush. I may have been as diplomatic as Conrad has recorded.[6] What I then said to him with the fervency of youth would seem to me a little bizarre now, had I not caught myself the other day, thirty years later, addressing a young author with much the same accents and convictions. But I spoke then with youth's ardent assurance. My thesis was that the life Conrad had witnessed on sea and land must vanish away into the mist and fade utterly from memory did he not set himself to record it in literature. And *Almayer's Folly* showed that he had the power. Conrad listened attentively, searching my face, and demurring a little. It seemed to me afterward that he had come to meet me that night partly out of curiosity and partly as an author who deep down desires to be encouraged to write. And the credo he heard matched his conviction that it was the thing that he could do that mattered. It was no doubt partly my curiosity about Conrad's life as a sailor in the Eastern seas that winged my words; and curiously the heavy, middle-class atmosphere of the National Liberal Club with its yellow encaustic tiles, cigar smoke, provincial members, political gossip from the lobbies, and business news on the tape, jarred less and less in the presence of this stranger who charmed one by something polished and fastidious in the inflections of his manner. Yes, he had 'the temperament'. Shortly after Mr Unwin's return we bade him good night and Conrad strolled some distance with me past the brilliantly lighted Strand. Our relations had been settled for good by this first contact.

We did not meet again for some weeks, when Conrad invited me to spend the evening with him at 17 Gillingham Street.[7] After dining in a private room at a Wilton Street restaurant where an obsequious Italian waiter dashed up and down the stairs all wreathed in smiles, I was introduced to Conrad's snug bachelor quarters. As soon as he had placed me in an easy-chair Conrad retired behind a mysterious screen and left me to study the cosiness of the small firelit room, a row of French novels, the framed photograph of an aristocratic lady and an engraving of a benevolent imposing man on the mantelshelf. On a little table by the screen lay a pile of neat manuscript sheets. I remained conscious of these manuscript sheets when Conrad reappeared and plunged into talk which ranged over things as far removed as the aspects of Malay rivers and the ways of publishers. Conrad's talk that night was a romance, free and swift; it implied in ironical flashes that though we hailed from different planets the same tastes animated us. To no one was the art of harmonising differences so instinctive, when he wished to draw near. To no one was the power of emphasising them more emphatic, when he did not. There was a blend of caressing, almost feminine intimacy with masculine incisiveness in his talk; it was that which gave it its special character. Conrad's courtesy was part of his being, bred in the bone, and serving him as a foil in a master's hand, ready for attack or defence. That first evening he took from the mantelshef and showed me the portrait of his mother with her sweet commanding eyes, and told me that both she and his father, a poet and translator of Shakespeare, had been arrested at the time of the Polish rising of 1862, and had afterwards been sent into exile. Of himself Conrad spoke as a man lying under a slight stigma among his contemporaries for having expatriated himself. The subject of Poland was then visibly painful to him, and in those early years he would speak of it unwillingly, his attitude being designed to warn off acquaintances from pressing on a painful nerve. Later he grew less sensitive and in a letter in 1901, he sketched at length his family history and connections.[8]

In response to this first confidence about his family, thrown out with diffidence, I gave him some idea of my own position, which at that time, as indeed later, was peculiarly isolated. A stranger to editors and to literary cliques I had no influence outside the publishing firm I worked for; but I could and did give new authors encouragement and practical advice about placing their work. My few literary friends were struggling young men, such as W. B. Yeats, men abler than myself and not so unskilled in the methods of success. My six years' work as a publisher's reader had taught me fully the anxieties and the hazards of the literary life; but youth believes instinctively that luck is on its side, and I had been lucky in finding authors for Mr T. Fisher Unwin.

However, to Conrad, ten years my senior, and incomparably more versed in worldly affairs, the ways of publishers, reviewers and editors were then an uncharted land, and his first view of New Grub Street, as he put it later to me, was 'as inviting as a peep into a brigand's cave and a good deal less reassuring'. When later that evening I had recurred to the subject of *Almayer's Folly*, Conrad suddenly picked up the pile of sheets from the little table and told me that he had embarked on a second book and that I should live to regret my responsibility for inciting him. This charming flattery was very characteristic of Conrad. Placing the manuscript in my hands he retired behind the screen and left me to glance through the pages. By the time he had reappeared with a bottle of Benedictine I had been captivated by the brilliant opening of *An Outcast of the Islands*. I exclaimed with delight at the following passage:

> They were a half-caste, lazy lot, and he saw them as they were – ragged, lean, unwashed, undersized men of various ages, shuffling about aimlessly in slippers; motionless old women who looked like monstrous bags of pink calico stuffed with shapeless lumps of fat, and deposited askew upon decaying rattan chairs in shady corners of dusty verandahs; young women, slim and yellow, big-eyed, long-haired, moving languidly amongst the dirt and rubbish of their dwellings as if every step they took was going to be their very last.[9]

Conrad, exhilarated by my praise, then described his idea of the downhill path of Willems and foreshadowed Aissa's part in the drama. The plot had already taken shape in Conrad's mind, but most of the action was still in a state of flux. Conrad's attitude toward this novel was from the first a strange blend of creative ardour and scepticism. He spoke deprecatingly of his knowledge of Malay life, but all the same the figures of Willems, Joanna and Aissa captivated his imagination. His sardonic interest in Willems's disintegration reflected, I believe, his own disillusionment over the Congo. I agree with M. Jean-Aubry that Conrad's Congo experiences were the turning-point in his mental life and that their effects on him determined his transformation from a sailor to a writer.[10] According to his emphatic declaration to me, in his early years at sea he had 'not a thought in his head'. 'I was a perfect animal,' he reiterated, meaning of course that he had reasoned and reflected hardly at all over all the varieties of life he had encountered. The sinister voice of the Congo with its murmuring undertone of human fatuity, baseness and greed, had swept away the generous illusions of his youth and had left him gazing into the heart of an immense darkness. So Willems's figure was not merely the vehicle for Conrad's sardonic irony, but through it Conrad had to express also his own 'romantic feeling of reality'; hence this character had to bear too great a burden both of feeling and commentary. I do not think that this criticism was ever formulated exactly by either Conrad or myself during the nine months in which *An Outcast of the Islands* came to me in batches. He was too engrossed in wrestling with his characters to see precisely the effect of all the parts in relation to the whole, and I was too enthralled by the strange atmosphere and poetic vision, and too intent on encouraging him to criticise Willems till the end was at hand. I well remember pencilling notes of admiration on the margins of certain pages, as on those poetical passages that conclude Part II. On the delivery of the final instalment, however, I criticised adversely the psychology of Willems's motives and behaviour just before his death at Aissa's hand; and Conrad agreed, with reservations, to my strictures and set to work to remodel various passages. I think now that my criticism was not so just as I imagined at the time.

However, to come back to that first evening at Gillingham Street, I recall that Conrad took alarm at some declaration of mine about the necessity for a writer to follow his own path and disregard the public's taste. His tone was emphatic. 'But I *won't* live in an attic!' he retorted. 'I'm past that, you understand? I *won't* live in an attic!' I saw then that it was essential to reassure Conrad about the prospects of *Almayer's Folly*. And I cited the names of various authors who, whatever they may have been doing, were certainly then not living in attics, public favourites such as Stevenson and Kipling and Rider Haggard – the work of the last-named, I remember, Conrad stigmatised as being 'too horrible for words'. He objected specifically to the figure of Captain Good, as well he might![11]

As I look back at that evening and at our subsequent meetings in little Soho restaurants, in Newgate Street, St Paul's Churchyard and in a Mecca café in Cheapside, I recall an atmosphere of humble conspiracy *à deux*, which infolded us. Conrad was then more obscure than any publisher's reader. At that time he was experiencing all the hot and cold fits and the exultations of literary creation, often thrown back and sceptical, but also boyishly eager while perfecting his strokes and broadening his effects as the novel grew under his hands; and I was taking this development of his genius for granted, being very enthusiastic over the romantic magic of his scenes. My part indeed was simple – to appreciate and criticise all that he wrote, and to ask for more, more.

While Conrad's brilliant charm arrested our notice in those early years, the depth of his creative vision eluded us. In his voice we heard the seaman and the artist speaking, but the poet, secretly inspiring the finest subtleties of his work, remained unseen. From what I gathered, then and since, of Conrad's parents I believe that from his mother he inherited his caressing sweetness, and from his father his sharp and sombre insight, with its fierce sardonic underplay. There were two natures interwoven in Conrad, one feminine, affectionate, responsive, clear-eyed, the other masculine, formidably critical, fiercely ironical, dominating, intransigent. Often the sweet mood would change in a flash, and with an upward fling of the head he would stare hard with wide-opened sardonic eyes at the perpetrator of some fatuity or sentimental falsity. His eyes would grimace ironically, and he would boil over suddenly while attempting to conceal his violent distaste; and the person who had awakened this mood would go away to circulate some alarming legend about his intractability. In the impetuosity of his prejudiced judgements, Conrad had a streak of Lieutenant Feraud, but also the contemplative wisdom and clarity of vision of Lieutenant d'Hubert, those two immortal creations of his own.[12] His fine courtesy kept his Polish impetuosity in check in those early years, but he resented bad manners when addressed, and I remember how the slighting remarks of a Mr N. at a National Liberal Club meeting in 1895 so chafed on him that he would have sent the speaker a challenge had the country been France. But unless offended or rubbed the wrong way he was as sympathetic and as softly responsive to people as a sensitive woman.

I remember being struck by this quality one day in the summer of 1897, when he had taken me for a sail in the boat that he shared with his old sailor friend, G. F. W. Hope, at Stanford-le-Hope.[13] The plan was to land at some jetty lower down the Thames, but the wind kept dying away on each occasion as we tacked and neared the bank, and we lay becalmed for over an hour in the hot glare. Hope disdaining to put out an oar, Conrad deferred with alacrity – like a young sailor boy – to his least wish and drew him out in talk with a fine tact, while whispering to me that to row the boat ashore was unthinkable, for such a proceeding would wound Hope's pride as a seaman!

Conrad's moods of gay tenderness could be quite seductive. On the few occasions I saw him with Stephen Crane[14] he was delightfully sunny, and bantered 'poor Steve' in the gentlest, most affectionate style, while the latter sat silent, Indian-like, turning inquiring eyes under his chiselled brow, now and then jumping up suddenly and confiding some new project with intensely electric feeling. At one of these sittings Crane passionately appealed to me to support his idea that Conrad should collaborate with him in a play on the theme of a ship wrecked on an island. I knew it was hopelessly unworkable, this plan, but Crane's brilliant visualisation of the scenes was so strong and infectious that I had not the heart to declare my own opinion. And Conrad's sceptical answers were couched in the tenderest, most reluctant tone. I can still hear the shades of Crane's poignant friendliness in his cry 'Joseph!' And Conrad's delight in Crane's personality glowed in the shining warmth of his brown eyes. When Conrad wished to surrender himself to anybody he did it single-heartedly in irresistible fashion. I remember on the occasion of a visit which he and Jessie Conrad paid to the Cearne in 1898, coming suddenly on him and my son David, aged six, sailing in the grass plot in a big zinc tub, rigged up with a broomstick, a table-cloth and a clothes-line. The illusion of a real boat was strangely complete, with Conrad shifting the sheet in the breeze while giving sharp orders to the boy crew in nautical language.

This gay buoyancy of spirit, while more in evidence in early years, contrasted curiously with the antithetic mental atmosphere of Conrad's sardonic brooding and disenchantment with life. The serious, contemplative stare Conrad's features often assumed in repose, with a shade of the saturnine, is well rendered in Miss E. M. Heath's portrait of him,[15] done in 1898, a likeness which he himself declared bore a strong resemblance to his father. The portrait does not however convey the extraordinary soft warmth of Conrad's eyes, which always struck me when talking with him. The painting was executed in a single sitting at the Cearne while I tasked myself to entertain him. One of my anecdotes drew from him the following: 'Yes, dear Edward. But have you ever had to keep an enraged negro armed with a razor from coming aboard, along a ten-inch plank, and drive him back to the wharf with only a short stick in your hand?' But to recur to the temperamental moods that blend in Conrad's creations and endow them with the most complex qualities, one may say that the Korzeniowski parental side, with its 'terrible gift of irony' rules, as astrologers put it, over the majority of the pages of *The Secret Agent*, and that his Bobrowski heritage rules similarly over most of the pages of *The Mirror of the Sea*. Of course these are approximate labels, but M. Jean-Aubry has shown that the letters to Conrad from his maternal uncle Thaddeus Bobrowski attribute certain of Conrad's traits to his Korzeniowski inheritance.[16]

One of the finest examples of the fusion of the two moods in Conrad's temperament, to my mind, is that example of his Polish virtuosity, his story 'The Duel'. That brilliant, gay, ironical, masterpiece has been underrated because the Anglo-Saxon is temperamentally unsympathetic to its qualities. I once witnessed a ludicrous interview between Conrad and a certain hard north-country Englishman who shall here be nameless. Conrad, for an admirable reason, was anxious to propitiate his host, but his ingratiating manner roused the Englishman's suspicions, and the latter became stiffer and harder, while Conrad struggled bravely to disarm his insular doubts. It was a relief to both of us when we had bowed ourselves out from this dour north-countryman's presence.

Great quickness of eye was one of Conrad's gifts. I remember while sitting one evening with him in the Café Royal I asked him, after a painted lady had brushed haughtily past our table, what he had specially noticed about her. 'The dirt in her nostril,' he replied instantly. On this acute sense rested his faculty of selecting the telling detail. It was an unconscious faculty, so he said. I remarked once of the first draft of *The Rescue*, that as a seaman he must have noted professionally the details of the rain-storm at sea described in Chapter III. Conrad denied this, and asserted that all such pictures of nature had been stored up unconsciously in his memory, and that they only sprung into life when he took up the pen.

That Conrad's memory had extraordinary wealth of observation to draw on I had an illuminating proof in *Heart of Darkness*. Some time before he wrote this story of his Congo experience he narrated it at length one morning while we were walking up and down under a row of Scotch firs that leads down to the Cearne. I listened enthralled while he gave me in detail a very full synopsis of what he intended to write. To my surprise when I saw the printed version I found that about a third of the most striking incidents had been replaced by others of which he had said nothing at all. The effect of the written narrative was no less sombre than the spoken, and the end was more consummate; but I regretted the omission of various scenes, one of which described the hero lying sick to death in a native hut, tended by an old negress who brought him water from day to day, when he had been abandoned by all the Belgians. 'She saved my life,' Conrad said, 'the white men never came near me.'[17] When on several occasions in those early years I praised his psychological insight he questioned seriously whether he possessed such a power and deplored the lack of opportunities for intimate observation that a sailor's life had offered him. On one occasion on describing to him a terrible family tragedy of which I had been an eye-witness, Conrad became visibly ill-humoured and at last cried out with exasperation, 'Nothing of the kind has ever come my way! I have spent half my life knocking about in ships, only getting ashore between voyages. I know nothing, nothing! except from the outside. I have to guess at everything!' This was of course the artist's blind jealousy speaking, coveting the experiences he had not had, and certainly he could have woven a literary masterpiece out of the threads I held, had he ever known the actors.

I may here note that Conrad's 'strong foreign accent' in March 1893 to which Mr Galsworthy has testified in his 'Reminiscences of Joseph Conrad', seemed to me only slight in November 1894.[18] But when he read aloud to me some newly written manuscript pages of *An Outcast of the Islands* he mispronounced so many words that I followed him with difficulty. I found then that he had never once heard these English words spoken, but had learned them all from books!

NOTES

Edward Garnett (1868–1937) was a reader for the publisher, Fisher Unwin, whose firm was publishing Conrad's first novel, *Almayer's Folly*. Conrad met Garnett on 8 October 1894 (not November, as recorded in the extract). Garnett was a source of invaluable advice and support to Conrad, especially in the early years of his career, and *The Nigger of the 'Narcissus'* is dedicated to him. Garnett was later to give similar assistance to John Galsworthy and D. H. Lawrence.

Conrad's gratitude to Garnett is perhaps best expressed in a letter which he wrote to him in 1923, acknowledging how 'in your feelings, in your judgments, your enthusiasms and criticisms, in all your fine reactions to that "best" which not every eye can see, you have been beautifully consistent, both in your subtle and your peremptory moods. . . . How much you have done to pull me together intellectually only the Gods that brought us together know.'

Garnett was a member of the distinguished Victorian family; he was the son of Richard, historian and librarian, the husband of Constance, a pioneering translator of Russian literature, and father of David, the novelist. The Garnetts moved to The Cearne, Limpsfield, Surrey, in 1896 and their home, to which Conrad was a frequent visitor, was an intellectual and literary centre.

1. Chesson's account is given on p. 83.
2. Sergei Stepniak and Felix Volkhovsky were Russian exiles and revolutionaries involved in the anarchist movements. The Garnetts offered them hospitality and liberal sympathy.
3. Wife of Muirhead Bone; see p. 167.
4. In fact, Conrad had begun his second novel, *An Outcast of the Islands*, in August 1894, a couple of months before meeting Garnett.
5. John Oliver Hobbes (Mrs Pearl Craigie, 1867–1906) and S. R. Crockett (1860–1914), both established Unwin authors.
6. See Joseph Conrad, *An Outcast of the Islands* (London: J. M. Dent, 1949) pp. vii–viii. Conrad misdated the conversation, which took place at their first meeting.
7. Garnett first visited Conrad at his lodgings in Victoria on 16 January 1895.
8. See Conrad's letter, dated 20 Jan. 1900, in *Letters from Conrad, 1895 to 1924* (London: Nonesuch Press, 1928) pp. 163–8.
9. Conrad, *An Outcast of the Islands*, p. 4.

10. See, for example, Gérard Jean-Aubry, *Joseph Conrad: Life and Letters* (New York, Doubleday, Page, 1927) vol. I, pp. 141–3.
11. Commander John Good is one of the explorers in *King Solomon's Mines* and other stories.
12. Characters in 'The Duel'.
13. For a note on Hope, see p. 9. The Conrads lived at Stanford-le-Hope from September 1896 to October 1898.
14. For a note on Crane, see p. 188.
15. E. M. (Nellie) Heath (1873–1962), Garnett's mistress.
16. Jean-Aubry, *Joseph Conrad: Life and Letters*, vol. I, p. 39.
17. During Conrad's trip to the Congo in 1890, he suffered severely from fever and dysentry. He began writing *Heart of Darkness* in December 1898, finishing it on 6 February 1899.
18. See pp. 62–3.

The Discovery of Joseph Conrad*

W. H. CHESSON

Sir, My attention has been called to a statement by you in *To-day* (page 45 of the April number) from which the reader would infer that the first favourable report written in Mr Fisher Unwin's publishing house on Mr Joseph Conrad's first published novel, *Almayer's Folly*, was from the pen of Mr Edward Garnett.[1]

As a matter of fact the first favourable report was written by me. My hand recorded the receipt by Mr Unwin of this romance on 5 July 1894, and when the author gently pressed for a decision it was I who decided that his work was too good to be surrendered to him, but must be submitted to Mr Garnett. Mr Unwin was on the Continent at the time, and remembers reading my report and agreeing thereupon to the acceptance of *Almayer's Folly*.

Needless to say, I have not the slightest inclination to pick one leaf of laurel from Mr Garnett's brows. He wrote, with admirable emphasis, 'Hold on to this,' after reading *Almayer's Folly*, and his opinion was the pure product of his own faculty of appreciation. Moreover, I owe to him the first praise accorded to my first book,[2] which he did me the honour to read in manuscript.

* *To-day*, vol. v (June 1919) p. 152.

NOTES

Wilfrid Hugh Chesson (1870–1952) was a novelist, biographer and critic, and at the time of receiving the MS of Conrad's first novel, *Almayer's Folly*, he was a reader for T. Fisher Unwin, a large London publishing house.

Conrad had submitted the MS on 4 July 1894 for publication in Unwin's Pseudonym Library, although it eventually proved too lengthy for that particular series. Fisher Unwin wrote to Conrad accepting his novel on 4 October 1894, the first typewritten letter he had ever received. *Almayer's Folly* was published on 29 April 1895.

1. For details of Edward Garnett, see p. 82.
2. W. H. Chesson, *Name This Child: A Story of Two*, published in 1894 by Fisher Unwin.

Joseph Conrad*

E. V. LUCAS

On an evening in 1895 I was dining alone at the Restaurant d'Italie in Old Compton Street, when from another table Edward Garnett beckoned to me, and when I joined him, introduced a friend who was with him as Mr Conrad, a ship's captain who had written a novel. The stranger was slight and foreign-looking, dark, bearded, with brilliant eyes and restless hands, and manners so punctilious, even ceremonious, that they made one's own seem like rudeness. On the table was a roll of galley proofs of his first book, *Almayer's Folly*,[1] then going through the press for Fisher Unwin, and I was told how his life at sea had been ameliorated and diversified first by the study of English and then by the effort to write it and to write romance. Conrad was very much the modest young author in demeanour, full of a charming self-depreciation (which he never lost, but which latterly was not always to be taken at its face value and, indeed, could be almost a weapon), and responding with almost embarrassing gratitude to wishes for his success. He spoke with a strong foreign accent, in sentences not too well constructed, so that when I came to read *Almayer's Folly* I was amazed. To the end his accent remained exotic, although his vocabulary of English words was more precise, if not richer, I suppose, than that of any English-born novelist now writing, and more sensitively managed.

* From 'Joseph Conrad', *English Life*, vol. III, no. 4 (Sept. 1924) pp. 247–8.

As he developed Conrad was less and less in need of advice, but at first it meant much to him, and had it not been for the accident that prompted a young Englishman to take a voyage as super-cargo on a merchant-ship, where he made friends with the chief officer – the young Englishman being John Galsworthy and the chief officer Joseph Conrad[2] – it is possible, indeed, that there might have been no *Almayer's Folly* at all. For it was John Galsworthy who not only encouraged the work, but passed the manuscript on to Edward Garnett, whose whole life has been spent in discovering gifts in others and fostering them, and who instantly discerned the genius in it.[3] I have a notion that John Galsworthy (who remained Conrad's beloved 'Jack' to the end) may not then himself have begun to write,[4] and that his talks with Conrad over de Maupassant and other craftsmen may have reacted on his own ambition. Conrad, who was always so much preoccupied with the workings of chance, must often have reflected with pleasure that it was the sea that brought them together.

When I came to know Conrad better – and he took lodgings in the same country neighbourhood, to be near the Garnetts[5] – he was more confident, or at any rate less diffident. I visited him less than I should have wished, for fear of cutting into his work, for he had none of the hack's regular hours; and sometimes he came over to us and took an incredible number of lumps of sugar in his tea, and talked more of the English countryside than of books. He delighted in domestic scenery. Melancholy always seemed to be brooding over him, but he had his fun, too, and I remember his enjoyment of some absurd burlesque titles which I once sent him, the only one which I can recall being 'A Narcissus of a Nigger; or, the Art of Darkieness'. Efforts to get him to express his real opinions of other writers were usually fruitless, although you could tell by his silences how the land lay. But on one occasion he went so far as to describe a certain publisher as a man of ' 'or-rible per-son-al-i-ty'. For the most part, however, he was smilingly inscrutable, and, no matter in what company, living his own life behind his mask, and always so polite as almost to terrify. He seemed at this time to be very nervous; his work tore him to pieces.

His next home was in remote Kent, in a village somewhere near Rye,[6] where I saw him once only, and then, except occasionally on his brief London visits, I did not meet him again till two years ago, under very unexpected conditions, for it was in the St Lawrence ground during the Canterbury cricket week.[7] For the most part this ground is a mass meeting of motor cars, but suddenly the modernity of the place was broken into by the notes of a guard's horn, and in rolled a coach-and-four driven by a benign gentleman in gold spectacles and a white hat, who might almost have come over from Dingley Dell. Behind him, on the next seat, was a distinguished bearded foreigner, tolerantly surveying the scene through a single eyeglass. When I came to look again I saw that the driver was J. B. Pinker,[8] the literary agent, since dead, and the distinguished bearded foreigner was Joseph Conrad. When the horses had been taken out and the vehicle was transformed into a private box, I joined the party, and for an hour or so sat with Conrad and did my best to qualify him to bat first for Poland. Cricket was strange to him, but he liked the crowd, and the excitement about such a trifle fed his sense of ironical humour. Again the thought struck me that there can be no defence like elaborate courtesy. I noticed that he had become much more restful; prosperity suited him; and, although grey, he was handsomer than ever, and his eyes as luminous. Indeed, as he grew older he became finer, suggesting not only that he was a man apart, a man of great distinction in whatever walk it might be, but a man of authority too. Yet never at any time should I have thought of him and the sea together. But for his gout, he said, he would be perfectly happy. He asked me to come back to Ashford then, but I couldn't; I said I would come directly I had a free weekend, but never found one, and now another regret is added to the increasing heap.

NOTES

Edward Verrall Lucas (1868–1938), journalist, essayist and critic. In 1893, he joined the staff of the *Globe*. Later, after a long connection with the publishing firm of Methuen, he became its chairman.

For a note on Edward Garnett, see p. 82.

1. Conrad received the first proofs of *Almayer's Folly* on Christmas Eve 1894, and the book was published on 29 April 1895.

2. For a note on Galsworthy's first meeting with Conrad, see p. 63.

3. Conrad himself sent the typescript to Fisher Unwin – see p. 41.

4. Galsworthy began to write in 1897, his first novel appearing the following year.

5. Conrad's home at The Pent, near Aldington, Kent, where the Conrads moved in 1898. The Garnetts had moved to The Cearne, Limpsfield, Surrey, in February 1896.

6. Lucas is referring to Capel House, Orlestone, near Ashford, Kent, where the Conrads moved in June 1910. Two other homes intervened between The Pent and Capel House.

7. John Conrad dates this event as occurring in August 1921.

8. For a note on J. B. Pinker, see p. 114.

Conrad in Cardiff*

ARTHUR MEE

A rising novelist has been staying at Cardiff for the last few days in the person of Mr Joseph Conrad. Mr Conrad was the guest of Mr Spiridion, at whose residence in Cathedral Road he was seen by one of our representatives. Mr Conrad is the author of *Aylmer's* [*sic*] *Folly* and other works, and his novels have appeared both in serial and book form. He is tall, dark and of decidedly Celtic appearance; and questioned as to the affinity between the Celts and the Poles – Mr Conrad is himself a child of that downtrodden and unhappy nation – he replied that they have much in common, the temperament of both being dreamy, poetic and romantic.

Mr Conrad himself has undergone many vicissitudes and strange experiences, which he doubtless finds of value in his present walk of life. His father took part in some political agitation, and (like many more of his countrymen) was consigned to Siberia, together with his family, the latter including little Joseph, a child of three or four years old. Mr Conrad's earliest recollections, therefore, are of the most dreaded of all the wide dominions of the Czar, and it is not surprising that he should entertain a hearty admiration for our own land of liberty. In this view, by the way, his host smilingly concurs.

'My father ought to have known,' is his observation, 'for he tried nine countries!'

Our representative gathered that Mr Conrad, like many another of his countrymen, had dropped his surname, the latter being not altogether pronounceable by English lips.

After a few years the Conrads were released from Siberia, and young Joseph then got into the English Navy, and subsequently into the mercantile service, varying his career with a lengthy sojourn in the interior of Africa. He was yet a seaman when the passion for writing took possession of him, and he found himself the wielder of a facile and fluent pen. The encouragement of friends determined him on his new career, and, though he is now by no means a young writer, he speaks of it with an enthusiasm that is contagious.

In the course of conversation, Mr Conrad took occasion to refer to an expression in 'Westminster's' notes of Monday,[1] where Dickens is

* 'A New Novellist [*sic*] on Dickens', *Western Mail* [Cardiff], 1 Jan. 1987.

spoken of as looked down upon by certain fashionable critics of the day. He does not think this view of Dickens is at all widespread.

'Dickens,' he said, 'still keeps up his popularity. I fancy he has left his mark, not because he is a caricaturist (as many people say), but because of his extreme simplicity, and his vividness of expression. His is not high art, but it conveys an exceedingly fine sense of humanity. I fancy that Dickens will never cease to be one of the masters: he is inimitable, and much more accessible to the general mind than Thackeray. He did not give a new form to English, but he used it as it had never been used before, and his very defects help to make up his greatness.'

As our representative left Mr Conrad took occasion to express his high opinion of the *Western Mail* as a bright and original paper, and this (he added) was the general estimate in the circles in which he moved.

NOTES

Arthur Mee, a journalist (unrelated to the popular author of that name) had the honour to be granted Conrad's first press interview. The Conrads went to Cardiff for a ten-day visit on 22 December 1896, staying with a Polish family. Their host was Józef Spiridion Kliszczewski, Conrad's contemporary and the son of a Polish emigré whom Conrad had met in 1885 (they were introduced by a mutual friend who was the only other Polish sailor Conrad ever knew). On Christmas Eve 1896, the patriotic Kliszczewski suggested that Conrad ought to write about Poland and its tragic history, but Conrad indignantly replied that he would lose his public if he were to write propaganda. Conrad may also have been angered that his host gave the interviewer some information about his Polish origin and his childhood in exile. Conrad and Kliszczewski do not appear to have met again after this Christmas visit.

1. Unidentified. Possibly the *Westminster Gazette* is meant.

A Visit to Conrad in 1897*

WINCENTY LUTOSŁAWSKI

In 1897 I was in London awaiting the publication of my first English book, on *The Origin and Growth of Plato's Logic.*[1] I thought then that I was the only living Pole who attempted to write in English. I knew nothing of *Almayer's Folly*, nor of *An Outcast of the Islands*, which had been published in 1895 and 1896, but which had to wait until 1907 for the first re-impression.

Then it happened that I met Henry James, the brother of my intimate friend, William James,[2] whose guest I had been in 1893 at Harvard. Henry James, when he heard of my forthcoming English book, said I ought to meet a countryman of mine living in Essex, who wrote remarkably well in English and had already published two fascinating novels dealing with life in Borneo. He spoke with rare enthusiasm of this new English writer of Polish nationality, although he was ordinarily rather sceptical, exceedingly difficult to please, and not at all encouraging for beginners. I asked him for an introduction to Conrad, which he gave me.

Immediately, I read the first two volumes of Conrad, and I noticed at once that only a Pole could have written them. In 1887, at the age of thirty, he had met Almayer in Borneo,[3] and he attached such importance to that accidental meeting that he wrote later in his personal record: 'If I had not got to know Almayer pretty well it is almost certain there would never have been a line of mine in print.'[4] Of course, this was an illusion. Conrad gave to Almayer an immortal fame, and he did it because he was a born writer, though he did not know it until after twenty years' activity as a mariner.

The slow awakening of a new vocation in Conrad's case was fully discovered for me by the long and passionate conversation I had with him when he was forty. It was due to his very high conception, as a Pole, of literary activity. He knew that writers in Poland had been, in the nineteenth century, the chief leaders of national life, as no practical activity was open to Poles in politics, the army, public education or any kind of office. Writing, authorship, was considered as a kingly function of the highest kind, implying a supreme knowledge of aims and means in order to lead the readers to do the right things in the

* 'A Visit to Conrad in 1897', *Blue Peter*, vol. x (Dec. 1930) pp. 638–40.

most difficult national circumstances of persecution, oppression and treachery.

Conrad, unaware of his great talent, had too much in him of the pessimism of Heyst, whom he pictured later in *Victory*, to trust himself as a mate in the ship of national destinies. Therefore he wrote in English for the English. But he waited until 1893 before he dared to show the first nine chapters of *Almayer's Folly* to W. H. Jacques, a Cambridge scholar, whom he asked whether the novel was worth finishing. He got the laconic answer, 'Distinctly.'[5] When he followed that advice in 1894, the subject had been maturing in his mind for seven years.

I could not know these facts when I spent a whole day in the British Museum reading Conrad's first novel, and another day reading a second volume dealing with the same persons and the same place. But I saw clearly that the *Outcast*, written later and complained of as 'tolerably bad work' in the author's letter to Edward Garnett (12 May 1895),[6] was far superior in literary craftsmanship to *Almayer's Folly*. We see a great difference in the working out of details, and especially in the love-story which, in *Almayer's Folly*, ends conventionally with a happy marriage, but in the *Outcast* takes on the tragic Conradian character which we find again in *Victory*, and in *The Arrow of Gold*, reflecting Conrad's own youthful experience at the age of nineteen, described forty years later.

Love as pictured in the *Outcast* is a tragic power, destructive of life, reason and happiness, inciting to every kind of violence, even between the lovers. In these oriental passions between persons of different race and education, we are far from the peaceful, settled family affections of English life – but such tragic passions have been peculiar to Poles more than to any other nation of Europe. Polish literature is full of such stories of tragic love between Poles and the children of their enemies of different race. There is no greater distance between a Malay wife and an English mariner than between a Polish girl and a German or a Muscovite. In reading the *Outcast* I saw that Conrad, like many of our writers, was disguising thoroughly Polish feelings under the garb of exotic conditions. Poles are as passionate and reckless as the Outcast.

Having read these first two volumes of Conrad, I wrote to him, and received and accepted his invitation to Ivy Walls, his farm-house residence in Essex.[7]

We had important things to say to each other which could not be said in English, and which, so far as I can judge from the available biographic literature, have never been repeated by Conrad. It will be sufficient to tell the truth about this memorable talk, which I remember as if it happened yesterday.

I came with a purpose. There was a very important link between us created by a similarity of exceptional circumstances. We were both glowing Polish patriots, induced to write in English. Neither of us knew at that time that we were starting a career as writers of English. Conrad still thought of returning to the sea; and I looked forward to using my philosophical knowledge in elaboration of a Polish conception of life for the Poles.

Conrad was five and a half years older, a man of forty,[8] while I had just begun the thirty-fifth year of my life. I was born on 6 June 1863, while Conrad was born on 3 December 1857, which according to the astrologers, corresponds to the greatest difference of type and innate character.

I was not aware at that time of this fundamental difference between us. But as soon as I introduced the subject, which was the chief aim of my visit, I clearly saw the enormous divergence of our outlooks. My purpose was to win Conrad for Polish literature, to convince him that such a great talent should not be wasted on a foreign language. I admired his mastery of English in his first two volumes, without being able to guess then that he would become a very great writer in that foreign language. But I soon discovered that Conrad did not believe in the lasting value of his writings. He wrote down his reminiscences under the form of stories, and he seemed unaware how his genius transformed the grey reality. He thought he simply repeated tales from hearsay. I could not convince him that he was a great artist. He had no conceit of any kind, nor the joyous certainty of real achievement. He disparaged his works, and said he was unworthy to write in his own language, after so many great Polish authors, whom he considered the greatest of all in literature.

He did not doubt that the great Polish writers were far superior artists to Walter Scott, Thackeray or Dickens, and his disparagement of his own works implied also a supposed inferiority of English literature and language compared with the language and literature of our own country.

He reproached me that I had myself written a book in English – why not in Polish, if I wanted him to write Polish? I answered that my book was for a narrow circle of Greek scholars, of whom I could not find half a dozen in all Polish lands, while his books were for millions of readers, who could learn from him how to stand the injustice of life without being thrown into madness.

I told him that the Poles needed such books very much more than the English readers, who had so many other authors. But all my pleading was in vain. He did not believe in his genius, he took his own writing as something accidental. Though he had published two volumes and was engaged on *The Nigger of the 'Narcissus'*,[9] he still looked upon seamanship as his real profession.

He fully admitted that it would be to him the most splendid destiny to become a great Polish writer, but he could not trust himself to give up the advantages won with such great efforts: British citizenship and the right to command British ships. He had just married an English wife,[10] whom he called 'my girl', and who soon was to give him two sons. He was hopelessly lost to Poland, though he remained unaware of having started on the strange and unique career of a great English writer.

If I could have convinced him that his first two volumes which I had read were masterpieces, then perhaps I could have won my case, for Conrad had a very strong feeling of duty. He did not acknowledge the duty to write in Polish, simply because he still looked upon himself as upon a mariner spending a spell of enforced unemployment in writing down his reminiscences.

My visit was, therefore, fruitless, and I hastened to return to my own work. At that period I used every moment of my time in London for research in the British Museum, preparing my future teaching in Poland.

I disliked the idea of being asked by Henry James, or anybody else, about that fateful visit, which could not be understood by my English friends. Therefore, I wired Conrad the next day asking him to keep my visit secret, and he must have felt in the same way, as he never mentioned that visit in his correspondence. Obviously he did not mention the object of our discussion to his wife, as she reveals by her account of that visit.[11]

To Conrad my visit had been the last test of his personal relation to the country of his birth and his ancestors. It was the voice of Poland calling back one of her lost sons, invoking the duty of a great writer to use his own language in order to reach the full size of his greatness.

Though I never saw Conrad again, and had no opportunity of reminding him of my prophecy that he would become a great writer, I have no doubt that he recalled this conversation in his thoughts many years later.

I mentioned my visit in a series of articles written in Polish on the emigration of talents – in which I pleaded the right of talent to emigrate if it could not find employment in its own country. This did not apply to Conrad, as a novelist of his kind could have written Polish, and even have lived in Poland. I wrote in No. 12 of the weekly *Kraj*, of 1899:

> It is worth while to consider whether our country really loses so much by the emigration of the most gifted of its inhabitants who, unable to find a suitable scope at home, look out for a wider field of activity abroad. Lately our countryman, Konrad Korzeniowski, won

distinction in English literature under the name of Joseph Conrad. His novels betray a Polish nobleman's imagination, grown in his travels through the isles of the Pacific. When I visited him on a farm near London, I asked him, 'Why do you not write in Polish?' He answered, 'I value too much our beautiful Polish literature to introduce into it my worthless twaddle. But for Englishmen my capacities are just sufficient: they enable me to earn my living.' Such an answer may appear as a paradox, but contains a truth which is insufficiently understood. Our literature is the work chiefly of noblemen, and corresponds to other than material needs. We are true artists and sing for our own pleasure. . . . But literary activity is justified not only by the highest ideal of beauty. Its scope is to spread thoughts and feelings, to move the masses. If Polish authors followed the example of Konrad Korzeniowski and mastered English as a world language, writing in English, and not in Polish, what they write in order to earn their living, they would win enough leisure to transmit to their countrymen their best thoughts in their own language.[12]

The above was written two years after my visit to Conrad, and after the publication of my first English book in 1897. Much later, in 1924, I followed his example, and since his death my most important books have been written and published in English. Though they could never reach such a large reading circle as Conrad's novels, they may be considered to pursue the aim to introduce Polish spirit into English literature. Thus the question at issue in our conversation of 1897, whether it is right for a Pole to write in English, has found its solution in the fact that I became an English writer, having been unable to convince Conrad that he ought to have been a writer in Polish.

NOTES

Wincenty Lutosławski (1863–1954), Polish philosopher and nationalist, was a student in London in 1897. He later taught in Cracow, Geneva, Lausanne, London, Paris and Wilna, where he was professor of philosophy from 1919 to 1928. He suffered a number of nervous breakdowns during his career.

Having received Conrad's address from Henry James, Lutosławski wrote to arrange the visit described here, which occurred on Sunday, 13 June 1897. He arrived six hours late, dined, went straight to bed and left very early the next morning. Conrad wrote to him in 1911, asking him to keep his 1897 visit a secret. Jessie Conrad recalls that Conrad described him as '"A queer customer if ever there was one"'.

1. Published in 1897 by Longman. Written in English, the book sought to establish the chronology of Plato's work.

2. William James (1842–1910), American philosopher and psychologist.

3. In 1887, Conrad met Charles William Olmeijer, a Eurasian Dutchman who had lived at Berau, Borneo, for seventeen years. Unlike his fictional counterpart, Olmeijer had eleven children, a Eurasian wife, and he was a successful trader. He died in 1900, aged fifty-two.

4. Joseph Conrad, *A Personal Record* (London: J. M. Dent, 1946) p. 87.

5. Ibid., p. 17. For details of W. H. Jacques, see p. 62.

6. *The Collected Letters of Joseph Conrad*, ed. F. R. Karl and Laurence Davies (London: Cambridge University Press, 1983) vol. I, p. 216.

7. The Conrads had moved to Ivy Walls, Stanford-le-Hope, in March 1897, and stayed until October 1898.

8. Conrad was thirty-nine years of age at the time of this visit.

9. Conrad had in fact completed *The Nigger* in the previous January, and it was to begin serialisation in August 1897. At the time of Lutosławski's visit, Conrad was working on 'The Return'.

10. Conrad had married Jessie on 24 March 1896.

11. See Jessie Conrad, 'Memories of Joseph Conrad', *Blue Peter*, vol. x (June–July 1930) pp. 304–9, 347–52.

Conrad's X-ray*

NEIL MUNRO

Following dinner at 179 Bath Street one night in September 1898, Joseph Conrad was entertained till one a.m. in a fashion which the novelist gleefully recounted in a letter to his friend Edward Garnett a few days later.[1] All the best 'celebrity' records in the doctor's private repertoire,[2] all the wizardry of Röntgen rays were turned on. I stood in front of a fluorescent screen behind which Conrad and the Doctor contemplated my ribs and back-bone, the more opaque portions of my viscera, my Waterbury watch and what coins were in my pocket. 'The rest of that promising youth was too diaphanous to be visible.'[3]

We had our hands X-rayed, and before we left for a stroll through the sleeping city which lasted till three a.m. we got the photograph prints of them. There may still be in Bath Street an X-ray photograph of Conrad's good right hand, for which George Keating, New York, the most inveterate collector of Conradiana, would give a lot of money.

* From *The Brave Days: A Chronicle from the North* (Edinburgh: Porpoise Press, 1931) pp. 113–14.

NOTES

Neil Munro (1863–1930), poet and journalist. Conrad met him on 27–8 September 1898 during his brief visit to Glasgow in a vain search for maritime employment. Munro's work had appeared alongside Conrad's in *Blackwood's Magazine*, and Conrad remarked shortly after this meeting that 'Munro *is* an artist – besides being an excellent fellow with a pretty weakness for my work.'

Munro is describing a visit to the Bath Street home of Dr John MacIntyre (1859–1928), a pioneer of radiology and phonography. He and Conrad had a mutual friend in Robert Cunninghame Graham.

1. Conrad's letter to Edward Garnett on 29 September 1898 gives the following account of his experiences in Glasgow:

> All day with the shipowners and in the evening dinner, phonograph, X rays, talk about *the* secret of the universe and the nonexistence of, so called, matter. The secret of the universe is in the existence of horizontal waves whose varied vibrations are at the bottom of all states of consciousness. . . . But, don't you see, there is nothing in the world to prevent the simultaneous existence of vertical waves . . . Therefore it follows that two universes may exist in the same place and in the same time – and not only two universes but an infinity of different universes – if by universe we mean a set of states of consciousness; and note, . . . *all matter* being only that thing of inconceivable tenuity through which the various vibrations of waves . . . are propagated, thus giving birth to our sensations – then emotions – then thought. Is that so?
>
> These things I said to the Dr while Neil Munro stood in front of a Röntgen machine and on the screen behind we contemplated his backbone and his ribs. The rest of that promising youth was too diaphanous to be visible. *The Collected Letters of Joseph Conrad*, ed. Frederick R. Karl and Laurence Davies, (Cambridge: Cambridge University Press, 1986) vol. II, pp. 94–5)

C. T. Watts has suggested that this experience provided the 'scientific' mechanism of *The Inheritors*, which Conrad and Hueffer were to begin two months later and which describes the undermining of civilisation by the dispassionate 'Fourth Dimensionists' who have always coexisted with human beings on a different plane (see *Notes & Queries*, vol. CCXII (July 1967) pp. 245–7).

2. MacIntyre had made the first recording of the Polish pianist, Paderewski.

3. A quotation from Conrad's letter to Edward Garnett, quoted in note 1 above.

Joseph Conrad as I Knew Him*

EDWIN PUGH

I believe I first met Conrad at some literary dinner. I was just then on the crest of a tiny little boom of my very own. There were, I know, quite a goodly few people keenly curious about me. I found myself being described in personal paragraphs as all kinds of an extraordinary creature. And in that way a certain interest in myself rather than in my work – the general public has never been very much interested in any of my work – became almost rampant in some strictly limited circles.

I had talked with several men and women, more or less famous in that little literary world of those days, and had suffered some severe buffetings under successive shocks of disillusionment. I was thinking of getting away by myself to readjust my sense of relative values.

And then, somehow, I was being introduced to Joseph Conrad.

He came at me with a sort of sinuous grace, with a sort of writhing servility; and he looked – it is the only word to use, if I am to translate my first impressions of Conrad accurately – simian. His head was a little askew and seemed somehow to be unduly sunken between his unusually high shoulders. His forehead, which was of a cold, shining whiteness, receded sharply from his heavy brows. The rest of his face was dully flushed, his cheeks thickly interlaced with tiny purplish veinings. And one had a feeling of forced geniality in the flash of his large white teeth through the bristling amplitude of his moustache and beard.

Then, as by a flashlight of inspiration, I had another impression – an impression of huge strength in reserve, of something smoulderingly fiery in his dark brown eyes, of pain and weariness and the sort of high courage and yet latent exasperation which all that kind of thing induces in the very bone, blood and flesh of all men who have seen and suffered and lived with a kind of savage pungency.

He was little known then. I had read hardly a line of his stuff. But in the instant we began to talk he was enthusiastically praiseful of

* 'Joseph Conrad as I Knew Him', *T.P.'s and Cassell's Weekly*, vol. II (23 Aug. 1924) p. 575.

H. G. Wells. Wells had been the first to extol in the *Saturday Review* his earliest books.[1]

'I didn't know,' said I, 'that Wells had ever done any literary criticism. I knew he was a thundering good judge of literature because he likes my stuff.'

'A thundering good judge – yes,' said he, with that strong inflexion of a foreign accent which he never overcame. 'He likes my stuff, too.'

Afterwards I went to stay with him for a week at his big stone house at Stanford, near Sandling Junction, which had some time before been occupied by Walter Crane, I think. It was called the Pent House,[2] and it crouched at the foot of a tall, precipitous hill. There was a wooden lintel over the doorway, and on that lintel was carved, presumably by Walter Crane:[3]

Want we not for board nor tent
Whilst overhead we have the Pent.

Along the extensive frontage of the house was a sort of veranda or stoep, which Conrad called his quarter-deck. And up and down that quarter-deck he and I paced together for miles at a time, talking swiftly, deedily, about all things mentionable and unmentionable.

He had travelled the world. He knew strange ports and portages of which I was abysmally ignorant. But I had travelled the world too, to his dark-eyed amazement. I knew France pretty well, mostly upon well-worn lines, and I had been in Italy and Germany, and so on. There was nothing to stir him in that.

What did stir him were my experiences in out-of-the-way parts of London. He had never before in his life met a man who knew burglars, prizefighters, underdogs of every type. He had never in his life met a man who knew any of the Chinks of Limehouse and Poplar. He was aristocratic in grain, as I am, and we felt that indefinable link between us, which made us understand and at the same time wonder how the lives of two such men as he and I should diverge so abruptly, so acutely, only to converge at last to that single point of contact.

He was, on the whole, a kindly-natured man, though very peevish and impatient when things went agley with him. He was, like me, by nature a silent man. But, again like me, under stress of excitement, he could talk prodigiously. And he had the talent, which nearly all writers of stories lack, of direct and dramatic narrative by word of mouth.

I can recall one tremendous story that he told me. I can remember particulary how, very late at night, with our first bed candles replaced by others, he concluded a description of a duel with sabres by tearing open his waistcoat and shirt and laying his breast bare.

And yet, in the ordinary way, he was most austerely haughty and restrained. He was then the aristocrat above all questioning; the child of ancient Polish rights and privileges. And in this connexion a queer story is told, for the authenticity of which I can vouch.

Somewhere, somewhen, somehow, a famous author,[4] Bart Kennedy[5] and Conrad came into conjunction; and this author, never extraordinarily remarkable for tact, observed that Kennedy and Conrad ought to know one another, 'because they were both sailors!' which of course inflamed the implacable resentment of each, and at the same time chilled their intercourse at its first inception.

Conrad was at that time only just beginning to get a precarious foothold on the slippery glissade of fame. He was then very eager to form friendships and to make acquaintance with those who, as it seemed to his inexperience, might help him on the way to success.

With his earliest friends he was almost embarrassingly frank and humble. It is said, in one or two of his obituaries, that he took to English as naturally as a duck takes to water, that he quite easily mastered the language in which he had elected to write, and that henceforth he had very little difficulty in expressing himself as fully and freely as his high ideals of style constrained him. That, bluntly, was never the case. I remember that after he had published six or seven books he was still puzzled and vexed by certain subtly simple words such as 'like' and 'as', 'who' and 'whom', 'that' and 'which'. I spent hours in discussing with him the finer differences between these words, their shades and nuances of meaning, and he wrought upon the examples I quoted or invented in agony and bloody sweat for days on end.

He was then always pressed for money. He envied me my facility, and wanted very much to do the sort of hackwork that I was doing to keep the pot a-boiling. And he could not. He was too great an artist to truckle to popular taste, even in the most legitimate way. His MSS, as I visualise them and as I see them mirrored before me in the stiff, angular calligraphy of his letters, were thick with interlineations and strewn with blanks or starred with French or other foreign words or phrases when he could not hit upon the right English word or phrase.

And then he had a dread of prolixity. 'This story of mine for *Blackwood's*,' he wrote to me, 'that was meant to be just a short tale, lengthens out like an anaconda. It seems as if it would never leave off uncoiling itself.' The story he referred to was *Youth*, one of the finest long–short stories ever written. And so it came about that for all his strivings and pains, his revisions, deletions, emendations and amplifications, his genius defied his craftsmanship, and forced him to work on lines altogether opposed to his very definitely formed and emphatically stated views of literary art.

And so, little by little, his favourite axiom, 'The style is the man', justified itself, and at last, very tardily, won for him that popular success which he had always so longed for and sought after.

Peace to his troubled spirit! He should have been a happy man. He lived a full life. And, above all, he had not only the noontide rapture of pursuing but the twilight calm of victory.

NOTES

Edwin William Pugh (1874–1930) was the son of a member of the Covent Garden Orchestra, and his mother was wardrobe mistress there. He began work at the age of thirteen in an iron factory and was later in a solicitor's office.

He published his first novel, *A Street in Suburbia*, in 1895, followed the next year by *The Man of Straw*. His reputation was that of a realist, absorbed in the sordid or grotesque characters of the London scene. His first meeting with Conrad which he describes probably occurred in Spring 1898.

1. Wells had reviewed *Almayer's Folly* and *An Outcast of the Islands* in the *Saturday Review*, on 15 June 1895 and 16 May 1896 respectively.
2. The Conrads had moved to Pent Farm (as it was properly called) in October 1898.
3. For a note on Walter Crane, see p. 112.
4. Pugh elsewhere identifies him as H. G. Wells (see his 'Big Little H. G. Wells', *New Witness* (1 Aug. 1919) p. 292).
5. Bart Kennedy (1861–1930), a novelist and former seaman.

Part V
Literary Friendships

Conrad Collaborates*

FORD MADOX FORD

Conrad came round the corner of the house. I was doing something at the open fireplace in the house-end. He was in advance of Mr Garnett[1] who had gone inside, I suppose, to find me. Conrad stood looking at the view. His hands were in the pockets of his reefer-coat, the thumbs sticking out. His black, torpedo beard pointed at the horizon. He placed a monocle in his eye. Then he caught sight of me.

I was very untidy, in my working clothes. He started back a little. I said: 'I'm Hueffer.' He had taken me for the gardener.

His whole being melted together in enormous politeness. His spine inclined forward; he extended both hands to take mine. He said: 'My dear faller. . . . Delighted. . . . *Ench . . . anté*!' He added: '*What* conditions to work in. . . . Your admirable cottage. . . . Your adorable view. . . .'

It was symbolic that the first remark he should make to me should be about conditions in which to work. Poor fellow: work was at once his passion and his agony and no one, till the very end of his life, had much worse conditions. On the last time I saw him, a few weeks before his death, he said to me: 'You see, I have at last now got a real study of my own. I can work here uninterrupted.' He was to do so little more!

He was staying at the moment of that visit up on the Chart to be near Mr Garnett. He had been living in the rather lugubrious village of Stanford-le-Hope,[2] on the estuary of the Thames amongst the Essex marshes. His poverty was like a physical pain, but his reputation as a writer was already enormously high. A week after the publication of his first book he stood absolutely in the front rank of English authors, yet the great public was extraordinarily slow to hear of him. I suppose it did not really do so till the publication of *Chance*, fifteen years after that date. And they were fifteen years of agonised labours and the most fell anxieties, the most desperate expedients. The highest note of his life was his passion for his work, the most dominant one that of being assured of having provided for his family. His tastes were of the least expensive; he was as happy playing dominoes in a city Mecca – a coffee house – over a cup of coffee as in any other situation in the

* From *Return to Yesterday* (London: Victor Gollancz, 1931) pp. 52–5, 201–3.

world. He would place on the marble table-top the winning domino of a series, his whole face lighting up with animation and triumph. Yet, since I never won one of innumerable games that I played with him, the triumph could only in the beginning have had any novelty for him.

In those early days he still had a great deal of the master mariner about him. His characteristic attitude was that, with his hands in the pockets of his coat and his beard pointing at the horizon. He strode, with the rolling gait of the quarter-deck, into a room or on to a terrace. He had the air of a Caliph entering a slave market – as if he could confiscate any of the beautiful slaves or do what he would with the view beneath his eyes. He was an unexampled *raconteur*. If his ambition in writing was, as he has said, 'before all, to make you *see*'[3] he could in telling stories, in his dusky and affectionate tones and with his singular accent, make you see almost anything in the world. It is to be remembered that he was Polish of very aristocratic ancestry. That was what gave a particular agony to his anxieties for his family's welfare. He sat almost in rags and groaned with the fear that his pen would not be able to provide, for his children and grandchildren, great mansions to withstand the snow, elaborately ornamented sleighs, blood horses, innumerable retainers and halls opening out, the one into the other, beyond the eyesight. I never heard him lament the shortages of the present. He was happy with, and even proud of the few poor things that he had. The old mare that he drove, Nancy, had such long ears that she had the air of a mule, but for him she was the most engaging of beasts with the most enlivening characteristics and the speed of a Rolls Royce amongst quadrupeds. His old harness and his old cart were of the noblest pedigree of such things. He never knew that he was shabby. If he had two odd gloves they would have been manufactured by the best maker Bond Street could show. But for his son the future must hold a Rolls Royce all of silver and clothes all from Poole who made for Edward VII.

But indeed he wore his old clothes with the air of a Prince and when he was behind Nancy you thought her the horse of the Cid, he so dominated all views. He had a singularly nice taste in cooking and in that respect fate was good to him. In the direst times of his poverty he yet had a table that was better than almost anybody's I have ever known. For with care, two eggs, a little butter, some potherbs and a few scraps you may eat as did Brillat Savarin, and Conrad had a devoted family.

Except for his unexpected, queer, rather stiff appearance, his sudden melting into oriental mannerisms, and the fact that his first speech was about conditions of work, I do not remember much more of that first visit of a man with whom I was destined to become extremely intimate and whose memory remains the most treasured of my possessions. I remember mostly his smile of satisfaction and enchantment at his son and my daughter as they climbed determinedly on all fours and wrestled like eighteenth-century cherubs on the sloping grass of Mr Garnett's property which was called The Cearne. I must have told him that I was writing a novel about Cuban pirates.[4] That the sequel will show. But I did not see him again during his visit to Limpsfield and he went away back to Stanford-le-Hope and its marshes.

* * *

I remember once we had been struggling with *Romance* for hours and hours, and he had been in complete despair, and everything that I had suggested had called forth his bitterest gibes, and he was sick, and over ears in debt, and penniless. And we had come to a blank full-stop – one of those intervals when the soul *must* pause to breathe and love itself have rest. And Mrs Conrad came in and said that the mare had trotted from Postling Vents to Sandling in five minutes – say, twelve miles an hour! At once, there in the room was Conrad-Jack-ashore! The world was splendid; hope nodded from every rosebud that looked over the window-sill of the low room. We were going to get a car and go to Canterbury; the mare should have a brand-new breeching strap. And in an incredibly short space of time – say, three hours – at least half a page of *Romance* got itself written.

That was how it went, day in day out, for years – the despair, the lamentations continuing for hours, and then the sudden desperate attack on the work – the attack that would become the fabulous engrossment. We would write for whole days, for half nights, for half the day, or all the night. We would jot down passages on scraps of paper or on the margins of books, handing them one to the other or exchanging them. We would roar with laughter over passages that would have struck no other soul as humorous; Conrad would howl with rage and I would almost sigh over others that no other soul perhaps would have found as bad as we considered them. We would recoil one from the other and go each to our own cottage – our cottages at that period never being further the one from the other than an old mare could take us in an afternoon. In those cottages we would prepare other drafts and so drive backwards and forwards with packages of manuscript under the dog-cart seats. We drove in the heat of summer, through the deluges of autumn, with the winter snows blinding our eyes. But always, always with manuscripts. Heavens, don't my fingers still tingle with the feeling of undoing the stiff buckles, long past midnight, of a horse streaming with rain – and the rubbing down in the stable and the backing the cart into the coach-house. And with always at the back of the mind, the consideration of some unfinished passage, the puzzledom to avoid some too-used phrase that yet seemed hypnotically inevitable.

So it went on for years – seven, ten, eleven – I don't remember how many. At any rate, it was after *Romance* itself was finished that Conrad wrote that 'Ford has become a habit', rather wondering at it because, he said, no one liked me.

My early job was to get Conrad's work over. I do not believe that any other person could have tackled it then, though later on Marwood[5] was quite as indispensable – quite as much of a habit. Given that you acknowledge that Conrad's professional career was fortunate from the date of our association, the conjunction must have been materially fortunate for him whether or no his work deteriorated. That it was fortunate for me I am sure, for if I know anything of how to write almost the whole of that knowledge was acquired then. It was acquired at the cost of an infinite mental patience, for the process of digging out words in the same room with Conrad was exhausting. On the other hand, the pleasure derived from his society was inexhaustible: his love, his passion for his art did not, I believe, exceed mine, but his power of expressing that passion was delicious, winning, sweet, incredible. When – but how rarely! – a passage went right or the final phrase of a long-tinkered episode suggested itself, his happiness was overwhelming, his whole being lit up, his face became serenely radiant, his shoulders squared, his monocle gleamed like rock crystal. It was extraordinary.

NOTES

Ford Madox Ford (1873–1939), novelist and critic. He was originally surnamed Hueffer, and changed it to Ford during the First World War. He came from Anglo-German parentage, and was a grandson of Ford Madox Brown, the Pre-Raphaelite painter. He met Conrad in September 1898 at the home of Edward Garnett, The Cearne, near Limpsfield, Surrey. Ford lived next door, indulging in his current passion for growing vegetables. When they met, Ford (who was Conrad's junior by sixteen years) had already published a novel, three collections of fairy tales, a volume of poetry and a biography. Their friendship, at times very close, lasted for more than a decade.

The idea that the two writers should collaborate was Conrad's, although it took a year for this decision to be implemented. Conrad's motivation was perhaps the wish to improve his English and overcome isolation. They eventually collaborated on *The Inheritors* (1901), *Romance* (1903) and *The Nature of a Crime* (1924). Such collaborations applied exclusively to works already begun by Ford, and Conrad's role was primarily to correct and polish the book.

Ford's reminiscences are well known for being highly imaginative, and should often be taken cautiously.

1. For a note on Edward Garnett, see p. 82.
2. Conrad had lived at Ivy Walls, Stanford-le-Hope, for the previous year.
3. Preface to Joseph Conrad, *The Nigger of the 'Narcissus'* (London: J. M. Dent, 1946) p. x.
4. The plot of *Romance* is based on the adventures of Aaron Smith, who had been a prisoner of Cuban pirates.
5. Arthur Pierson Marwood, who came from a Yorkshire county family, met Conrad in 1905. The friendship was to prove of great value and importance to Conrad.

'More the student than a sea-captain'*

FRANK HARRIS

One day I picked up a new book by a new author. *Almayer's Folly*, by Joseph Conrad. I had not seen the name before, but a glance at the first page told me that the man was a writer. At about the same time a Mr Low came in (a brother of Sidney Low),[1] a very able writer. I threw him the book and said: 'There seems to be good stuff in that.'

He took it with him and in a few days sent me a murderous review. I got another copy of the book and read it. After reading it, I sent the review back to Low, saying it was altogether wrong: Joseph Conrad was a good writer and as a newcomer should be praised and not condemned, standing, as he did, high above the ordinary!

Then I sent the book to H. G. Wells.

After a week or two Wells blew in boisterously. 'What a book', he cried, throwing it down on the table. 'Thanks very much for sending it to me. That sort of stuff makes one's task as a reviewer pleasant, but I am afraid you will think my review far too long and far too eulogistic. I have written pages about Conrad, not columns, and I have praised him to the skies. Will you stand it?'

'First-rate,' I cried, 'just what I had hoped from you. I sent the book to a man who crabbed it. After all, a great reviewer should be a star-finder and not a fault-finder.'[2]

For some reason or other, I never met Conrad until the autumn of 1910,[3] fifteen years later. Talking one day with Austin Harrison of the

* *From My Life and Loves*, ed. John F. Gallagher (London: W. H. Allen, 1964) pp. 704–5. First published in three volumes, 1922–7.

English Review,[4] Conrad's name came up and I asked: 'How does he look? What age is he? Has he any foreign accent? Is he a great personality?' – a stream of questions.

Harrison declared that Conrad knew me, always spoke warmly of me, and ended by proposing that we should motor down to his cottage in Kent.[5]

We did so the very next Sunday.

Conrad met us most cordially, was eager to record that the review in the *Saturday Review* had given him reputation. I had thought from his photograph that his forehead was high and domed, but it was rather low and sloped back quickly. He was a little above middle height and appeared more the student than a sea-captain. Both he and his wife were homely, hospitable folk, without a trace of affectation. But Harrison's presence prevented any intimacy of talk, and the nearest I got to Conrad was when I asked him for a recent book, *The Mirror of the Sea*.[6] He stipulated that I should send him my latest in exchange, and under the dedication to me he wrote the first and last verses of Baudelaire's magnificent poem comparing man to the sea. He repeated the last line:

O lutteurs éternels, ô frères implacables![7]

with a note of bitter sadness I thought characteristic. His French, I noticed, was impeccable.

Since then I have read most of Conrad's books, but I have never rated him at all as highly as Wells did.

NOTES

Frank Harris (1856–1931), English author and editor of the *Evening News* (1882–6), the *Fortnightly Review* (1886–94) and the *Saturday Review* (1894–8). A man of extrovert arrogance who made many enemies, he acquired a scandalous reputation, and his undoubted flair as an editor was obscured by his boastful self-aggrandisement.

1. Sidney James Mark Low (1857–1932), journalist and historian, at this time editor of the *St James's Gazette*.

2. For a note on H. G. Wells, see p. 112. His unsigned review of *Almayer's Folly* appeared in the *Saturday Review* of 15 June 1895 and noted that the novel is 'exceedingly well imagined and well written, and it will certainly secure Mr Conrad a high place among contemporary story-tellers'.

3. The meeting occurred in October 1910.

4. Austin Harrison (1873–1928), son of Frederic Harrison. Conrad was about to begin publishing *Under Western Eyes* in the *English Review* in December

1910 and had been closely involved in the new journal's foundation.

5. Capel House, near Ashford, Kent.

6. Published 1906.

7. 'O eternal wrestlers, O implacable brothers.' Baudelaire's poem '*L'Homme et la mer*' from *Les Fleurs du Mal* (1857) begins appropriately: '*Homme libre, toujours tu chériras la mer! / La mer est ton miroir*' [O free man, you will always cherish the sea! The sea is your mirror].

'*Wat* shall we do with *thesa* things?'*

H. G. WELLS

At first he impressed me, as he impressed Henry James, as the strangest of creatures. He was rather short and round-shouldered with his head as it were sunken into his body. He had a dark retreating face with a very carefully trimmed and pointed beard, a trouble-wrinkled forehead and very troubled dark eyes, and the gestures of his hands and arms were from the shoulders and very Oriental indeed. He reminded people of Du Maurier's Svengali and, in the nautical trimness of his costume, of Cutcliffe Hyne's Captain Kettle.[1] He spoke English strangely. Not badly altogether; he would supplement his vocabulary – especially if he were discussing cultural or political matters – with French words; but with certain oddities. He had learnt to read English long before he spoke it and he had formed wrong sound impressions of many familiar words; he had for example acquired an incurable tendency to pronounce the last *e* in these and those. He would say, '*Wat* shall we do with *thesa* things?' And he was always incalculable about the use of 'shall' and 'will'. When he talked of seafaring his terminology was excellent but when he turned to less familiar topics he was often at a loss for phrases.

* * *

He came into my ken in association with Ford Madox Hueffer and they remain together, contrasted and inseparable, in my memory. Ford is a long blond with a drawling manner, the very spit of his brother

* From *Experiment in Autobiography: Discoveries and Conclusions of a Very Ordinary Brain (Since 1866)* (London: Gollancz, 1934) pp. 615–16, 617–19, 621–2.

Oliver, and oddly resembling George Moore the novelist in pose and person.[2] What he is really or if he is really, nobody knows now and he least of all; he has become a great system of assumed personas and dramatised selves. His brain is an exceptionally good one and when he first came along, he had cast himself for the role of a very gifted scion of the Pre-Raphaelite stem, given over to artistic purposes and a little undecided between music, poetry, criticism, The Novel, Thoreau-istic horticulture and the simple appreciation of life. He has written some admirable verse, some very good historical romances, two or three books in conjunction with Conrad, and a considerable bulk of more or less autobiographical – unreality. As a sort of heir to Pre-Raphaelitism, he owned among other things a farm called The Pent at the foot of the Downs above Hythe; it had been occupied previously by Christina Rossetti and Walter Crane the artist; and he had let it to Conrad;[3] Conrad wrote about the *Heart of Darkness* and *The Secret Agent* on a desk that may have creaked to the creative effort of *Goblin Market*; and thither Hueffer and I walked to our meeting.

One goes downhill to The Pent, the windows of the house are low and my first impression of Conrad was of a swarthy face peering out and up through the little window panes.

He talked with me mostly of adventure and dangers, Hueffer talked criticism and style and words, and our encounter was the beginning of a long, fairly friendly but always rather strained acquaintance. Conrad with Mrs Conrad and his small blond-haired bright-eyed boy, would come over to Sandgate,[4] cracking a whip along the road, driving a little black pony carriage as though it was a droshky and encouraging a puzzled little Kentish pony with loud cries and endearments in Polish, to the dismay of all beholders. We never really 'got on' together. I was perhaps more unsympathetic and incomprehensible to Conrad than he was to me. I think he found me Philistine, stupid and intensely English; he was incredulous that I could take social and political issues seriously; he was always trying to penetrate below my foundations, discover my imaginative obsessions and see what I was really up to. The frequent carelessness of my writing, my scientific qualifications of statement and provisional inconclusiveness, and my indifference to intensity of effect, perplexed and irritated him. Why didn't I *write*? Why had I no care for my reputation?

'My dear Wells, what is this *Love and Mr Lewisham about*?'[5] he would ask. But then he would ask also, wringing his hands and wrinkling his forehead, 'What is all this about Jane Austen? What is there *in* her? What is it all *about*?'

I remember a dispute we had one day as we lay on the Sandgate beach and looked out to sea. How, he demanded, would I describe how that boat out there, sat or rode or danced or quivered on the water?

I said that in nineteen cases out of twenty I would just let the boat be there in the commonest phrases possible. Unless I wanted the boat to be important I would not give it an outstanding phrase and if I wanted to make it important then the phrase to use would depend on the angle at which the boat became significant. But it was all against Conrad's over-sensitised receptivity that a boat could ever be just a boat. He wanted to see it with a definite vividness of his own. But I wanted to see it and to see it only in relation to something else – a story, a thesis. And I suppose if I had been pressed about it I would have betrayed a disposition to link that story or thesis to something still more extensive and that to something still more extensive and so ultimately to link it up to my philosophy and my world outlook.

* * *

I had, I have, few 'complexes'. I would almost define education as the prevention of complexes. I was seeing myself as fas as possible without pretences, my *persona* was under constant scrutiny, even at the cost of private and secret sessions of humiliation, and not only was I trying to avoid posing to myself but I kept up as little pose as possible to the world. I eschewed dignity. I found therefore something as ridiculous in Conrad's *persona* of a romantic adventurous un-mercenary intensely artistic gentleman carrying an exquisite code of unblemished honour through a universe of baseness as I did in Hubert Bland's man-of-affairs costume and simple Catholic piety.[6]

When Conrad first met Shaw in my house,[7] Shaw talked with customary freedoms. 'You know, my dear fellow, your books won't *do*' – for some Shavian reason I have forgotten – and so forth.

I went out of the room and suddenly found Conrad on my heels, swift and white-faced. 'Does that man want to *insult* me?' he demanded.

The provocation to say 'Yes' and assist at the subsequent duel was very great, but I overcame it. 'It's humour,' I said, and took Conrad out into the garden to cool. One could always baffle Conrad by saying 'humour'. It was one of our damned English tricks he had never learnt to tackle.

Later on he wanted Ford Madox Hueffer to challenge me. If Conrad had had his way, either Hueffer's blood or mine would have reddened Dymchurch sands. I thought an article Hueffer had written about Hall Caine[8] was undignified and I said that he had written it as if he was a discharged valet – or something equally pungent. Hueffer came over to tell me about it. 'I tried to explain to him that duelling isn't done,' said Hueffer.

NOTES

H. G. Wells (1866–1946), novelist, critic and sociologist, first met Conrad in 1896, and their friendship lasted for about a decade until a growing estrangement set in. Even at its height, it had always been an uneasy friendship, given their differences in politics and temperament. The breach seems to have begun in 1907, but the decisive episode may have been the publication of Wells's *Tono-Bungay* (1909) which contains a vicious portrait of Conrad as the captain of a ship, a Romanian Jew accused of bribery and incompetence. Conrad is recorded by Hugh Walpole as saying that 'the difference between us, Wells, is fundamental. You don't care for humanity but think they are to be improved. I love humanity but know they are not!'

1. Svengali, a mesmeric German-Polish musician, is a character in George du Maurier's novel *Trilby* (1894). Cutcliffe Hyne was the author of a highly popular series of short stories describing the adventures of Captain Owen Kettle, published in 1898 and 1899.
2. For details of Ford (Hueffer), see p. 106. Oliver Madox Hueffer was two years younger than his brother. George Moore (1852–1933) was an Anglo-Irish novelist.
3. Ford's aunt had married William Michael Rossetti, brother of Christina Rossetti (1830–94), whose writing desk was part of The Pent's furniture. Her poem, *Goblin Market*, appeared in 1862. Walter Crane (1845–1915), the artist, and his wife had rented The Pent in July 1898, and had recently vacated it when the Conrads moved in, on 26 October 1898.
4. Wells's home in south-east Kent, about two miles west of Folkestone.
5. Wells's novel about the career of a young socialist was published in 1900.
6. Fabian and rake, husband of E. Nesbit, children's author.
7. Conrad probably met George Bernard Shaw about the turn of the century.
8. Hall Caine (1853–1931), popular novelist.

Some Personal Memories of Conrad*

ARNOLD BENNETT

I first met Conrad about 28 years ago (I pretend to neither accuracy nor industry, but I am sure that the meeting occurred towards the end of the last century), at the house of H. G. Wells. Even then, from the

* From 'Some Personal Memories of Conrad: "Cad" as a New Word: His "Twilight"', *Evening Standard*, 3 Nov. 1927, p. 7.

way he talked, one could perceive at once and all the time that creative writing for him was not a literary pursuit, but a sanguinary war, in which victories were won at an enormous cost. His working days were terrible. The most suitable epitaph for the artist in him would be that which Francis Adams wrote for his own life as a whole:

Bury me with clenched hands
And with eyes open wide,
For in storm and struggle I lived,
And in struggle and storm I died.

At that period Conrad's command of colloquial spoken English was rather imperfect. Even towards the end of his life he could not utter ten words of English without betraying by his accent a foreign origin. Then, he was still more spectacularly a foreigner. Nor did he really understand English literature, which nevertheless he read eagerly and admired much. I remember his dramatic declaration that Milton was not first-rate. (I will not be sure, and I do not wish to traduce a friend; but my recollection is that H. G. Wells supported him in this deplorable position.) It would have been too onerous a business for me to defend *Paradise Lost*, but I did raise my poor shield over those unsurpassed masterpieces, *Lycidas* and *Comus*. No! Conrad would have none of Milton. He called Milton 'woolly'. I never mentioned Milton to him again.

But a still stronger, and a more fantastic, instance of the gaps in his knowledge and comprehension of English occurred when we were discussing some trifling literary scandal. Somebody – I forget whom, but it was no doubt Henley[1] – had referred to R. L. Stevenson as 'a man of three letters'. (There are writers who cannot keep off the classics.[2]) Conrad took me aside and said 'Of course, I know the Latin reference, but Stevenson was never a thief. What English word is meant? Is it "pig?"'

I said: 'The word has not been printed, but I think it must be "cad".'

'"Cad"?' he said. 'What is that? I have never heard the word.'

At first I could not believe this, but he positively assured me that he really never had heard the word 'cad.' He had already written one first novel in English. True, it was dotted with locutions which, while more or less correct, no Englishman would have enjoyed.

I remember another meeting, accidental, in the office of the late J. B. Pinker, his agent and mine.[3] He was very melancholy. He needed, but did not want, a change. I suggested some new form of activity – I forget what. He shook his head sadly. '*Non!*' he replied in French. '*Le pli est pris.*' To translate this as 'The crease is formed' would be ineffective. One could only render it: 'I'm in the groove and can't get out.' This brief remark affected me as much as a phrase in the letter which accompanied his gift to me of a copy of *The Rover*. '*Twilight lies already on these pages*.'[4] It did.

My last meeting, also accidental, with Conrad was at the house of a mutual friend, Mme Alvar.[5] I had not seen him for some years, and for a few minutes he failed to recognise me. Then he suddenly came across the room to me and gripped my shoulders with both hands. His dark eyes were burning into mine, his broad shoulders shaking. 'My dearrr Bennett,' he said, in his earnest, formidable voice. 'You have been my faithful friend for 25 years, and I do not recognise you! Forgive me.' Believe me, I was profoundly touched, and could scarcely speak to him.

NOTES

Arnold Bennett (1867–1931) published his first stories in 1890 and his first novel, *A Man from the North*, eight years later. Very popular and successful in his own time, he is best known now for *Anna of the Five Towns* (1902), *The Old Wives' Tale* (1908) and *Clayhanger* (1910). Conrad's first letter to Bennett is dated 1902, and they had probably met through their mutual friend, H. G. Wells.

1. For details of W. E. Henley, see p. 188.

2. A 'man of three letters' is a thief (Latin *fur*). The classical allusion is to Plautus's use of this phrase in his *Aulularia*.

3. James Brand Pinker (1863–1923) was born in England of a modest family background. Initially a journalist and editor, he began as one of the very first literary agents in January 1896. H. G. Wells soon began to use his services and he was joined by Conrad in 1899. Pinker also acted as agent for Stephen Crane, Henry James and Arnold Bennett. Later, he had a difficult time with D. H. Lawrence, who described him as 'that little parvenu snob of a procureur of books'. To Conrad, however, he was simply 'the Pinker of agents', looking after all his commercial affairs until his death and often advancing him large sums of money and equally generous supplies of support and encouragement.

4. Conrad's letter to Bennett, dated 5 December 1923, is quoted in G. Jean-Aubry's *Joseph Conrad: Life and Letters* (New York: Doubleday, Page, 1927) Vol. II, p. 308.

5. According to the menu, signed by Conrad, Bennett and Maurice Ravel, the composer, this dinner was held on 17 April 1923 at the home of Mme Alvar, a well-known hostess.

Conrad and the Royal Bounty Fund*

HENRY JOHN NEWBOLT

I first met Joseph Conrad at the Savile Club – then housed in Piccadilly. There on Saturday afternoons a small symposium of half a dozen writers and artists was often held after lunch in the second drawing-room and lasted perhaps for one, two, or even three hours. It was on one of these occasions that someone introduced me to Conrad. I had for some time read both long and short stories by him and I looked at him with fascinated interest – he had repelled me by *The Nigger of the 'Narcissus'* but not so much as he had attracted me by *Lord Jim*. In this last work I saw a modern writer instinctively reproducing patterns of the Greek world – not one but two at once, for the book begins with the sombre religious feeling of an Orestean tragedy, and then sails away into an Odyssey of the Far East.

The man himself did not disappoint me. One thing struck me at once – the extraordinary difference between his expression in profile and when looked at full face. In both aspects it was an Oriental face: but while the profile was aquiline and commanding, in the front view the broad brow, wide-apart eyes and full lips produced the effect of an intellectual calm and even at times of a dreaming philosophy. Then came a sharp surprise. As we sat in our little half-circle round the fire, and talked on anything and everything, I saw a third Conrad emerge – an artistic self, sensitive and restless to the last degree. The more he talked the more quickly he consumed his cigarettes, rolling them so fast one after another that the fingers of both hands were stained a deep yellow almost as far as the palms. And presently, when I asked him why he was leaving London after a stay of only two days, he replied that he could never be more than a day or two in London, because the crowd in the streets so terrified him. 'Terrified? – by that dull stream of obliterated faces?' He leaned forward with both hands raised and clenched. 'Yes, terrified: I see their personalities all leaping out at me like *tigers*!' He acted the tiger well enough almost to terrify his hearers: but the moment after he was talking again wisely and

* From *My World as in My Time: Memoirs of Sir Henry Newbolt, 1862–1932* (London: Faber & Faber, 1932) pp. 300–6.

soberly as if he were an average Englishman with not an irritable nerve in his body.

Some months after this I heard a gloomy account of his health from my friend, William Rothenstein,[1] and this was followed up by a letter two days later.

9 *June*, 1904

My dear Newbolt,

I saw Conrad again yesterday – he really is in a very bad state of mind, and, I learn, very hard pressed at the moment. Could you advise me whom to approach, or help yourself in any way? I am sorry to bother you in the matter, but an artist's life is a precarious one, and I never cease to marvel myself that more of us are not in Conrad's position. I feel sure, and he feels sure, that if he can tide over the present difficulties he will be all right: but his nerves are in a terrible state, and his wife is pretty seriously ill with heart trouble, and help would do a great deal just now.[2] Your advice would be most useful. Sincerely yours,

W. Rothenstein.

I had by this time known Rothenstein long enough and well enough to be able to read all that was concealed in his letter as well as all that was revealed. He had, of course, as a true descendant of St Martin, divided his own cloak with Conrad – or perhaps given it all – and he was now regretting that it did not suffice to clothe the man completely. What was needed was to find a source of bounty, not more generous, but more copious, and I had no doubt where and by whom it could best be found. I moved accordingly and a fortnight later Edmund Gosse[3] wrote to tell me that he had had a long talk with the Prime Minister, Mr Balfour,[4] who asked to see some of Conrad's books and was vaguely favourable to the idea of a pension.[5] The letter ended by putting to me the crucial question – 'Can you, with perfect tact, discover what Conrad's attitude would be?'

My heart sank heavily – I had been inquiring into Conrad's antecedents and from all I heard it seemed unlikely that a man of his birth and spirit would ever accept anything that could be regarded as charity, public or private. The pseudonym by which he was known in England, was only the most modest fraction of a resounding name in the history of Poland: Teodor Joseph Conrad Korzeniowski was the only son of Apollo Korzeniowski, poet and patriot, translator of Shakespeare, head of an ancient and wealthy landed family, and for years of exile a victim of Russian tyranny. His character was said to be fiery, especially upon the point of honour and independence, and I expressed my doubts to Rothenstein with some emphasis. He was far more optimistic – he knew what I did not, that our friend had already accepted a donation from a well-known public fund.[6] He wrote a few days later: 'Conrad is evidently greatly touched by your and Gosse's proposal, and is very willing to have the application made.' Gosse also wrote that 'the Chief is manifestly affected by the romance of Conrad's life' and after some delay I was relieved to hear again from Rothenstein as follows:

> My dear Newbolt,
>
> Gosse wrote me the good news to-day: I don't think the offer of help could have been made in a more thoughtfully delicate way than in Gosse's form of Balfour's excellent proposal.[7] As a matter of fact a sum such as that proposed will be of far greater use to Conrad at the present moment than a pension would be, and I have not the smallest doubt of Conrad's accepting it most gratefully and joyfully. I don't think we need have any fear on that score. I owe you many thanks for having in the first instance approached Gosse on the subject. I have written to Conrad this evening and sent him a copy of Gosse's letter, and we shall no doubt hear without delay from Capri.[8] Conrad writes that he has been suffering from influenza and unable to get any work done in consequence. His wife is getting on, however, very satisfactorily, and the copy of Gosse's letter should do much to cheer him. Yours always sincerely,
>
> W. Rothenstein.

To a certain point this was a true forecast: acceptance followed at once, but it was acceptance under a misconception. Conrad in fact wrote from Capri, and wired for some money – he was delighted with the grant, and wished to be able to use some of it *immediately* in order to get back to London at once. There was some prospect of the Stage Society producing a little play of his, and he thought it might lead to commissioned stage work for himself.[9]

Unfortunately the grant was expressly intended to promote the 'permanent benefit' of the recipient, and was to be administered in that sense by Rothenstein and myself. Still more unfortunately, Gosse's letter had given the impression that the money would be forthcoming at once, and at Conrad's disposal. On 16 May I received a note from W. R.: 'Could you meet me at the Vienna café at 4 o'clock to-morrow afternoon? I have heard from C. who has taken the arrangement rather badly.[10] . . . Yrs in haste, W. R.'

By 23 May[11] Conrad was back in London and urgently desiring to see me. He had already seen Rothenstein, and Rothenstein was 'worn out by the time he left, having argued with him until late into the night'. I had a very similar experience on the 25th when I spent the afternoon in a discussion with Conrad, which he summarised in a long letter written the same evening. Two passages from it are enough to show the force of his contention and the reasonableness of our caution.

Pent Farm,
Stanford, Nr. Hythe,
25 *May* 1905.

Dear Mr Newbolt,

In my view of the grant made to me I start from the principle that the first and main intention has been to procure for me the ease of mind necessary for tranquil and steady writing, in which – and in which alone – is to be found a radical and complete remedy for my difficulties.

It is this thought which emboldened me to urge so earnestly the advisability of allowing me the sum of £250 at once, in order to pay certain very pressing debts. I trust that after our conversation you take the view that they have not been incurred recklessly: at most perhaps indiscreetly, and if indiscreetly then only in part so. The pressure of circumstances must be taken into account. Besides there is the fact that provision was made to meet them (not quite completely but in considerable proportion) at the end of last year, when the aggravated state of my wife's health, necessitating an operation of a serious kind and a sojourn abroad under rather expensive conditions, diverted the moneys destined for my creditors. In this I had but little option. Life is uncertain (mine from the actuarial point of view is not a very good risk) and I admit that the dread of having to leave, perhaps, a woman completely and painfully crippled, with a small child and with no means of support, left but little inclination for the cool consideration of ways and means and consequences. The detail of debts is as follows . . . total £298.[12] By sitting very close all the next month I think that with £250 I may be able to manage. Though of course it will be managed under stress. . . . All these affairs are very miserable: but the point, as I venture to state it with all the deference and gratitude imaginable, is that if I have been judged worthy of that favour there can be no harm of applying it in the way in which its beneficent effect will be most felt. Never, perhaps, an unexpected help had been more timely. The view also may be taken that those debts being for the *most part* the result of my wife's illness, the grant pays for her cure; which is in fact the feeling I first had when the news reached me. And what greater relief could be given to a man?

I trust you will forgive this interminable letter. I wished to state my case fully, for the matter is of great and urgent importance to me. I can't thank you sufficiently for the sympathy with which you listened to me this afternoon. You have in that interview given me the great moral support of your commendation of my work heard from your own lips. It is a great thing. Sometimes a few words have a magical effect. I look forward with increased belief in my work. I am my dear Mr Newbolt, Always yours faithfully,

Jph. Conrad.

I intended buying your latest book[13] tomorrow before going home to the Pent; but I venture now to ask you to send me a copy – inscribed – *à charge de revanche* – as the French say.[14] I'll send you my *Mirror of the Sea* as soon as it comes out – a pinch of my chaff for your solid grain – but one gives what one has.

Rothenstein and I consulted together and decided that we must agree to provide the £250 for payment of debts: but to ensure that we should only pay such debts as were justly due, and that the proper receipts should be forthcoming, we proposed to employ a solicitor in this part of the business. To this Conrad made the most strenuous objection – he thought that it looked like making a composition with his creditors, and that it would tarnish his credit as a man of honour. I sympathised with his feeling: it was the kind of obstacle I had been expecting from the beginning. But I was more haunted than Rothenstein was by the spectre of the law. We were in some sort Trustees: we were agreed on paying the debts: but we were asked to hand over money not to the creditors direct but to the debtor himself. I had no shadow of mistrust about Conrad's intentions – he had been frank with us, he was evidently a man of fine instincts and strong character. But if anything should go wrong – under 'pressure of circumstances' – we should have to face inquiry, and inquiry would show that we had paid away a large part of our trust money, although we knew from Conrad's own statement that only six months before, when provision had been made to meet these debts the pressure of circumstances had 'diverted the money destined for my creditors'. What reply could we make? How could we say that we had acted for the beneficiary's 'permanent benefit'?[15]

NOTES

Sir Henry John Newbolt (1862–1938), barrister and poet, best known for rousing nautical and patriotic ballads such as 'Drake's Drum' in *Admirals All and Other Verses* (1897). He was devoted to public and honorary service, and he served on the committee of the Royal Literary Fund. He met Conrad in 1904 but they never became close friends.

1. For details of William Rothenstein, see p. 146.

2. At this time, Conrad was very concerned about his wife's health; a valvular defect in her heart had recently been discovered, and she was still troubled by lameness and neuralgia, to the extent that Conrad feared that she would be a 'helpless cripple. . . . Half the time I feel on the verge of insanity. The difficulties are accumulating around me in a frightful manner' (letter dated 5 April 1904; see *The Collected Letters of Joseph Conrad*, ed. F. R. Karl and Laurence Davies, vol. III (Cambridge: Cambridge University Press, 1988), pp. 128–9). In addition to his family's health and financial difficulties, Conrad was trying to concentrate on *Nostromo*, which he finished in August 1904.

3. Sir Edmund William Gosse (1849–1928), author of *Father and Son* (1907). In 1904 he was Librarian of the House of Lords and Secretary of the Royal Literary Fund.

4. Arthur James Balfour (1848–1930) became Prime Minister in July 1902, resigning in 1905.

5. The official name of the Fund from which Conrad received his grant of £500 is the Royal Bounty Special Service Fund, which awarded money either in trust or for the purchase of a life-insurance policy.

6. In July 1902 Conrad had received a grant of £300 from the Royal Literary Fund.

7. Conrad received Gosse's official notification of the £500 grant on 11 April 1905 and the money was paid out to the trustees on 3 May 1905.

8. The Conrads had left for Capri in January 1905, mainly for the benefit of Jessie's health.

9. The Stage Society had not summoned Conrad to return home, and the date of his departure from Capri had always been fixed for mid-May. His urgent request for £150 shows that he was seriously in debt. In June 1905, five performances of *One Day More*, a one-act play, were given at the Royal Theatre.

10. Conrad's letter to Rothenstein has not been preserved. He must have heard about the appointment of Newbolt and Rothenstein as trustees before leaving Capri, and he wrote to Gosse on 16 May 1905 that 'the whole affair has assumed an appearance much graver and more distressing than any stress of my material necessities: the appearance of "Conrad having to be saved from himself" – the sort of thing that casts a doubt on a man's sense of responsibility, on his right feelings, on his sense of correct conduct'.

11. The Conrads arrived back at The Pent on 18 May 1905.

12. In addition to his obligations to friends such as Ford, Galsworthy, Pinker and Rothenstein, his debts totalled more than £450.

13. *The Year of Trafalgar*, published earlier that month.

14. 'Provided that I may do the same for you.' *The Mirror of the Sea* was published in October 1906.

15. Newbolt and Rothenstein agreed to pay off Conrad's pressing debts without the assistance of a solicitor. The total came to £260 (including £50 bank overdraft, £45 rent, £60 medical fees and £85 tradesmen's bills). The rest of the grant was paid in instalments of £15–20 until April 1906.

'The greatest stickler for uprightness'*

NORMAN DOUGLAS

Yes; I liked Harris,[1] though he once did victimise me in a small way. He had a powerful new car; wouldn't it be good fun to run down, both of us, to see his friend Joseph Conrad at Orlestone in Kent?[2] That was in 1914 or 1915.[3] I thought it strange that Frankie, with his reputation of a perfect immoralist, should be on terms of intimacy with Conrad who was the greatest stickler for uprightness I have ever known; little I dreamed that he was simply using me to get another sight (with a view to future 'copy') of Conrad whom, as I afterwards heard, he had met just once before, when he ran down to Kent with Austin Harrison on some other pretext. On the way there he told me of his past life in Japan, as a rivetter on Brooklyn bridge, as a cowboy, and I cannot remember what else. The moment we set foot in the house I saw that something was wrong.

Conrad managed to scrape up a polite greeting and then, after three minutes, went upstairs to sulk in his room and not to emerge again till Harris was off the premises. He did this on his usual and only too justifiable plea of gout, saying to me, as I accompanied him up the stairs: 'I should like to know why you bring this brigand into my house. Am I never to see the last of him?'

That earlier impression, apparently, had not been favourable. Whether Harris got any 'copy' out of the family I cannot say, but so far as Conrad was concerned it was a misspent afternoon – doubly misspent, because on the way home we ran into a police trap, and Frankie was afterwards fined for exceeding the speed limit.

NOTES

George Norman Douglas (1868–1952) was living on Capri when the Conrads visited there in 1905. A former diplomat, Douglas was at that time pursuing his interest in botany. Conrad was later to help him with the beginning of his

* From *Looking Back: An Autobiographical Excursion* (London: Chatto & Windus, 1934) pp. 416–17.

literary career. During school holidays, Conrad and his wife looked after his son, Robin, who was four years older than John Conrad, and, indeed, they paid for his education. Conrad remained a loyal friend to Douglas until the latter's sexual behaviour became a matter of public scandal; Douglas was arrested in 1916 on a charge of molestation, but he jumped bail before the trial and took up permanent residence overseas.

1. For details of Frank Harris and his previous visit to Conrad in the company of Austin Harrison, see pp. 107–8.

2. Capel House, Orelestone, near Ashford, was the Conrad's home from 1910 to 1919.

3. Of this visit, Jessie Conrad wrote that 'it was one occasion on which Joseph Conrad went completely off the deep end, as the boys would say, without any warning, and sparks flew for some moments. These three men arrived early one Sunday afternoon, and coffee was brought at once. I stayed in the room some half-hour or so and Frank Harris, to everyone's surprise, rose and without a word to either of us, coolly rang the bell for more coffee. The impertinence nearly took my breath away, and the air was tense for a few moments. Then some remark made by that extraordinary man, who must have forgotten he was in an English drawing-room, brought Norman Douglas to his feet with a bound. But consummate gentleman as he was always, in his dealings with a woman, he merely offered me his arm and led me to the door' (Jessie Conrad, *Joseph Conrad and His Circle* (London: Jarrolds, 1935) p. 97).

The Flurried Years*

VIOLET HUNT

Once that autumn [1908] the editor[1] and I were asked to a quiet dinner with a poetess – now Lady Dilke[2] – and her husband, and he called for me. It was foggy, the worst day of the year. We were eating quails stewed in wine, with little green grapes in the cocottes with them. Suddenly the editor let out that he had left Conrad at home in Holland Park Avenue,[3] sitting over the fire with a bad cold. He was not allowed to hide his light under a bushel any longer, and the telephone was used. But Conrad – on the telephone I heard his queer, foreign voice – refused to stir out in the fog, but was going straight to bed. The editor drew a vivid picture of the great man sitting, full of aches and pains, grouting there in the lonely flat over a dying fire, and leaving even that poor comfort for the colder one of the cubicular bedroom. I thought that Joseph Conrad – his two *Christian* names, as it happens – must

* From *The Flurried Years* (London: Hurst & Blackett, 1926) pp. 31–2, 52–3.

be very fond of Joseph Leopold[4] to put up with the bedroom, but, then, he was used to the cabins of merchant ships.

This was probably during one of his darker days – a fit of toothache, perhaps; one of those evil hours that come to authors round about the *enfantement* of a masterpiece.[5] For they are all to be masterpieces, and that is why the merest, tiniest essay costs the writer of it so dear. Conrad would think nothing of writing to me or the editor a letter headed with, or in the corner, 'Pray for me these days!' And we knew at once it was a question of literary parturition.

* * *

Once I spoke of Love by name to Henry James and got, sweetly enough, snubbed. As for Conrad, he got quite cross when once, *en tête-à-tête*, I invited him to take some interest in that sort of thing for my sake. He spoke to me just as he used to speak to the editor, asking, with lifted eyebrows and savage twist of the upper lip: 'What object, what purpose, could be served by the creation of equivocal situations – juggling with the realities of life?'[6] That was just what Love was, and nothing else, the creator of equivocal situations. Art was the only reality of life. He himself did not go in for love-affairs, except of course, the master affair of all. He did not envisage the fact, I suppose, that other literary existences, imagining themselves capable of including more than one, are ruined by the swelter entailed by plurality of emotions.

It was never any use asking him to take sides, to speak to this or that person, to engineer *raccommodements*. The very atmosphere of arrangement and possible compromise seemed terrible to him: 'I can't breathe in situations that are not clear.' He abhorred plots and suspicions; 'They are neither in my nature, my tradition, or my experience.' 'Happy man!' I said. 'No, I am not *fine* enough for them', he maintained whose work it was to create situations, not unravel them – especially in his society *intime*; and with a lovely shrug and a smile, as of an infant at bay, he murmured: 'We are just a pair of silly innocents.'

NOTES

Isobel Violet Hunt (1866–1942) was a novelist and short-story writer. She was the eldest daughter of Alfred Hunt, the painter, and her parents were intimates of Browning, Ruskin, Rossetti, William Morris and all the Pre-Raphaelites. Her first novel was published in 1894. She had a brief affair with H. G. Wells and, in 1908, had recently begun a long relationship with Ford Madox Ford, whose wife refused to grant him a divorce. All three members of this triangle tried to gain Conrad's support and sympathy, and the messy personal life of Ford contributed greatly to the cooling of Conrad's friendship with him. In a letter to John Galsworthy, in March 1912, Conrad mentions 'the great F. M. H. [Ford] who was here shortly after New Year with the somewhat less great V. H.'

1. Ford Madox Ford (Hueffer), who in 1908, had founded the *English Review*, an outstanding monthly journal which attracted much new talent. At the beginning, Conrad participated in all its administrative and editorial activities. For details of Ford, see p. 106.

2. Ethel Clifford, who had published two volumes of verse, married Sir Fisher Wentworth Dilke in 1905.

3. Ford's apartment at 85 Holland Park Avenue, London served as the office of the *English Review*.

4. Ford Hermann Hueffer adopted the additional Christian names of Joseph Leopold Madox. He changed his name by deed pool in 1919 to Ford Madox Ford.

5. In September 1908, Conrad began writing the reminiscences which appeared initially in the *English Review* in 1908–9 and were later published as *A Personal Record* (New York: Harper & Brothers, 1912) and as *Some Reminiscences* (London: Eveleigh Nash, 1912).

6. This and the following quotations from Conrad are virtually identical to sentiments which Conrad expressed in a letter to Ford, dated April or May 1909 [see Zdzisław Najder, *Joseph Conrad: A Chronicle* (Cambridge: Cambridge University Press, 1983) p. 348). Many of Conrad's letters to Ford have survived in the form of copies made by Violet Hunt.

Joseph Conrad: A Reminiscence*

CECIL ROBERTS

It is to chance, despite the banal philosophy of the opportunists, that most of us owe our richest experiences, and it has certainly been to chance that, in my journeying up and down the face of the earth, I have owed the most cherished moments of contact with those rare beings who, dowered by providence, out of the stress of their own sensitive personalities in conflict with life give back to us an interpret-

* From 'Joseph Conrad: A Reminiscence', *Bookman* (NY), vol. LXI (July 1925) pp. 536–42.

ation whose truth we can no better describe than as the divination of genius.

Of such men, pre-eminently, was Joseph Conrad. Our own happy contact was brief and fragmentary, but for some reason richly affectionate, almost in the nature of that perfect bond between master and disciple described by Plato in his *Republic*. Looking back, I see the beginning of so rich and fortunate an experience in chance, unless mortal conceit permits one to think the divinity that shapes our ends was here working for mine.

One evening I sat in the pleasant studio of Alvin Langdon Coburn,[1] which overlooks the river at Hammersmith Mall. I was examining the amazing gallery of notabilities created by his camera. A photograph of Joseph Conrad caused me to offer my tribute of admiration, whereupon a lady sitting obscurely in one corner of the studio began to talk as one of the scribes. She knew Joseph Conrad and spoke authoritatively.[2] She was an American journalist, a kind creature whose name, I am ashamed to confess, I have now forgotten but whose kindness enriched my life, for with a dangerous generosity she promised that I should meet Conrad.

Promises of this nature fill me with doubts. In the first place, I question the good faith of the promises; secondly, I hesitate before lending myself to that selfish curiosity which causes us to crowd about a famous man, trading upon our own indebtedness to his genius as a claim to personal inspection. What possible interest would Joseph Conrad have in an obscure, ambitious young man, and in what observation of good taste could I lend myself to an intrusion which arose more from the generosity than the tact of my hostess? But human frailty assented to her design. She promised, I hoped.

A few weeks passed, and I had dismissed the promise as one of those pleasantries that pass with the tea cups, when I received a card to say that she was giving a house warming in her new flat off Bedford Square, to which Joseph Conrad might come. 'And might not', I concluded, but accepted, since her kindness and her charm were sufficient rewards of themselves.

I found the flat, an attic storey, on the fifth floor of one of those stiff-fronted houses whose exteriors give no indication of their roominess within. But the accommodation was certainly crowded on that winter's afternoon of a dreary February in 1918. My hostess's daughter, two or three young actresses and a couple of American university students, full of curiosity, packed the small cheerful room into which I was drawn through the hospitable aroma of toast-making. We chatted and laughed, and my hostess said she hoped Mr Conrad would come. We all hoped, but disguised the meanness of our spirit from the nervous anxiety of our hostess. Conrad the elusive, Conrad the recluse, was he to be captured and held in this attic box whose high windows looked on the yellow sunset glow of a fog-shrouded day? A knock, a cry of welcome, and the good soul felt delivered. The Master had arrived.

I watched him, furtively, from the bay of the window into which I was wedged. While recognition was easy and complete, since photographs had truly conveyed that head – like an inverted triangle with its long jaw, pointed beard, and semi-Mongolian eyes sunk beneath dark, defined eyebrows – I was surprised by the nature of the man. A master of seascapes, familiar with the moods of the Seven Seas and the stranger moods manning the ships upon those seas, a sea captain, an eye witness of strange happenings on the borderlands of civilisation, he was wholly unmarked by experience, unchanged by environment. For this man of medium height and compact body, trimly attired in a double-breasted blue serge suit, with reflective monocle swinging on a thin cord, was a figure of complete civilisation. The Polish aristocrat and not the sea captain entered the room, as I had seen him, racially dominant while nationally disinherited, entering the drawing-rooms of the Faubourg St Germain, driving in the Prater, or enjoying the sunset from the Pincio.

I accounted him then, in surmise, as I learned him to be in familiarity later, a prince among men. That is the testimony of all who knew him, a testimony which sprang neither from the glamour of fame nor the written evidence of genius, but simply and spontaneously from the regality of his mental and physical presence. As Muirhead Bone defined him, as truly by pen as by pencil, 'Centuries may come and go before anyone so gifted, so strange, and such a charming human being as Joseph Conrad comes this way again.'[3]

I had yet to learn that charm, but the singularity was apparent at once. Half an hour elapsed before the movement in that flat found me standing and talking to Conrad. He told me afterward that I had rescued him – by a frontal attack with teacups and tea – from the wearisome catechism of an earnest but tactless young man bent on the dissection of genius, and in the same complaint I heard a protest against this exposure to an assembly.

I had no superiority in most respects over the guest I had dispossessed, but I steered my bark cautiously through the ruffled waters of a mind whose depth I had no means to fathom. Of his work, his achievement, it would have been presumption to speak; his own tireless, meticulous taskmaster, he knew well his triumphs and defeats. I spoke nothing of these, in question or tribute, but with an egotism irrepressible in youth and tolerable only in that period because it is inconsequent and spontaneous, I told him of some experiences, since I was fresh from visits to the Grand Fleet and the Dover Patrol. I had caught his interest at once. He told me the war had overwhelmed his power of expression, so that he had been unable to complete a series of articles on the mine-sweepers which the Admiralty had sought him to do.[4] 'I write with difficulty, with agony, in this hour of indecision', he said. This inability, I saw later, was of the very essence of his genius. He was the alchemist, not the photographer, transmuting, not recording, observations to the fabric of a dream in which shape and substance were lost, from which potent suggestion and atmosphere arose. His human creatures, in love or anger, never sought words for expression. In that saga of a woman's heart, *The Rescue*, the word 'love' is never mentioned in its four hundred pages, despite the theme.

So we talked until both grew conscious that duty to a hostess was in danger of eclipse; but as we parted he expressed a wish that we should meet again and, to my surprise, named an evening for dinner at his flat. The manner of his expression was characteristic of his exquisite courtesy, his innate kindliness – if I was not too busy, if I should care, he said. Then he went, leaving me with a bounding heart, a sense of grateful, incredible wonder – if I was not too busy, if I should care! I saw my hostess was as baffled as I. The great god Chance is full of vagaries.

Before the momentous evening arrived, a note was delivered at my rooms. It was from Conrad. 'I think it fair to warn you,' he wrote, 'that we will have on Sunday two dear ladies, great friends of ours, but who will certainly be in the way of the good talk I promised myself to have with you. My wife has just told me of these invitations. However, if you have the necessary courage, we will be delighted to see you at seven o'clock on Sunday next.'

Dear ladies, or dreadful Amazons, they could not have deterred me. It was the custom of Conrad, who at that time was living at Orlestone, to make a yearly excursion to London. He had rented a furnished flat in Hyde Park Mansions, Marylebone Road,[5] and it was there I arrived on this memorable Sunday evening. The party was a small one, but friendly and of a family nature, so that the sense of visiting was soon lost. Conrad himself had the rare art of conferring distinction on those with whom he spoke, his choice of words, his deferential air, dismissing any nervousness one might feel in stating an opinion. The two old ladies certainly did not spoil our evening, and for that they prevented our 'good talk' I was subsequently grateful, when Conrad suggested another visit in a few days.

That first evening enabled me to see Conrad as he declared, in a memorable passage, he could never be seen, namely – 'Conrad *en pantoufles*. It is a constitutional inability.'[6] That was true of the writer, but the man I then saw was certainly Conrad 'with his boots off' in the bosom of his family. The loving admiration that sounded in every mention of his wife, his vigilant attendance upon her wants, the pride with which he confidentially assured me 'Jessie' was a marvellous cook, the benediction that sounded in his voice as he pronounced this name of his wife, these revealed the personal Conrad, the Conrad for which you will search his books in vain, since no evidence or personal rumour of the man invades his prose or intimidates his style.

There were others, besides the two dear ladies, who were bent upon preventing a good talk between us, although the talk was good, bright and lengthy as we gathered later in the little sitting-room: the Germans were busy above us in the night sky, and a muffled roar from the St Pancras district told us of the drama overhead. Afterward, when I had departed, I realised that while I had seen Conrad the man, he had as yet divulged no aspect of the novelist. Our talk had been of everything but books, of anything but Conrad. Later I might be rewarded, but I respected his reserve and the charm of his hospitality too deeply to intrude on this intimate domain of his inner life. But would he remember our reunion, or was I never to hear Conrad speak of what, in a life of such varied experience, came nearest to him, the passion for self-expression?

A few days passed, and then another note: 'Next Friday is our last in Town and it is Edward Garnett's evening.[7] E. G. has done a lot for literature in the '90s and anyway is an interesting and worthy personality. If you would like to meet him come in about seven and we will have a three-cornered talk.'

Mrs Conrad once again sustained her reputation as hostess and cook, a rôle resulting later in a small volume of recipes in which a preface proclamed the faith of one who had tested the recommendations.[8] 'Edward', as he was affectionately called, quizzical and quiet, listened more than spoke, ruminating over some point of discussion prior to my advent, which point proved afterward to be upon a new work in hand.[9] Dinner finished, Mr Garnett, with much fond shepherding, was helped to gather papers and apparel for his departure. Mrs Conrad quietly disappeared, and we were alone in the dining-room.

My mind faithfully preserves every detail of our long conversation, unblurred through the crowded interval of my life since then. The strange indelible quality of Conrad's personality was even more potent than I realised, and its potency was commingled with a singular diffidence, with a secret doubt that amounted at moments to a private agony of apprehension. I stumbled upon it by accident and I leaped into his heart by a chance expression.

Our talk had turned to the art of writing, and he questioned me closely upon my own experience regarding the speed of composition, the need of revision, the fluidity of ideas. He confessed he had never known the pleasure of writing, only the ardour that drove him to it, and that his progress was painful, a long wrestling with the spirit within. 'Perhaps that is because I began late, when experience checked the singleness of youthful thought. I have never been fluent. Easy writing – and I do not say it cannot be good writing – is not possible to me. My success seems in proportion to my effort, to my striving. I feel that generalship has brought me whatever victories I may claim – if any.'

I watched his face as he pronounced the last two words, with a sadness, a quiet resignation that surprised me.

'If any?' I repeated, the surprise in my voice.

He had risen and stood, one foot resting upon the fender, one hand adjusting the position of the black marble clock on the mantelpiece, his face looking into the fire.

'You may think I am childish, perhaps,' he said, very slowly and quietly, so that I seemed to overhear his thoughts, 'but I could be content if I could think something of mine, something however small, might endure a while. One has expressions of immortality – there are my boys – but one's writing is one's own immortality, if it can be achieved.'

I expressed my surprise that he could doubt his own achievement. Could he not feel assured, I asked. Had he not realised that his recognition, no popular one in its beginning, was soundly based, that his work had an enduring quality by virtue not only of its singularity of treatment but also because it appealed neither through sensation nor cleverness?

'My dear young man – if I could think that . . .' he answered, and then, fixing his eyes steadily upon me as I sat there on the opposite side of the fireplace, 'In what book do you feel I have done this?'

'*Nostromo* undoubtedly', I said, without hesitation.

There was a silence, during which he looked again into the fire, and I quietly observed him, the fine tenuous hand, the long Slavonic head. His hair was straight and dark, with a greying trimmed beard and thin moustache. The droop of the lids over the eyes gave him an imperious expression, and the skin, lightly furrowed with lines that marked the impress of nervous tension and high sensibility, had a yellow tinge which is the legacy of those who have braved the tropic suns. In this face its colouring may also have taken something from the fever that attacked him in the Congo and which, one felt, had reduced the strength of a highly strung but resilient constitution. There were moments when he bore a similarity of type, though not of detail, to his friend R. B. Cunninghame Graham, or 'Count Roberto' as he called him, but he had not the dash nor the suggestion of the dandy which characterises Graham.[10] The deep steady eyes, with their direct look, impersonal withal as a bird's eyes, so that you learned nothing of him while he seemed to learn all about you, the extraordinary length of the jaw from ear to chin, fine and emphasised by the high cheek bones, so that with his tight parchment skin he had a forceful resemblance to the mummied head of a Ptolemy – all these combined to give his appearance, added to a princely bearing in manner and deportment, a distinction that marked him as one apart, yet gave no clue to the *métier* of his distinction.

Observing him in this ensuing silence, I saw a change, a softening in the eyes, a less acute air in his manner. He turned towards me, murmuring, half to himself: 'My poor *Nostromo* – you think that? My dear young man, you have touched me as you cannot realise. Why did you say *Nostromo* of all my books? Tell me.'

I told him and he listened carefully, so that I found myself embarking upon an analysis of Conrad that left me amazed at my audacity when I had finished.

'Listen,' he said, 'you shall know a secret, if it interests you, which I could not have told to you except for those words of yours. *Nostromo* is my best book, it is more Conrad than anything I have written, that is, in the sense that it embarks on my greatest imaginative adventure, and that it involved the severest struggle. No work cost me so much, and, achieved, gave me such satisfaction. I stand by *Nostromo*, out of the frailty of flesh, hoping it may last a while for a memorial. And yet it did not succeed with the public. They will not have my poor *Nostromo*. They prefer *Lord Jim*.'

He said this sadly, not bitterly, but henceforth I was conscious that my opinion had stirred him, and when I left the house I wondered upon the uncertainty of human ambition. Conrad, in the world's eyes pre-eminent, successful, reaping already the homage and attendant signs of tribute that presage immortality, seeking assurance of and comforted by the opinion of an obscure young man. That my unguided selection of *Nostromo* had touched him I knew, by the closing incident of that meeting. As I was about to leave, in the early hours of the morning, he asked me to wait in the hall a moment, and, returning, bore in his hand a book which he placed in mine, extracting at the same time a promise that I should reciprocate the gift with a book of poems I had just published.[11] That was the *beau geste* of the Master. His own volume – it was a copy of *Nostromo* – bore a prized inscription. A few days later I fulfilled my promise, with diffidence. Never again shall I exchange such dross for gold.

NOTES

Cecil Roberts (1892–1976), poet, novelist, journalist, traveller and wit, was born in Nottingham. After a brief spell in the Civil Service, he entered journalism as a Special Correspondent with the forces in the First World War. In 1920 he was appointed editor of the *Nottingham Journal*.

His first volume of poems, with a preface by John Masefield, was published in 1913, and he won considerable critical acclaim when he began writing novels ten years later. He became an established best-seller in the 1930s with *Pilgrim Cottage* and *Victoria Four-Thirty*. He later travelled extensively in the United States on lecture tours and eventually settled in Italy, where he died at the age of eighty-four. He met Conrad, as he describes, in February 1918, when he was twenty-five years old.

1. Alvin Langdon Coburn (1882–1966), pioneer portrait photographer.
2. This would appear to be Grace Willard (see p. 47).
3. See p. 167.
4. In the last quarter of 1916 Conrad made several North Sea voyages with the Royal Navy as an observer in the war effort. He subsequently wrote 'The Unlighted Coast' for the Admiralty, probably in December 1916, but it was published only posthumously, as it had no propaganda value. Conrad did not follow through with his original plan to write more articles for the Admiralty.
5. In November 1917, the Conrads rented a flat in a boarding house at 4C Hyde Park Mansions, Marylebone Road, London, not far from Jessie Conrad's nursing home, where she was undergoing medical tests on her leg. They returned to Capel House, Orlestone, in February 1918.
6. Joseph Conrad, *Notes on Life and Letters* (London: J. M. Dent, 1949) p. vi.
7. For a note on Garnett, see p. 82.
8. Conrad wrote a preface for his wife's *A Handbook of Cookery for a Small House* (London: Heinemann, 1923).
9. Conrad at this time was working on *The Arrow of Gold*, about which Garnett was positive and encouraging.
10. For a note on Graham, see p. 234.
11. Probably Roberts's *Twenty-Six Poems*, published in November 1917 by Grant Richards.

Everyman Remembers*

ERNEST RHYS

Since we had last met, my host was a little older, a little greyer, and his old enemy, podagra,[1] had got under his guard. But he was in spirit undiminished; though he might growl now and again at an enemy that had attacked him first while he was at sea years ago, and had kept worrying him ever since.

* From *Everyman Remembers* (London: J. M. Dent, 1931) pp. 261, 262–6, 267–8.

On the table by the fire lay a novel he had been reading when I arrived. 'Edith Wharton', he said, with the zest of a connoisseur, as if one should say, 'a blue picotee'.[2]

When we talked, then and afterward, of his contemporaries, I found him keenly interested in what they were doing, and fully alive to a sense of their fellow craftsmanship and their new modes. It was not any mere literary test he applied, but one that in the novel, in the tale, must always come first: the human factor.

He spoke of the younger writers and their amazing cleverness.

'But,' said he, 'some of them do not seem to think you need to be kept *engaged* all the while. There are dull pages; the story drags. You have to whip up your interest. That does not do. Every page must be alive.' He resumed with a droll look of dismay: 'Some people say "I find Conrad dull." Eh? I do not know. I try to make every page tell – every sentence. When that fails . . .' He made a gesture of abdication that was not at all final.

* * *

'Do you make a scenario of a story before you set about writing it? Or do you simply pitch on a character like Lingard or Almayer,[3] or your other-self in *The Arrow of Gold*, to serve as *agent provocateur*?'

Conrad had an agreeable way of treating his inquisitor. He looked, with a cryptic look, at his Kentish wood fire – across the smoke of the cigarettes.

'No, I have my psychological aim, first of all. That is quite distinct in my mind. Then I look about for some event, some personal adventure, or if you like some catastrophe, *pour motiver*[4] my chief characters. But I never lose sight of my real aim.'

Later on, we resumed our talk in another room. I was troubled by an uneasy feeling that I was a treacherous guest, conspirator to steal the elixir of this magician, like Hussuf in the *Arabian Nights*. How far was it English in essence? Remember, Conrad was only twenty-one when he first reached English shores and landed at Lowestoft;[5] then he spent five months in a coaster, the *Skimmer of the Sea*, between that port and the Tyne.[6] He could not speak a word of English when he landed; though the Red Ensign had already cast its spell over him. He learned seamanship and English on the *Skimmer*. It was his mariner's university.

But there was no hesitation on his part. He did not even adopt English. 'It was I who was adopted by the genius of the tongue.' The capture was swift and inevitable. The very idioms of English, he declared, affected his temperament and fashioned his 'still plastic character'. Now, having followed him through some forty sea voyages from the first Lingard book to the last, and from the Nigger to Belarab,[7] we see how natural the adoption was. We can make out both his seaman's and penman's pedigree which begins with the English novels he read in Polish versions – among them *Nicholas Nickleby*. 'It is extraordinary,' he says, 'how well Mrs Nickleby could chatter disconnectedly in Polish.'[8] A novel of Anthony Trollope was actually the ritual-book used on the eve of Conrad's Anglican baptism.[9] . . . Another forebear, not so surprising because of the seaman strain, was Captain Marryat, who 'created a priceless legend', and yet another was Fenimore Cooper, who wrote 'before the great American language was born'.[10] In his cordial appreciation of the two, Conrad declared *sans réserve*[11] that they 'shaped' his life.

These old standards help us to take what we might call 'the departure' in his career. He learned their narrative device, but he broke with their literary mode. What is it in him – this consummate sailor, this reshaper of the Ship Adventurous – what is it that has so taken hold of a public that is forgetting Marryat's *Midshipman Easy* and Fenimore Cooper's *Pilot*?[12]

Presently we fell to discussing the art of the satirist; then that of the caricaturist. Hogarth he spoke of with vehement appreciation; but the caricaturists – no! He disliked their attitude, their mode of ridicule, their art of derision. The caricaturists are of a day; the day goes, and they perish. But the great satirists – Cervantes, Rabelais, Hogarth – lie by their dilatation of human nature. They look to its substance, its essential virtue and vice, not to its accidents. One harps on such things because of a perverse desire to get into a master craftsman's workshop, find his measure and surprise him at his craft. But it is not so easy.

'One knows,' he said, speaking of the *via media* of the imagination, 'one knows well enough all mankind has streamed that way. It is the charm of universal experience from which one expects an uncommon or personal sensation – a bit of one's own.'

Which of the English novelists, I asked, counted to him most for stimulus, in his sense of narrative, when he was beginning to write? He did not hesitate.

'Dickens and Thackeray. And of the two, Dickens easily first!'

'What of the later men? George Meredith?'

'No! Meredith's books are too glittering, too *éblouissant*[13] as the French say.'

* * *

Conrad had one decided *bête noire*: no other than Bernard Shaw. Possibly the antipathy dated from the time of the War when Shaw was amusing himself at the expense of the English soldiers and their friends at home, which affronted Conrad in his regard for his adopted country and his Polish sense of the dignity to be observed in matters of life and death. Still, one is left puzzled by it, and reduced to quoting a friend of both men who once said in explanation: 'Ah well, you see, Conrad had the strain of the Polish aristocrat in his blood, while Shaw is – well, Shaw is Shaw.'

Some little while after that Canterbury pilgrimage, when I wanted if possible to get out of Conrad the right to reprint one of his short stories in a collection of such things, I remembered how eagerly he had spoken of Hogarth and decided to use that as a base means of securing his consent. Hanging over my mantelpiece was a Hogarth print, one of the 'Idle Prentice' series, in which the godless youth is putting off in a boat attended by a gaol chaplain and rowed by a boatman as ugly as sin.[14] A great little cartoon – it seemed the very thing to gain Conrad's good will. So I sent it off to him with a letter asking him if, when it had put him in a congenial mood, he would think of letting me include one of his stories in the contemplated book. He replied very cordially, but not a word about the story. It served me right for having given a gift with an ulterior motive.

I did not see him again until the day of the meeting in Bedford Street to arrange the memorial to W. H. Hudson, which afterward created so much heart-burning over the Epstein figure of Rima.[15] Conrad was slipping away before the end, after a delightful speech by the late Lady Grey, when, knowing how rarely he was in London then, I followed and caught him at the door. There I reminded him how he had evaded my question about the short story and he shook his head. 'But,' said he, 'I hung up that Hogarth on my wall, and do you know what? It keeps me straight.'

NOTES

Ernest Rhys (1859–1946) was one of the first three members of the Rhymers' Club which was established at the Cheshire Cheese tavern in 1889, and where he later met W. B. Yeats, Lionel Johnson and Ernest Dowson. Rhys's principal achievement was his founding of 'Everyman's Library', the series of literary classics which he produced with the support of the publisher, J. M. Dent.

Rhys had met Conrad during the war. The visit which he records here occurred in November 1920. Rhys had been commissioned to write an article on Conrad, which was later published as 'An Interview with Joseph Conrad', *Bookman* (NY), vol. LVI (Dec. 1922) pp. 402–8.

1. Gout of the foot.
2. A rare kind of carnation.
3. Both feature in *Almayer's Folly* and *An Outcast of the Islands*.

4. 'In order to motivate'.
5. 10 June 1878. Conrad was twenty years of age.
6. July–August 1878.
7. Lingard appears in *Almayer's Folly*, *An Outcast of the Islands* and *The Rescue*. Belarab is a character in *The Rescue*.
8. Joseph Conrad, *A Personal Record* (London: J. M. Dent, 1946) p. 71.
9. Conrad mentions in *A Personal Record* that he may have been reading a Trollope novel on the evening before he began writing his own first novel (ibid., p. 73).
10. 'Tales of the Sea', in Joseph Conrad, *Notes on Life and Letters* (London: J. M. Dent, 1949), pp. 55, 56.
11. 'Unreservedly'.
12. Captain Frederick Marryat, *Mr Midshipman Easy* (1836) and James Fenimore Cooper, *The Pilot* (1823).
13. 'Dazzling'.
14. William Hogarth, 'The Idle 'Prentice Turned Away and Sent to Sea', *Industry and Idleness* (1747) pl. v.
15. William Henry Hudson (1841–1922), novelist. This meeting was held on 28 November 1922 at the office of Hugh R. Dent, the publisher. The nude figure of Rima by Jacob Einstein (see p. 172) was regarded as obscene by the popular press. It is situated in Hyde Park.

The Diary of Hugh Walpole*

Jan. 23 [1918] Conrad even better than I had expected – looking older, very nervous, rather fantastic and dramatic somehow – his eyes I think – 'an intellectual Corsair'. He talked eagerly, telling me all kinds of things about his early life. Delighted when I said I liked *Nostromo* best, although he said *The Nigger* was *the* book! Cursed the public for not distinguishing between creation and photography. His final quarrel with Wells[1] was: 'The difference between us, Wells, is fundamental. You don't care for humanity but think they are to be improved. I love humanity but know they are not!'

June 2 [1918] Great and glorious day. Conrad simply superb. A child, nervous, excitable, affectionate, confidential, doesn't give you the idea anywhere of a strong man, but *real* genius that is absolutely *sui generis*. Said *Green Mirror*[2] fine – no holes to be picked – but I need more resonance. Said only thing was to be a 'glorious story-teller'. Said all

* Rupert Hart-Davis, *Hugh Walpole: A Biography* (London: Macmillan, 1952) pp. 168, 171, 176, 179, 186, 187, 195, 215, 236, 286.

'isms were rot. Said end of *Secret Agent* an inspiration. Wrote nearly all *Romance.*[3] Doesn't think end of *Victory* anything but inevitable. Wanted to put *everything* into *Lord Jim.*

[September 1918] A very happy day, although Conrad is in many ways like a child about his various diseases, groaning and even crying aloud. He said some interesting things: about Gissing[4] turning over the manuscript of *Amy Foster* and saying in a melancholy voice: 'Ah! I envy you that!' About *Romance*, that it was originally written by Hueffer and called *Seraphina.* Conrad expanded it, writing the entire whole of 'Casa Riego' and the 'Guitar' book.[5] That he can't read Wells, Bennett or Galsworthy – in fact, reads no one now. That it's his ambition after the war to get a yacht and sail down the Thames. That he has never studied any technique and doesn't think one should.

[January 1919] Conrad said many wonderful things about the book;[6] that he was astonished at its art, that it was wonderfully level, that it had true style, etc. I listened as in a dream. I was with him all day. He gave me a wonderful account about his time with the drunken captain on the *Riversdale.*[7] He said he got only £250 for *Under Western Eyes*, £750 apiece for the next three novels by Dent. Spoke of Harold Frederic as 'a gross man who lived grossly and died abominably'.[8] Said Verloc's shop[9] was where Leicester Galleries now are; said 'easier to have an intellectual friendship with a Chinaman than with an American'.

[March 1919] The usual delightful but rather tiring day, as Conrad insists on talking the *whole* day through, never reads or walks or sleeps. . . . Conrad said: 'The damnation of our profession is that it has no artistic security. There's not a masterpiece in the world but you can pick thousands of holes in it if your digestion's out of order – but if a carpenter makes a good box it *is* a good box!' Also: 'Journalists, like labour leaders, only shout up their professions in order to get out of them.'

Aug. 10 [1919] Most jolly day, although the female guest was extremely trying. How I hate most women. How conceited and egoistic and unhumorous they are! Terrifically hot and we sat under a tree in the garden all day almost without moving. Conrad in great form. Annoyed with the reviews of *The Arrow*, especially Lynd's.[10] Said I was the only younger novelist who had drive and breadth enough to be a great one. Said the only thing to be in literature was a tramp. Said his favourite books to re-read were Hudson's *Patagonia* and Wallace's *Malay Archipelago*. Scoffed at *Typee*.[11]

July 18 [1920] Jolly day. Conrad very cheerful. Really has started the Napoleon novel.[12] Showed me some of the second chapter and I was surprised to see how many foreign phrases there were in this first draft. I am thus the first person in the world, after his typist, to meet Cosmo and Henrietta. When I criticised Mrs Travers[13] a little, he said: 'Of course, *mon cher*, it is not very good. I did my best work long ago.' Cunninghame Graham and Lawrence, the Arab man,[14] came down. The latter mild, small, modest, with fine eyes. Said the legend about him all untrue. Talked of printing and the Crusades.

July 19 [1920] More that Conrad said yesterday: That all this talk about technique was absurd, but that you must write just as well as you can and take every kind of trouble. That F. M. Hueffer belittled everything he touched because he had a *small* soul. Got very angry as usual at the mere mention of Americans or Russians, both of whom he detests. More delighted than I have ever seen him at being asked to advise some Liverpool ship men about a training ship for boys.[15] Again at lunch spoke of *Nostromo* and one or two short stories as his best work.

[October 1921] Much odder than I've ever known before, bursting into sudden rages about such nothings as the butter being salt, and then suddenly being very quiet and sweet. Never cross with me save in a sudden tirade about publishers. . . . Too many women in this house and too many secret feelings.

On October 20 [1923] Hugh went down to spend what proved to be his last week-end with Conrad. Richard Curle and G. Jean-Aubry were of the party, and Paul Valéry came to luncheon.[16] Hugh recorded 'jolly talk in the evening, mostly damning everyone, but Conrad's eyes lit over Fenimore Cooper and over Proust, who stirred him to deep excitement'. On the Sunday the old man was 'in great form, saying to me that I must be absolutely myself, the only thing that mattered to get myself free. Very dear he was this time and tender. Certainly happier, I think, since America, where he liked the praise.[17] He remembers snubs like more mortal men!'

[February 1928] Conrad never said anything very interesting in his last years; he was too preoccupied with money and gout. He was only thrilling when he lost his temper and chattered and screamed like a monkey.

NOTES

Sir Hugh Seymour Walpole (1884–1941), novelist, published his first book in 1909, and he was to write some forty-two novels and volumes of short stories. The four parts of his Herries saga, published in the early 1930s, were the most popular with his vast reading public. He was knighted in 1937.

Walpole published one of the first critical books on Conrad in 1916, although he did not meet him until 1918. This first meeting, at a luncheon party in the Carlton Hotel, London, is described in the initial extract from Walpole's diary. In the following year, Conrad was to call the 35-year-old Walpole '"the most intimate of my younger friends"'.

1. Conrad's friendship with H. G. Wells is described on p. 112.
2. Walpole's *The Green Mirror* (London: Macmillan, 1918).
3. During his collaboration with Ford Madox Ford on the writing of *Romance* (1903), Conrad's role was chiefly to correct existing text and add fragments to the novel.
4. George Gissing (1857–1903), novelist.
5. 'Casa Riego' is Part Third and 'Blade and Guitar' is Part Fourth of *Romance*. Conrad's description here of his role in the writing of the novel is much more accurate than his earlier claim which Walpole cited.
6. Walpole's *The Secret City* (London: Macmillan) had been published on 17 January 1919.
7. Conrad joined the *Riversdale*, a clipper, as second mate in September 1883, sailing from London to Madras, where he left the ship in April 1884. Conrad had quarrelled with the Captain, whom Conrad had accused of being drunk.
8. Harold Frederic (1856–98), American author and journalist, a friend of Stephen Crane. In 1898 he suffered a stroke of paralysis which proved fatal. As a devout Christian Scientist he had refused medical attention. At the inquest into his death, his daughter testified that he was insane, but the jury did not agree.
9. In *The Secret Agent*, Verloc's shop is located in Soho, London.
10. Robert Lynd's review of *The Arrow of Gold* had appeared four days earlier in the *Daily News* (London).
11. W. H. Hudson, *Idle Days in Patagonia* (1893); Alfred R. Wallace, *The Malay Archipelago* (1869); Herman Melville, *Typee* (1846).
12. *Suspense*.
13. In *The Rescue*.
14. For notes on R. B. Cunninghame Graham and T. E. Lawrence, see pp. 234 and 218.
15. In July 1920 Conrad was asked by the Ocean Steam Ship Company, a large Liverpool shipping business, to advise on the planned construction of a sailing ship to be used in the training of boys for the Merchant Marine.

16. Paul Valéry (1871–1945), French poet, had met Conrad in the previous year and visited him in October 1922. For a note on Richard Curle, see p. 229. Gérard Jean-Aubry (1882–1950) was a critic and Conrad's biographer.

17. Conrad visited America in May 1923.

Part VI

Under Artists' Eyes

'Writing is a treadmill'*

WILLIAM ROTHENSTEIN

Ford Madox Hueffer, coming in one day while I was drawing Hudson,[1] suggested I should draw Conrad, and seeing Conrad shortly afterwards, for Conrad was living at The Pent, the farmhouse where Crane had stayed, which now belonged to Hueffer,[2] he spoke to him about sitting. Whereupon Conrad asked me down for a week-end. The Pent was a small farmhouse, with farm buildings round it. It provided modest quarters for Conrad, his wife and little boy, and a room where he could put up a friend. The walls were hung with drawings and cartoons by Madox Brown.[3]

One sees more of a man by staying with him for a week-end than by meeting him a dozen times at London parties. Conrad had met few painters and was curious about the painter's outlook on life. With his piercing eyes and keen, deeply-lined bearded face, in some ways he looked like the sea captain, but his nervous manner, his rapid, excited speech, his restlessness, his high shoulders, didn't suggest the sailor. I accepted him at once as an artist; never, I thought, had I met anyone with a quicker apprehension, with such warmth of intellectual sympathy, sympathy which came half-way to meet everything one said. This warmth, not uncommon between young artists, was rare in a man so much my senior as Conrad was; but as a practising artist I was, Conrad pointed out, *his* senior; for I had begun to paint before he had thought of writing.

On the Sunday, Wells, who was then living at Sandgate, was expected to lunch.[4] We waited and waited, looking out across country; each time Conrad caught sight of a distant figure he would say, *le voilà*! But Wells never came. Well, I must meet him later, Conrad said, and must get to know his friend, Jack Galsworthy, too. 'Of course you couldn't have heard of Jack.[5] Our first meeting was when I ordered him out of the way; he was a passenger on my ship, you know; he is such a good friend; but insists on writing, poor fellow. Writing is a treadmill; he doesn't know it yet. I shall be coming up next week to see Pinker[6] – Pinker is my agent; he believes in me – wants to pull me out of my difficulties – an idealist, you understand. You must meet

* *Men and Memories: Recollections of William Rothenstein 1900–1922* (London: Faber & Faber, 1932) pp. 41–4, 157–8.

Pinker too. And may I bring Jessie? She would like to meet your dear wife.' And before the visit was over we had become fast friends. We met again very soon. Conrad wrote generously about the portrait I did of him during this visit.

Pent Farm
Stanford, Near Hythe
Kent.
13*th Oct* 1903.

My dear Rothenstein –

You are exceedingly kind. My wife is delighted with her Hudson both as to work and the inscription. You have got the man there in a striking way. We are impressed for as it happens we have both seen him in just that way; or, may be, the force of the rendering imposes your conception of the personality. Anyway it is triumphant.

Of myself in black and white (I mean without colour) I do not speak. Hueffer prophesied to me how effective it would be – and it is.

I am so profoundly satisfied that I cannot help fearing you've flattered me – not in feature *vous concevez* – but in the suggestion. At any rate I accept your vision of that head, eagerly. The contemplation of it *m'a remonté le moral*:[7] for you must know I have been tormented by gout for three weeks and brought morally, intellectually, temperamentally to the lowest ebb.

P.S. Have you found that Pinker can be of any use to you? Or is he no good?

Through my painting, through my desire to wring all I could out of my subject, to aim at what was beyond me, rather than to achieve an easier and more attractive result, I could sympathise with Conrad's difficulties. For Conrad wore himself out in his struggle for *le mot juste*, for words that should glow with a white heat; Conrad would often despair, and one needed all one's energy to pump faith and hope into him. He was then writing *Nostromo*, and working himself into a fever. In addition he suffered terribly from gout, and his wife, Jessie, had trouble with her knee. 'I can't get anything out of myself quickly,' he said, 'it takes me a year of agony to make something like a book – generally longer. And, my dear fellow, when it is done there are not more than twenty people who understand *pourquoi on se tue pour écrire quelques phrases pas trop mauvaises*.'[8] There was always an element of strain in Conrad – an excitability, which may have been individual, or may have been Polish – I cannot say. Perhaps something of each. But I sympathised with him acutely in his desire to impress the passion of life on to his pages. This sympathy was, I think, the basis of our friendship; for Conrad seemed to understand what I too was aiming at in my painting. It was a fascinating friendship; Conrad's charm, his mental energy, were inexhaustible. And Conrad understood everything; in him I had at last met a man of a passionate nature, who yet understood that a sane view of life is not a matter of compromise; but, as the *mot juste*, the phrase which shows neither weakness nor exaggeration, is the quest of the writer, so the sane opinion, the just action, are the signs of the enlightened man.

I leaned more towards radicalism than Conrad, and he often brought me up sharply with a contemptuous remark. Conrad was, by birth and by choice, an aristocrat; he believed that the object of life was the perfection of individual conduct – the education of man's own spirit. For panaceas of human perfection he had neither patience nor respect. Social idealists, pacifists and their like roused his anger. Hence he couldn't abide Bernard Shaw. Conrad knew that Cunninghame Graham[9] was more cynic than idealist, that he was by nature an aristocrat, whose socialism was a symbol of his contempt for a feeble aristocracy, and a blatant plutocracy.

While Conrad was extremely courteous and understanding by nature, his nerves sometimes made him aggressive, almost violent; and like most sensitive men, he was strongly affected, either favourably or disagreeably, by others. Poor Conrad was always in difficulties over money. His books brought him insufficient for his needs; needs which were perhaps not quite so simple as he believed them to be. There was an extravagant side to Conrad, characteristic, I thought, of his former profession; he was like a sailor between two voyages, ready to spend on land what he couldn't aboard-ship; and he had a wife in one port only, for whom nothing was too good. His gallantry to his Jessie was a true sailor's chivalry. What others had, she should have too.

* * *

Conrad had an aggressive side, which his friends overlooked, because of his obvious genius. Yet Conrad was nervous and sensitive, and he could be very irritable. I mentioned earlier how prejudiced he was against Masefield's work.[10] He was still more hostile to Shaw; and once when I told him that Max didn't like Proust, he burst out against Max;[11] yet another time I heard him judge Proust sharply. But when he liked people he would admit no faults; indeed, he was inclined to flatter – perhaps this was a Polish trait – both in speaking and writing. Poor Conrad; he suffered much from gout, which racked his nerves and depressed his spirits. At times it took all one's energy to pump life and hope into him; for he was cheered by his friends' faith in his work. Not that he lacked faith in himself; measuring himself against his contemporaries, he knew his own power. But he strained after an unattainable standard of perfection, and the effort to reach it often exhausted him.

NOTES

Sir William Rothenstein (1872–1945), painter and Principal of the Royal College of Art, was a Yorkshireman of Germanic extraction. He attended the Slade School of Fine Art at the age of sixteen. Between 1889 and 1925, he completed more than 750 portrait drawings (including Verlaine, Einstein, and T. E. Lawrence among many others) in his great series of contemporary portraits. He served as an official artist in the Great War, recording the Front in France, and he was an unofficial artist for the RAF in the Second World War. He was knighted in 1931.

In the summer of 1903 he made his first visit to Conrad, as recorded in the extract, and his work on that occasion is the earliest known portrait of Conrad. It is now in the National Portrait Gallery in London. The visit was the beginning of a long friendship, and on several occasions he proved to be of great assistance to Conrad in his financial troubles.

1. For details of Ford Madox Ford (Hueffer) and W. H. Hudson, see pp. 106 and 135.
2. Ford's ownership of The Pent is described on p. 112.
3. Ford Madox Brown (1821–1893) was a painter and grandfather of Ford Madox Ford.
4. H. G. Wells – see p. 112.
5. John Galsworthy had begun to write in 1897. His first meeting with Conrad is described on p. 112.
6. J. B. Pinker – see p. 114.
7. 'has restored my morale'.
8. 'why one kills oneself to write some not too bad phrases'.
9. For details of Cunninghame Graham, see p. 234.
10. John Masefield (1878–1967), Poet Laureate from 1930.
11. Max Beerbohm (1872–1956), artist and parodist.

Conrad's Dislike of the Camera*

CARINE CADBY

Joseph Conrad hated being photographed, and had successfully avoided it for years. It was Perceval Gibbon[1] who at last persuaded him to let himself be photographed, and suggested that it need not be by the regular professional of his dislike, but by someone he had been in the habit of meeting at the Gibbons' place at Trosley.

And when it came to the point Conrad was an heroic sitter. He made us tell him beforehand just what to do to make things easy, and he struggled hard not to show how much he disliked it. He could control his body, but his expression was one of such enduring sadness that no exposure could be made.

It was really *Typhoon* that saved the situation and made the portraits a success. In talking about the book, the photographer's helper remarked that the part she had enjoyed most was the correspondence of the sea captain and his suburban wife. Luckily, this appreciation pleased Conrad, because these letters had never received any notice from reviewers or been commented on by friends, and he confessed to a weakness for them himself. He grew so interested in discussing them that the camera was forgotten and his expression was once more the old Conrad.

A year or so later, an American publisher was urgently asking for photographs of Conrad taken in his own surroundings, and Mrs Conrad wrote inviting us down to their place near Ashford.

Unluckily the day was one of November's worst: thick and dark. The Conrads' house, too, was old, with low-pitched rooms and small windows, a real twilight of the gods: impossible conditions for photography, and the photographer's heart sank.

It was really Conrad himself who saved the day from disaster and the negatives from blackness. He soon understood that only a long exposure can make up for want of light, and so he forced himself to keep the pose wanted, and, what was even more to the point, with a normal, natural expression, for longer than the photographer thought

* 'Conrad's Dislike of the Camera and How it was Conquered by Will Cadby', *Graphic*, vol. cx (1 Nov. 1924) p. 728.

it possible for anyone to keep motionless. At first it was difficult for us all, for we hated having to interrupt him and bring his mind back to the camera, but soon he grew interested in seeing how long he could keep absolutely still. He certainly was surprisingly good at it; and for such a highly-strung individual it was remarkable. Mrs Conrad beat him, however, and when she was giving us our coffee she stood like a statue, the sugar tongs poised in her hand, for over sixty seconds.

When we reached home the photographer insisted on developing the negatives at once. 'They can't possibly be any good', he said as he shut himself in the dark room. An hour afterwards, however, he called through the door the glad news, 'They're all right, thank God; he could keep still!'

NOTES

Will and Carine Cadby took two photographs of Conrad in formal pose in September (not November) 1913, at his home, Capel House in Ashford, Kent. Alfred A. Knopf, a young assistant at Conrad's American publishers, Doubleday, Page & Co., had proposed making a publicity pamphlet that would include a formal portrait of Conrad, together with some informal snapshots, to assist sales of the forthcoming *Chance*. Conrad described the Cadbys in a letter to Knopf as 'a couple in great repute as photographers. Very artistic' (see John S. Lewis, '"Artless Photos": Two Previously Unknown Photographs of Joseph Conrad', *Conradiana*, vol. 8 (1976) pp. 203–8). John Conrad gives an amusing account of the poses in his *Joseph Conrad: Times Remembered* (Cambridge: Cambridge University Press, 1981) pp. 62–4.

The earlier sitting which Carine Cadby describes must presumably have taken place during 1912.

1. Reginald Perceval Gibbon (1879–1926), gifted writer, war correspondent and motorcycle enthusiast. The Gibbons lived at Trosley in Kent, and Jessie Conrad described Gibbon as 'perhaps the closest and for both Joseph Conrad and for me, the most intimate' of their friends. Conrad met him in 1909.

'Conrad lives in the country with his cook!'*

JO DAVIDSON

Though style be the man the books may be a mask. I don't know whether the little sketch of Joseph Conrad that I give in the words of Jo Davidson, the American sculptor, can add anything of more than passing interest to what the reading public knows of the man Conrad. I presume not. But it is at any rate a glance at the man behind the books.

'I love Conrad and so do you,' said Davidson as he gave a final dig at one of the buttons on his clay model of General Diaz. 'So then let's talk about him.'

It was a *negligée* conversation, rather early in the morning, in the studio in the avenue du Maine, where there are busts of General Foch, Pershing, Diaz and some of the younger Frenchmen who may one day want to be Premier. Davison was lounging in a corner behind a glowing stove.

'The striking thing for me about Conrad,' said Davidson, 'was the way I found he approaches his work. He uses life as a point of departure. For instance, I was curious about how he got his characters for *The Secret Agent*. He told me that he used to go to restaurants in Greek Street or Dean Street or 'So' Square,[1] where he watched the types – anarchists, agitators, charlatans, wretches of all sorts or just arch-individuals of our genus fellow man. He didn't talk with them. He just sat looking, studying, reflecting on them. If he saw a man with certain striking characteristics, with a certain sort of face, he didn't try to break into the man's life story. It wasn't necessary. He'd simply work it out to his own satisfaction that the man was a character and then he'd work out to his further satisfaction what sort of character did belong, ought to belong, with that sort of face.

'Any one who reads *The Secret Agent* must see, I think, how the method leads by the way of the imagination to something profoundly real. It's a world Conrad makes, using life as a source of reference, as a sculptor might use a model not for ideas – he gets them, or he ought

*M. K. Wisehart, 'Joseph Conrad Described by Jo Davidson', *Sun* (NY), 2 March 1919.

to, out of himself – but to refer to for the facts that are noted and may never be transcribed. It struck me that Conrad works like a painter, who goes into the country and sits down to look at a landscape. He hasn't any notion of copying it. If he feels like it he's going to make something of his own out of the facts before him; he won't hesitate to put a tree where it's needed – in a word, what he sees begins to take form for him. He sees the picture; he'll do the arranging. There, roughly, is what struck me about Conrad's method as I learned of it from him.

'There's this about Conrad. He's all artist – that means in an important particular he's Godlike. It's one way with most of humanity and another way with God. Humanity looks at a man, decides whether it thinks the man right or wrong, and so hates and despises or dislikes and neglects him. If humanity doesn't like a man it criticises him. Again, humanity may take a liking to a man, decide he's the right sort of man; then humanity praises him. But God looks at a wretch or a saint and says, "Isn't he a beautiful wretch – a real character!" or "Isn't he a lovely saint!" It's all the same. God loves the wretch and the sinner as much as he loves a lovely saint. It's humanity, not God, that is rigid and intolerant. God and the real artist take the same point of view; they're detached, sympathetic, so far as criticism is concerned. So Conrad. If he makes a wretch he doesn't love him less than he does his good characters; he may care for the wretch a little more. He doesn't dislike any character he ever made; has no preference among them on the ground of their being saints or sinners. So far as his books individually are concerned he made me feel that *Under Western Eyes* is the one that means most to him.

'It's still vivid in mind the first time I arrived at the station when I went down from London to his house in Kent. Conrad met me with a flivver,[2] a real American flivver, but the most battered, rattling, rusted flivver I ever expect to see. A stocky man, with extraordinary broad shoulders, he had on a derby hat that was pulled down so far it rested on his ears; and he had on a short, heavy, reefer coat. I got into the flivver. It was not acting well. Conrad at the wheel, trying to be polite in conversation over his shoulder while jabbing levers of the machine that went this way and that and seemed more inclined to go astern than forward, was a revelation. The way Conrad drives an automobile makes me think he would be a good captain of a ship.

'In speech he is not fluent; he gestures continually and completes phrases with gestures. He speaks English in fact with a slight accent – not so well as he speaks French. When I asked him why he didn't write in French he said, "Oh, it's much more difficult. English is so plastic – you can do anything with it!"

'His manner is nervous and he moves about continually. During sittings he was never still. He talked a good deal. What did he talk about? Well, it was in 1914. He was aware that the war was on, but he wasn't distraught; he didn't talk excitedly about it. He talked about – books, news? What the deuce do men talk about? Neither books nor news, everything!

'I didn't hear anything about his preferences in books, but he's most sympathetic toward any work brought to his attention – toward the work of all other men. It was just like him to answer as he did when asked to express an opinion on the best American book he had read in the past year that he had read so few he couldn't comment. He's frank. For one thing, I suppose, he talked about the process of making a bust. He was much interested in the process; and I may say that he never once tried to tell me how I ought to go about what I was doing. It was a great pleasure to have him assume that I knew what I was up to.

'You'll notice – if you notice it at all – that the bust shows his head pushed far forward. That's characteristic. His shoulders are mighty and broad and the head is set far forward, strikingly so. The skin of his face isn't that of a litterateur. It's the skin of a man branded by all sorts of weather year in and year out – rough, an inch thick if it's epidermis at all. He has extraordinary eyes – deep – deep and velvety – but sharp. They're like two holes in his head. In making the eyes it seemed I couldn't dig in deep enough to get them.

'He writes as the mood strikes him. When he has written a page longhand his wife typewrites it. He writes at all hours and when he finishes a page he is eager to see how it looks in print right away. I dare say his wife has had a request to copy a page at 3 a.m. It wouldn't be surprising.

'His wife, Mrs Conrad – Jessie – is a remarkable woman. Conrad is her baby. She looks after him, talks of him in the most loving and good humoured way – regards him, I dare say, as the greatest genius in the world – and I'll not be the one to dissent from that point of view. She is as protecting in her care of him as anything implied in the reminiscences. He is a man of imaginary ills. Sometimes he thinks many things are the matter with him – rheumatism, &c. He may tell you about his ills. He probably will. If he does you'll surely have a special remedy and he'll try it. His room is full of the bottles he has tried to the despair of his wife. In this particular, it seems, she lacks control; for Conrad will have his special remedies. Moreover, with three servants in the house he won't eat unless his wife cooks for him. The maids may cook for everybody else, but not for Conrad; his wife does that. Always with good humour. She is short and plump and has a rare good humour.

'Conrad is not a man to go to town much. If you want to see Conrad you go where he is; he's a great man, he's interesting and people are always going out there. It was with a quick smile of amiable humour that Mrs Conrad remarked one day in an enlightened manner: "You know they say in town that Conrad lives in the country with his cook!"

'Conrad takes great delight in his boys. One is in the navy. The other is John, a youngster. He was nine when I knew him;[3] and the father found great amusement in anecdotes they tell of John. John came home from a neighbour's one day and said, "Mamma, isn't it too bad father didn't write the Bible?" When his mother asked "Why?" he said: "Because then it would be on everybody's table and would have been through so many editions!" I dare say the notion was particularly striking for Conrad for other reasons than the youngster's notion that his father's authorship would have increased the circulation of the Bible. Appreciation of Conrad was none too fast in coming and there was a time when there were not three maids in the house.

'At the age of eight Conrad's John saw *Quo Vadis* in the moving pictures. When a striking figure in that presentation came upon the scene John exclaimed, "Mamma, Mamma, who's that??" She told him that the figure was Christ. "Who?" he asked. When she told him that the man was Jesus he cried, "Oh, yes, I know now. But I didn't recognise him by his surname!"

'Besides being an author Conrad is a father. You can say he's like all fathers if you want to.'

NOTES

Jo Davidson (1883–1952), American sculptor, was introduced to Conrad by Grace Willard. The bust was unveiled in April 1916.

1. Soho Square, London.
2. A cheap motor car.
3. In 1914, John was eight years of age.

The Conrad who Sat for Me*

WALTER TITTLE

A cold thrill of apprehension passed over me as I opened the door to leave my apartment on the morning of August 4.[1] Gazing up from the front page of the newspaper that lay on the threshold was the face of Joseph Conrad. Having left him a few months previously at his home in England, I felt that news about him was not likely to be good news. During the previous autumn and winter I had witnessed his sufferings, and since my departure the letters I received had but slight improvement to record. No new novel was forthcoming, I knew, to bring him so soon again into the world's headlines, and another visit to America was impossible. I seized the journal hoping against hope, but my surmise was right. Joseph Conrad was dead.

Well I knew that the world was grieving for its irreparable loss, but mine was a personal sorrow. He had allowed me to taste of the friendship of which his great heart was capable, and sweeet was the quality of the friendship of this man of fire and tenderness. To few people was this privilege accorded, simply because he had not surplus strength to expend in a multiplicity of attachments. Of necessity he was on the defensive against new acquaintances, however desirable and pleasant they might prove to be, and often did I marvel, as did he, at the fortunate circumstance, recorded in a previous article,[2] that favoured me. Comparative solitude was imperative to this tortured body that for years had lagged, perforce, behind his energetic soul, and great was the anguish of the brain, filled with creations demanding birth from a body too frail to endure the travail.

This creative impulse seemed merciless in its exactions, colouring its possessor's every act. Repose was almost an impossibility for him; in conversation, laughter and gesture, a vast amount of precious nervous energy was invariably consumed. At times he would be the gayest of the gay, burning up any additional strength that might have accumulated as the result of a more fortunate night's rest than was usual with him, and often in the midst of his gaiety an expression of hopeless anguish would appear upon his face, to be expelled with an obvious effort that finally would resolve itself into a brilliant smile. Sometimes when we were alone the smile would fail, and once, after a most violent attack

* *Outlook* (New York), vol. CXL (1, 8 July 1925) pp. 333–5, 361–2.

of coughing that left him weak and gasping for breath, he confided to me his fears that he had not long to live.

'I don't want my family to know about this,' he said. 'It would give them added cause for worry, and would do no good, but I am sure there is something vitally wrong with me here', touching his chest. 'I would like to live longer, life is so short at best; there is so much work to do, and so little time and energy with which to achieve it. Not only would I like to live to excel my previous literary efforts, but I want to see my family well provided for and my boys matured and fully established before I pass on.'

I endeavoured as best I could to convince him that his trouble was due to nervousness from overwork, and that rest and relaxation would restore him to health. He seemed to be eager to grasp some hope from what I said, but the effort was only partially successful.

'I am convinced that it cannot be that I work too much, I really am able to achieve so little, and, besides, hard work never hurt anybody. It is something else. Sixty-five is a critical age for many men. If a man gets past this period, he may live quite a while longer. Perhaps I shall, but I doubt it, seriously. How I envy you the twenty years immediately ahead of you! Make the most of them, my dear; they are the best and most productive of one's life. What wouldn't I give to be your age again! We always think that if we had our work to do over we could do it so much better.'[3]

In view of Mr Conrad's vivid and vital personality and abundant nervous energy, I had a conviction that his health surely could be restored in some way; I was convinced that this supposed 'crisis of the middle sixties' could be passed with normal health to follow. And, apparently, my confidence in this belief had its effect upon him to some degree. More than a year and a half after this first discussion of his physical difficulties, I arrived at his house for a week-end visit. I had seen him quite often in the interval, but on this occasion we had planned the making of another sketch of him. He was not at the door to greet me on my arrival, as had been his unfailing practice, and I was taken at once to his room, where he was confined. He was seated in a wheel-chair beside the bed, and extended his hands to greet me.

'I owe you an apology, my dear', he said. 'I have been in bed for days. I just got up a few minutes ago in order to be able to receive you respectably. I have been quite ill. I will have to go back to bed in an hour, and I fear there will be no chance to sit to you this time. So, you see, I have got you here under false pretences; I hope you will forgive me. I could have sent you a telegram and told you the situation, but I just could not bring myself to do it. You do buck me up so, and I could not resist having you. You will forgive me, won't you?'

I proceeded with the 'bucking up' with all my heart, full of sympathy for his sufferings, and was still able to believe the encouraging things that I said. But before that visit was over my faith in his ultimate recovery was shaken quite a bit by a confession from Mrs Conrad. The doctor had told her that his heart was acting badly, and that his constant sufferings were having a weakening effect upon it. From that time onward I looked upon him with different eyes, concealing from him the added anxiety that was born of this disclosure.

Work being impossible for him at this period, we had long conversations morning, afternoon and evening during the days of this visit, and I now look back regretfully to a remark that Mr Lloyd Osbourne[4] made to me at about this time.

'You are most fortunate in your friendship with Conrad', he said. 'He is more difficult to meet than the King of England. Let me give you a bit of advice; write down everything that he says to you, so the rest of us can have the benefit of it at some future time. If you neglect making your notes carefully and promptly, most of it will escape you. I advise you as one who had a similar experience.' This warning bore scant fruit in comparison withu the possibilities; my notes were few and very far between. I could not think of our talks in the light of 'copy', and the bulk of what was said has, I hope, sunk into my subconsciousness to be salvaged at a later time. Mr Conrad and I joked about my being his pictorial Boswell; I wish I had been a more thorough verbal one as well.

The modesty of the man concerning his achievements was complete and sincere. Before his visit to America[5] I had voiced the hope that he would make the journey to my native land, assuring him that a royal welcome awaited him there at the hands of hosts of admirers. Betraying again the often-observed fact that he was unable to believe in his fame, he flouted the idea that there could be a very wide knowledge of him in America, saying that he was not a writer of great popularity, and had a distinctly limited public. It would be pleasant to visit our shores, he thought, but the probability of making the trip was very small. That he was destined to make the voyage so soon neither of us dreamed at the time, nor did we think of the surprise he was to receive concerning his modest estimate of his fame. I met him on board the ship at the time of his arrival; the story of that visit is known to every one now. Royalty could not have been received with more distinction or enthusiasm, and Mr Conrad was amazed, I am sure, at the hordes of reporters, cameramen, reception committees and the public in general that greeted him. I smiled as I left him moving slowly down the crowded pier, almost eclipsed by huge bunches of American Beauty roses, all that his arms could hold. His unbelief in his fame was being shattered!

An additional amusing example of this phase came at the time when the manuscripts of some of his books were sold at such amazing prices.[6] I sent him one of the first of the newspaper announcements, expressing regret that so little of the money realised went to him. I received in reply a gay and cordial letter in his unique handwriting that discussed everything but the cutting that I had sent until a tiny postscript after the signature: 'That Quinn sale was an enormous stunt, wasn't it? It will make me famous!'

Despite the greatness of his achievements, mention to him of his work revealed him always apologetic to himself for not having done better justice to the vision of his conceptions. All sincere artists know the disappointment of comparing a finished work with the vividness of the dream that inspired it. I, from experience, had come to the conclusion that, when most successful, we capture about one-third of the beauty that drives us to the labour of creation. Mentioning this to Mr Conrad, I found him in agreement.

'You are right,' he said; 'I have estimated the proportion that can be captured at about thirty-five per cent.' It behooves us, then, that our conceptions be of ever-increasing beauty.

One day in my studio in London, as my famous sitter divided his time between the model-stand and a place of vantage behind me where he could observe over my shoulder the application of the colour, I asked him how he was coming to feel about *The Rover*.[7] He had previously expressed himself as unable to judge it satisfactorily, the task of its production having been too recent. How I wish I had a sketch of him as he looked at that particular moment, huddled in his chair, gazing at the skylight with an eagle-like intensity, his monocle raising a huge welt above his drooping right eyebrow from the muscular contraction of his forehead, and magnifying grotesquely the eager eye behind it. The cold top light accentuated with utmost vividness every hollow and salience of his rugged face; no carving at Chartres could have rivalled him in intensity.

'What do I think of *The Rover*?' His head was plunged into his hands, and he sat for a moment in an attitude of deepest dejection. Returning to an erect posture, he seemed to recall himself from the melancholy train of thought that my question had occasioned.

'*The Rover*? Well, I'll tell you – I have not yet made up my mind about it. It worries me. It is going wonderfully well both here and in America, and the reviews have been excellent,[8] but I cannot come to a satisfactory conclusion about it myself. I cannot decide if it is one of my best works. Perhaps I shall know later. It may be the best of the lot, but for the moment I am very much at sea about it. Which is my best book? Again, I don't know. They are all so different. I can never resist the temptation to experiment, and can never write in the same way twice. *Nostromo* is my biggest canvas, my most ambitious performance. Perhaps it is the best. I do not know. Dickens and Thackeray always wrote in a consistent style. They had established methods, and one book resembled another, so that comparison is possible. This is not the case with me. With each effort I want to try something new. This makes immediate comparison very difficult, almost impossible.

'*The Rover* is hardest of all for me to judge, naturally, as it is the most recent. What an amount of labour it cost me, and labour under such difficult conditions! I had to stop repeatedly because of illness; I wrote the thing at least eleven times. And I never use a stenographer much; the work must be done so largely by hand. I can dictate the first rough draft, and then begins endless re-writing. The labour of it fatigues me so; I hate to write! I do it only when an idea comes to me so strongly that I cannot resist it. Otherwise it would be impossible for me. I write when a story demands telling so strongly that there is no further possibility of postponement. I am not a literary man. Literary men can write about anything, often with equal facility. I am not one of those clever and accomplished people.'

'But you are missing a golden opportunity for the sale of a valuable by-product', I replied, jokingly. 'I refer to the classic custom of writing American impressions. Many Englishmen visit us for ten days or a fortnight, and come away with sufficient material to classify us completely, and tell exactly what is wrong with us in every way. What they have not observed the imagination usually supplies; and there's money in it! The market is well established, and I would like to see you benefit by it. We read these critiques with the same incomprehensible avidity with which we consume imported lectures and ice-cream sodas.'

'What you say is undoubtedly true, but that sort of thing is not possible for me. I cannot sit down in cold blood and write for profit. I can produce only creative work, and that only when the desire to write is so strong that it takes complete possession of me and resistance is impossible.'

The progress of the portraits interested Mr Conrad very much, and as the likenesses developed he displayed much pleasurable excitement.

'Artists, and even photographers, have a way of smoothing me out and making me look too nice and polite. I see that you are going to represent me as the rough old sea-dog that I am. There is nothing smooth about my face. Feel my temples, how deep and narrow they are; now my cheek bones, and see how they project. And feel how my head broadens abruptly over the ears; the back of my skull is nearly circular. Now my chin, feel how rugged and prominent the bones are. Paint me to look as I am – an old pirate with hooded eyes, like a snake! You laugh? Well, I was virtually a pirate once. I commanded that filibustering ship in *The Arrow of Gold*, you know, and was nearly captured many times.[9] I know that you have caught my attitude exactly in these pictures; my father used to sit like that. And see how my waistcoat has crept up!' He laughed his approval. 'Capital! I could never keep it down. You were worrying a while ago about the length of the nose. Don't change it, because you have it exactly. That's the Korzeniowski nose absolutely. I don't know which of the two I like better, they both seem so utterly like me. First I prefer one, then the other. This background of the gray, cold sea is an excellent idea. You may not have been conscious of it, but you have introduced a fine bit of symbolism here; you show the ocean and the seaman who came out of it to the land. The pale-yellow light on the horizon suggests that there was hope for better things for the sailor when the land called him. The front view has quite an air about it.' Meditatively, 'My dear Tittle, do I look as great as that? Don't you think that our friendship has prepossessed you in my favour?'

A great luxury this for an artist, when all too frequently one's sitters wish to be glorified. Of the two portraits, the latter-mentioned one proved to be the favourite with Sir James Barrie,[10] who came to my studio to see them and my paintings of Mr Bernard Shaw. 'It is so like him as he used to sit talking with me by the hour in my studio,' he said. 'Always so nervous and intent on the subject in hand. I used to like to imagine that he was really a pirate, who at any moment was likely to leap from his chair and stick a knife into me!'

* * *

As I painted my sitter talked, part of the time on the subject of art, encouraging me often by questions to discuss the branch of it that provides my vocation. Between poses he examined many prints and paintings that were in the studio, praising with the utmost generosity my product and outlining a most alluring future for me.

'You are most fortunate to have such a thorough grounding in the technique of your art,' he said, 'in these times when technique is so blatantly scoffed at by so-called modernism. It is most important, and I find a command of it indispensable in my own work; for, after all, my dear, technique comprises about sixty per cent of any art, doesn't it?' I spoke of the iconoclastic tendencies of these same modernists, who, while some of them are really achieving something for art, limit and blind themselves by sweeping condemnations of all points of view save their own. By many of them Velasquez is described as a mere painter of surfaces, Dickens is beneath contempt, and many other titans destined for the ages simply do not exist. It makes one feel that in their destructive generalisations they seek to dignify themselves in their own and others' eyes.

'Dickens is very great and will live when such critics are long forgotten,' he replied. 'A really big mind, and one for which there is hope for achievement in art, should be able to appreciate all that is, or ever was really good in art, treasuring each performer for his particular qualities of excellence. Taste is fickle, and changes in different periods, appreciation veering away for a time from one set of goods to another. Sometimes it is in error altogether for a while, but eventually it must inevitably return to all things that possess really great qualities.'

Luncheon was served in the studio by an Italian *restaurateur*, the proprietor coming personally, filled with excitement at the prospect of a glimpse of the novelist. He had seen an account in the newspapers of Mr Conrad's sitting to me, as well as Mr Shaw, and begged that he be allowed to see the latter, too. I told Mr Conrad beforehand of the literary penchant of our *cuisinier*, whom he gratified beyond measure by a bit of chat over the menu. Probably because it is one of my pet detestations, I tried to dissuade my guest from beef à la mode, convinced that the restaurant could provide something more palatable. Great was my amazement when the argument was concluded, victoriously for Mr Conrad, by a pathetic dissertation on his part of his passion for this particular dish, long unsatisfied, and threatened in this moment by the determined ogre, myself, trying to thrust my will between him and his stomach's desire. So beef à la mode was the foundation of our repast, and we proceeded with it at once on its arrival.

Light is precious in London, especially in winter, and I found it impossible to restrain myself from seizing every moment between courses and when not actually engaged in eating to work upon my portraits. 'Now, my dear, are you trying to kill yourself with paint poisoning?' my sitter protested. 'Look at that rag you have there, and at your hands! Go and wash them at once.' He seemed really alarmed, and as I was about to comply to pacify him he laughed heartily. 'No, no, don't go. I was only joking. Get all the painting done that you can.'

'I am so sorry you could not come to the studio when I was sitting, Jessie, dear', he said later to his wife when I was again with them at Bishopsbourne. 'It was such fun to see Tittle putting the colour on the canvas, and on himself as well. Even during luncheon he was constantly up and down, like a jack-in-the-box – now a mouthful of food, now a stroke of the brush, all over the place at the same time. I was quite impress-ed by him!' The little peculiarity of accent noted was a constantly recurring one.

The sartorial side of the portraits was one to which Mr Conrad gave some attention. He presented me with a neck-tie of black and red checks, asking that I use it in one of the paintings. We also made a careful survey of his wardrobe to choose clothing that would fit harmoniously into the colour schemes.

'You see, when I show you my clothes like this I am trying to impress you with my wealth. Having got several new suits from my tailor recently, I just must show them. Here is a brown one that pleases me very much. What do you think of it for one of the pictures?'

I expressed preference for grey and blue for the two portraits, though it was evident that my sitter had his heart set upon the brown. I explained that the other shades were better suited to the schemes of the pictures in hand, Mrs Conrad agreeing with my choice, her opinion being supported by Miss Hallowes, Mr Conrad's secretary. With mock despair he succumbed: 'No one likes my brown suit, and I do so much! Jessie insults it, Tittle bites my head off about it, and now Miss Hallowes picks on me too. I'll have to fight for my life soon!' I pointed to the unfinished portraits, and then to him:

'There are three of you, you see, so we three must combine.'

'Well, you'd better look out,' he replied, laughingly, 'or I will take back that tie I gave you.'

There came to Mr Conrad's house one day a young writer whose first book was just off the press. He was an employee of the Foreign Office, and a mission on which he had been sent to some out-of-the-way spot had provided material for an unusual chronicle that had attracted some attention. He came to question my host most minutely about all details of his method of work, apparently thinking that a faithful following of the same routine would be a long step toward producing results similar in excellence to those achieved by the great writer. Mr Conrad answered his queries with painstaking patience, there being evident in his manner a feeling of the futility of giving this sort of information, and finally pointed out to his inquisitor the simple truth that should have been obvious to him from the beginning, that no blanket rules can possibly apply in the matter of method in writing. It may be interesting to know the varying ways in which writers proceed in the making of their products, but a procedure that is perfect for one will probably, in all its details, be suitable to no one else. Consequently each writer must experiment until he evolves the manner of work best adapted to his own peculiar needs, and thus achieve his own salvation.

In one of our conversations Mr Conrad discovered to me a deep-seated aversion to the cinema. We had been talking about different phases of humour, and the various devices, literary and otherwise, that can be depended upon to produce laughter, from the subtlest of them to common slapstick. I told him of a variety comedian in Paris who had reduced me, through laughter, to an almost helpless state by the smashing of hundreds of dishes in ingenious and unexpected ways.

'Yes,' he exclaimed, 'isn't it curious? When you see a performance like that, at first you think, "How silly!" and as the thing is repeated again and again you laugh harder and harder. He was a great psychologist who first discovered this secret about humour.' I then mentioned Chaplin as a master of slapstick and the art of clowning, and, to my surprise, found no concurrence from Mr Conrad at all. He said that he did not find him funny, only vulgar, and that his work possessed no virtue whatever. From this he launched into a real tirade against the films.

'They are absolutely the lowest form of amusement. I hate them!' he said, with quite a considerable show of heat. 'They are stupid, and can never be of real value. The cinema is not a great medium. It merely affords entertainment for people who enjoy sitting with thought utterly suspended and watching a changing pattern flickering before their eyes. Shadowgraphs in pantomime[11] are much better.'

I argued that surely all the virtues possessed by good pantomime could be appropriated for the films; but even this he would not grant, nor would he agree with his wife when she championed slow-motion pictures as a form providing both amusement and instruction. Supporting her claim, I cited the analytical value of golf strokes, boxing and other sports depicted in this way, which elicited the objection:

'There is no value in a gesture except at full speed. I like to see a blow delivered in boxing, but I hate to see it analysed. As for golf, no two swings are ever alike, anyway. One kind of motion picture might be of some value if the producers would not spoil it. I have seen several so-called educational films that pretended to show a process of manufacture, beginning with the raw material and ending with a finished product. But no stage of the thing was ever completed. As soon as I began to be interested the scene would invariably change, skipping most essential steps in the sequence of production, and taking the thing up again at an advanced stage. It was most amazing, maddening, and not in the least informing. Why, I am ashamed of you two for having a taste for anything so bad!' and the discussion ended in laughter.

During the months immediately preceding my departure Mr Conrad's health continued to be quite bad, and the periods of relief between his painful attacks of asthma and gout were fewer and shorter. His hands and feet succeeded each other into heavy pads and bandages, emerging by slow degrees, ending in woollen socks and gloves to avoid the possibility of chill. Perhaps a more moderate climate would have spared him much of this; I myself suffered from an attack of influenza and resultant rheumatism because of the penetrating damp and cold, but Mrs Conrad pointed out the fact that Kent is noted for the longevity of its inhabitants, citing for example a man who was then supplying them with milk and butter, making his daily rounds over the countryside at the age of ninety-six.

'That simplifies matters', I said to her husband. 'Just stay in Kent. You are a mere stripling.'

'Well, I'm staying,' he replied with a smile. 'But won't you let me go to the south of France for a little while? I do so want to go!'

During this last period work was almost an impossibility for him. His suffering left him but little energy. We had often spoken of some friends of mine who had a country place at no great distance from Bishopsbourne, in whom Mr Conrad showed considerable interest, having other friends in common with them. But to a suggestion that they motor over to see him his tired face abetted his spoken objection:

'I am sorry, but I cannot meet new people. They are charming, I know; I have heard much about them. But I cannot enlarge my circle of friends. It consumes time and energy that I am unable to spare. Besides, I am a sailor, not a society man. I could sit on a wharf in Marseilles and talk to an old salt with pleasure, at any time. I can always get on with people like that, but not with everybody.'

My last visit to Bishopsbourne was on 10 February 1924. On this occasion Mr Conrad's condition was so greatly improved that I was full of hope for a permanent betterment, which he and Mrs Conrad seemed to share. My departure for Paris *en route* to America was set for four days later, and I did not think that this was the last time I would see him. He was in a reminiscent mood during much of our conversation, and reviewed the period since our first meeting in a most kindly and affectionate way, regretting my departure and advising that I divide my time between England and America. During the last hour and a half we were together I produced a piece of copper that I had in my pocket and made a dry-point sketch of his profile as we talked. A hasty tea concluded, I was motored off to Canterbury, my heart warm from hearty hand-clasps and many good wishes for the future.

NOTES

Walter Ernest Tittle (1883–1966) was born in Ohio and moved to New York and London as magazine illustrator and later portrait painter. He first met Conrad in the Curzon Hotel, Mayfair, in July 1922. He did two oils, two lithographs and a copper dry-point etching of Conrad (one of the oils is now in the National Portrait Gallery, London). Conrad appreciated Tittle's portraits of him above all others, and he chose one of them as the frontispiece for the Dent Collected Edition of his works. Although their friendship was not of long standing and they saw each other infrequently, Tittle would visit the Conrads when he was in England, and he was the first to greet Conrad on his arrival in New York in May 1923.

1. Conrad died on 3 August 1924.

2. Walter Tittle, 'Portraits in Pencil and Pen, III: Joseph Conrad', *Strand Magazine*, vol. LXVII (June 1924) pp. 546–50.

3. Conrad was sixty-five years of age in 1922, and Tittle was thirty-nine years old.

4. Lloyd Osbourne (1868–1947), an American author, was the son of Fanny Van de Grift, later the wife of Robert Louis Stevenson.

5. Conrad visited America in May 1923. For descriptions of his arrival in New York, see pp. 175–80.

6. In November 1923, John Quinn, an American collector, sold the many manuscripts which he had bought from Conrad over the previous thirteen years. The auction, at the Anderson Galleries in New York, made sensational headlines, and the prices realised (perhaps boosted by the publicity of Conrad's visit earlier in the year) were extraordinary. The top price was $8100 for the manuscript of *Victory* (which Conrad had chosen for his public reading in New York), while *Chance*, for example, fetched $6600. Quinn made a ten-fold profit.

7. Tittle painted a portrait of Conrad, now in the National Portrait Gallery, on 6 January 1924. *The Rover* had been published six weeks earlier. Tittle had previously done an etching of Conrad on 12 November 1922.

8. Reviews of *The Rover*, in fact, were usually respectful or valedictory at best, and Conrad himself, in a letter to his agent, acknowledged the 'note of disappointment' in the novel's reception.

9. For details of Conrad's experiences in the *Tremolino*, see p. 180.

10. Sir James Barrie (1860–1937), author of *Peter Pan* (1904) and *The Admirable Crichton* (1902).

11. Shadowgraphs are silhouettes made by casting a shadow, usually of the hands, on a lighted surface.

An Artist's Impression*

MUIRHEAD BONE

The soul of Conrad is embodied for ever in his books, but there was a formality when he spoke of himself there – an unconscious bit of formal sea manners where a captain must always remember he is captain first, or the result of the deliberation with which he used the English language, or perhaps of the mature age at which he began to give us his confidences when so expert a psychologist could gauge all its effects on us. Whatever the reason I was not prepared for the exquisite quality of that personality as a human being – its humour, gaiety, irony and tenderness – when, after long years as a reader, I became a friend. We crossed to America together last year in the Anchor liner *Tuscania*, from Glasgow, and her captain being my brother the 'Brassbounder', and an old friend of Conrad's,[1] the voyage was very memorable to me. It was the first time J.C. had been on a large modern liner, and the handling of her had his close attention. There was a heavy head wind against us as we cleared from Moville after taking Irish emigrants aboard, and with a pitch-dark night it was not easy getting under way again. I remember Conrad peering from the ship's high bridge and telling me we were the height of a full-rigged ship from the sea and all these decks were like an immense spread of canvas catching the wind. My brother, proud of his ship, tried artfully to trap Conrad into an admiration for her, but the mere size of modern liners gave him no pleasure. He had none of a Kiplingite enthusiasm for material powers – with him it was Man and the Elements, with the apparatus always a bit inadequate. I remember his turning back from the big engine-room – very little of it had sufficed him, – and only becoming happy again talking to David, in the captain's room, of all the sailing-ships and small tramp steamers of their mutual acquaintance and what had become of them. They ran over their names most lovingly; odd or to me very ordinary names which to these two seamen for some mystic and unfathomable reason seemed beautiful, exactly right and strangely appropriate, and David was able to tell Conrad most of their fates – for their fates seemed all to have been settled in one or other of the Seven Seas. The talk was an odd mixture of the traits of sailors and

* 'The Soul of Conrad: an Artist's Impression', *Manchester Guardian Weekly*, vol. XI, no. 6 (8 Aug. 1924) pp. 124–5.

the traits of ships and the traits of owners, and the continual skipping from the one to the other had something baffling to the landsman. They made the discovery that one of them was master of one of the old Loch Line sailing-ships when the other was first mate of another.[2]

I was trying to draw them, talking so, and was delighted that sometimes they would sit for long in the immobile way in which people sit who are looking into the past. Then a call from the bridge above, and my brother would obediently tap out his pipe and leave us. On the bridge my brother was very careful to instruct all his officers to speak of 'Captain' Conrad, and I think it pleased him. David would not admit that with the passing of the sailing-ship training the merchant officer had declined in any way, but the two old wind-jammer skippers agreed that they were 'different', and would never know a peculiar something *they* had known – and leave it at that. The author of *The Mirror of the Sea* (which my brother said was so exact in its observation of the sea that he wanted it to be a textbook in the navigation schools) did not seem to me to spend much time on this voyage looking at seascapes, but I dare say he sized up things quickly and knew exactly what was happening without appearing to look. He would screw his head (which was deep-set on his shoulders in a very characteristic attitude) slowly round and look upwards at the sky with a slightly whistling and quizzical expression which the artist in him and the seaman in him had compounded from all the skippers and all the sea experience he had ever met. He took such attitudes quite unconsciously, but with an inimitable 'finality' which was a joy for the artist to behold. At such a moment he looked what a naval officer would call 'a wise old bird', but one who had the humour and the artistry to be exactly right. Our camp chairs and rugs, carefully put out every day for us, were never used, and indeed I cannot imagine him with his thick-set, precise figure sprawling on a camp chair. He wearied a little of the *Tuscania*'s endless decks and hamperings everywhere; accustomed to a ship where you could from the master's stand take in everything and her position on the sea with a glance of the eye, he felt here, I imagined, that he was helpless and carried along. I remember him saying 'It is hotel life, but I don't like hotel life, and it is no improvement when it is floating.'

Four days off New York we ran into fog and, crossing the lanes of ships from Southampton and Liverpool at the same time, the captain's anxious time set in, and after this there were no more long chats in the captain's room. Day after day, on our way down to the saloon for meals Conrad would glance at the sky and tell me we would see nothing of the captain today. In this unendingly grey Atlantic I recalled the mutual enthusiasm with which in one of our talks the two sailors spoke of the Mediterranean – 'Deep water and no fogs!' They chanted it like a sailor's litany. One day the captain sent for us and explained the working of his ship in the fog. Though nothing could be seen of them the *Tuscania* was now one of a group of ships constantly giving their bearings to each other by wireless, and these new methods, which he had never known when at sea, interested Conrad deeply.

The fog did me a good service, for sharing Conrad's cabin and unable to sleep because of the foghorn set, timed for short intervals over our heads (we had the deck 'suite'), we sat up at nights and he talked. He admired French literature, above all Anatole France; the Russians less, like the Pole he was. He told me of his sea days, of the moment when he first felt sure he would get promotion. . . . One day he had ordered the men working at the sail on deck to put it away for he saw the weather would change, and his order being heard by the captain below through the open skylight, Conrad heard him growl to the mate 'That second officer knows the weather.'[3] 'That cheered me up', he explained. 'For he was a silent man, and I had never known before how he took me.'

Sometimes I would catch Conrad unawares, and he had that look of an eloquent orator haranguing an unseen audience which someone once suggested to me was the secret of the extraordinarily cogent and eloquent English some foreigners attain (though no one, of course, has ever risen to the heights of Conrad in this) – *i.e.*, that they are always 'justifying themselves' in the choicest phrases they can, to their own minds. Conrad was a natural king among men – W. H. Hudson[4] is the only other I have ever known who had this compelling quality. Sometimes it came on me with overwhelming force that this man had first lived a life of toil and danger and responsibility and then begun a second life as a writer – beginning before the mast again as it were. The tremendous effort of all this had certainly borne him down. It gave one a tremendous respect for him that the materials for his art had been gathered at such a cost. His fever on the Congo which weakened all his after-life was what he paid for *Heart of Darkness* – that incomparable poem of the tropics.

Once I said to him, 'Well, how now, Ulysses?' He smiled and said, 'How odd you should say that. . . . They used to call me Ulysses at Marseilles in the old days. . . . They joked at me then, but I have made my voyage.' He had a great and touching admiration for 'Don Roberto' (Cunninghame Graham) and in his eyes 'Edward' (Garnett)[5] could do no wrong. He shared in the excitement as our landfall approached, the soundings which brought up a pebble and a little sand from Atlantic's floor, and I see his wise old head bent over the chart as David explained the successive soundings which should bring us up the submarine stair till we were before New York.

The fog had lifted, and it was a calm evening when we made our

American landfall, Fire Island Lightship – Conrad's first sight of North America. We entered New York harbour at dawn next morning, and before we reached quarantine we stood on the quiet bridge looking down on the excited emigrants on the fo'c'sle below. Manhattan was rising and rising – a wonderfully beautiful rosy glitter in the sunny air. Conrad murmured, 'Like a dream.' Half his life was a waking dream, I think. Then the 'ship reporters', but above all the photographers, swarmed aboard. Fortunately Christopher Morley[6] was there and interpreted Conrad to the others with the wise instinct for which he is famous. Conrad needed it. Anyone less able to 'tell a story' as a man, and to a reporter, I have never come across. Just before we berthed I soothed a kinema operator who was not pleased with his man because he would *not* 'wave his hat to the Statue of Liberty'. It was a flushed and rather angry Conrad who muttered as they all surrounded him, 'It's like a dream' – in a very different tone from that of the earlier morning. Then came aboard his American publisher and host Frank Doubleday,[7] and after that the landing-stage where I caught the long queue of a Polish deputation waiting with bouquets, and it gave me a start to remember that he was not only a British seaman and one of the greatest of English writers but a Polish notable as well. Centuries may come and go before anyone so gifted, so strange, and such a charming human being as Joseph Conrad comes this way again.

NOTES

Sir Muirhead Bone (1876–1953), water-colour painter and etcher. He was the first official war artist to be appointed in the First World War, and he was a leading force behind the foundation of the Imperial War Museum. He met Conrad in Glasgow on the day before their departure for New York on 21 April 1923. They sailed together in the *Tuscania*, captained by Bone's brother, David, and they arrived in New York on 1 May 1923. Muirhead Bone was knighted in 1937.

1. Sir David William Bone (1874–1959), elder brother of Muirhead. He first went to sea in 1891, and rose to become Commodore of the Anchor Line, which owned the *Tuscania*. In 1916, he was Commander of the *Cameronia* when it was sunk in the Mediterranean, with the loss of 130 troops. He wrote many books and articles about life at sea, and Conrad wrote to him after the publication of his first novel, *The Brassbounder*, in 1910. The two men met in Liverpool in 1919. David Bone was knighted in 1946.

2. Conrad sailed as third mate in the *Loch Etive* on a round trip from England to Sydney, 1880–1. Bone had sailed round the world in the barque, *Loch Ness*, many years later.

3. Conrad sailed in five ships as second officer, between 1881 and 1887.

4. For details of W. H. Hudson, see p. 135.

5. For details of Cunninghame Graham and Edward Garnett, see pp. 234 and 82.
6. See p. 180.
7. See p. 188.

Joseph Conrad*

JACOB EPSTEIN

Muirhead Bone[1] had arranged that I should do a bust of Conrad for him. I had desired, ten years before, to work from him and had spoken to Richard Curle[2] about it, but had been informed by him that Conrad could not sit for me owing to the intervention of a painter 'friend'. At the time I was deeply disappointed and dropped the idea, but in 1924 the commission was finally arranged. My admiration for Conrad was immense, and he had a head that appealed to a sculptor, massive and fine at the same time, so I jumped at the idea of working from him at last. After a meeting in London it was arranged with him that I should go down to his place at Oswalds, near Canterbury, and – at my suggestion – should live in an inn in a nearby village while working on the bust. This arrangement always suits me best, as I prefer to be free outside my working hours.

I set out from London on a cold March morning, feeling somewhat ill and down-hearted. I hated working away from my studio, amidst uncertain and perhaps disagreeable conditions. Before beginning a work I am timid and apprehensive. What will the lighting be? A good start is everything, and with a subject like Conrad I wanted to do justice to myself. My taxi contained my working materials, stands, clay and working tools. It seemed a long journey to Kent, I arrived towards dark with snow falling. Conrad met me and we arranged the room in which I should work, where I unpacked my baggage. I was then conducted across a park to the village of Bridge and the inn where I was to stay. This inn seemed to be of the gloomiest and coldest type. The whole mood of the place, with the sodden country-side, promised a cheerless beginning.

The next morning I began the work. At the end of the sitting I did not know what to think of it, and felt altogether wretched. In the

* From *Let There Be Sculpture: An Autobiography* (London: Michael Joseph, 1940) pp. 89–94.

evening I wired for my five-year-old Peggy Jean to come. The second day, on the arrival of Peggy Jean, things looked better. Conrad was an absorbing study. He took posing seriously and gave me good long sittings until one o'clock, when we lunched and talked. Conrad from the beginning called me *Cher Maître*, embarrassing me by this mode of address from a much older man who was a great master of his own craft. His manners were courtly and direct, but his neurasthenia forced him at times to outbursts of rage and irritability with his household which quickly subsided. I already had a fairly clear notion as to how I should treat the bust. A sculptor had previously made a bust of him which represented him as an open-necked, romantic, out-of-door type of person.[3] In appearance Conrad was the very opposite. His clothes were immaculately conventional, and his collar enclosed his neck like an Iron Maiden's vice or garrotter's grip. He was worried if his hair and beard were not trim and neat as became a sea captain. There was nothing shaggy or Bohemian about him. His glance was keen despite the drooping of one eyelid. He was the sea captain, the officer, and in our talks he emphasised the word 'responsibility'. Responsibility weighed on him and weighed him down. He used the word again and again and one immediately thought of *Lord Jim* – the conscience suffering at the evasion of duty. It may have been because of my meeting him late in life that Conrad gave me a feeling of defeat; but defeat met with courage.

He was crippled with rheumatism, crotchety, nervous and ill. He said to me, 'I am finished.' There was pathos in his pulling out of a drawer his last manuscript to show me that he was still at work.[4] There was no triumph in his manner, however, and he said that he did not know whether he would ever finish it. 'I am played out,' he said, 'played out.'

We talked after the sittings, mostly in the afternoons when we had tea together and Conrad was full of reminiscences about himself. We were usually alone. There, in this country house, he seemed to live alone although the house was filled with servants. A few visitors came at the weekends, but he appeared a lonely, brooding man, with none too pleasant thoughts.

He was a good sitter, always strictly punctual, and he stuck to the stand, giving me plenty of opportunity for work and study. I was with him for twenty-one days. Once, while posing, he had a heart attack, and felt faint. His manservant brought him a stiff whiskey and he insisted on renewing the sitting. I had no hesitations while at work, owing to his very sympathetic attitude. A doubtful, or critical attitude of the sitter will sometimes hang like a dark cloud over the work and retard it. Conrad's sympathy and goodwill were manifest, and he would beam at me with a pleased expression and forget his rheumatism and the tree outside the window at which he railed. The tree was large and beautiful, but to Conrad it was a source of misery.

The house was roomy, and set among low hills. To Conrad it was a prison set in a swamp. He must move. He must find another house. He would set out in his car. One step from the door to the sealed vehicle to search for the new house. No outdoors for him. The sea captain hated out of doors, and never put his nose into it.

To return to the bust; Conrad had a demon expression in the left eye, while his right eye was smothered by a drooping lid, but the eyes glowed with a great intensity of feeling. The drooping, weary lids intensified the impression of brooding thought. The whole head revealed the man who had suffered much. A head set on shoulders hunched about his ears. When he was seated, the shoulders gave the impression of a pedestal for the head. His gnarled hands were covered with woollen mittens, and his habit of tugging at his beard when in conversation or in thought gave me the idea of including the hands in the bust, but Conrad recoiled from so human a document.

On anything connected with the plastic arts Conrad frankly confessed ignorance, although perhaps to flatter me he attempted to draw a parallel between the processes of building up a work of sculpture and that of writing a novel. Of music he said he knew nothing, nor did it interest him; but he admitted being impressed by the sound of drums coming across the waters in Africa at night.

The walls of his house carried a few indifferent family portraits in oil. He turned over lovingly the family portrait album of his ancestors. His father, Korzeniowski, was a distinguished literary Pole, who had suffered under the Czar, photographs of himself very young; these showed him as being extremely handsome.

We usually had tea in his small, cosy study. On one occasion, as there was company, I recall having tea in a large, grand, shuttered room with French furniture very conventionally arranged. Conrad was strongly feudal in his ideas and when I complained of the servile attitude of the villagers round about, he said that they were happier so. My reference to the villagers was occasioned by an incident which happened at Bridge. I had remarked on the astonishing velocity of a racing-car which had driven through the village at race-track speed scattering children and chickens. At the local barber's I mentioned this, and ventured to remark that the children were in danger of their lives. The barber said that in fact several children had been killed, but that the racing magnate had paid the parents handsomely, and all the villagers looked to him for employment. The report that Conrad refused a knighthood because it was offered by a Socialist Government, would, if true, bear out my observation about his feudal cast of mind.[5]

I looked at Conrad's bookshelf. He had not many books. In no sense a library. A complete edition of Turgeniev in English.[6] We talked of books and, expecting him to be interested in Melville's *Moby Dick*, I mentioned it, and Conrad burst into a furious denunciation of it. 'He knows nothing of the sea. Fantastic, ridiculous,' he said. When I mentioned that the work was symbolical and mystical: 'Mystical my eye! My old boots are mystical.' 'Meredith? His characters are ten feet high.' D. H. Lawrence had started well, but had gone wrong. 'Filth. Nothing but obscenities.' For Henry James he had unqualified admiration. Of his own novels he said it was a toss up at one time as to whether he would write in English or French. He emphasised the amount of labour he gave to a novel to get it to satisfy himself.

At a few of the sittings Conrad dictated letters to the secretary. His English was strongly foreign with a very guttural accent, so that his secretary frequently failed to get the right word, which made Conrad growl. I would try and detach myself from the work to listen. His composition was beautiful. Sentence followed sentence in classic 'Conrad', totally unlike his conversational manner, which was free, easy and colloquial.

The work on the bust was nearing completion. One day at the end of the sittings, Mrs Conrad appeared at the door to see it. She gave one glance and fled. A wife, a lover, can perhaps never see what the artist sees. The fact, at any rate, is that they rarely ever do. Perhaps a really mediocre artist has more chance of success in this respect. When George Bernard Shaw was sitting to me, I asked him why he had given sittings to a very incompetent artist. Shaw exclaimed: 'Why, he is a fine portrait painter – my wife, on entering the room where the portrait was, actually mistook it for myself.'

Conrad's own opinion about my portrait of himself was conveyed in a letter he wrote to Richard Curle, his biographer and literary executor. 'The bust of Ep. has grown truly monumental. It is a marvellously effective piece of sculpture, with even something more than masterly interpretation in it. . . . It is wonderful to go down to posterity like that.'[7] Later Sir Muirhead Bone offered the bust to the National Portrait Gallery. It was refused.[8]

At last the bust was completed. I wired my moulder to come and carry it away to London to be cast. I said goodbye to the old Master and travelled with the bust. Five months later I opened a newspaper and read that Joseph Conrad was dead.

NOTES

Sir Jacob Epstein (1880–1959) was the son of Jewish immigrants to New York, where he studied drawing and illustrating before his departure for Europe in 1902. He settled in Camden Town, London, in 1905 and was naturalised six years later. His early sculpture (such as his 1912 carving for the tomb of Oscar Wilde) was the object of much puritan criticism, and his decoration for the new British Medical Association building in the Strand (1908) was closely inspected from the scaffolding by the Bishop of Stepney, who declared its nudity to be inoffensive. Between 1916 and 1929, he became established as a modeller of portrait bronzes, and his works portray such figures as Einstein, George Bernard Shaw, the Emperor Haile Selassie and, later, Winston Churchill. In his later years he received numerous public commissions. He was knighted in 1954.

Conrad sat for Epstein in late March and April 1924. Epstein's sculpture is widely regarded as the most impressive portrait of Conrad.

1. For details of Muirhead Bone, see p. 167.
2. For details of Richard Curle, see p. 229.
3. By Jo Davidson. See p. 152.
4. *Suspense*, unfinished at the time of Conrad's death.
5. In May 1924 Conrad declined the offer of a knighthood from the Labour Prime Minister, Ramsay MacDonald. There is no evidence that Conrad refused the offer because it was made by a Socialist government. Perhaps, like his friend John Galsworthy in 1918, who had similarly refused a knighthood, he thought it inappropriate for an artist to accept such honours, or perhaps he believed that the acceptance of a new title would be a rejection of his ancient family heritage. He also declined five honorary degrees.
6. Constance Garnett, wife of Conrad's friend Edward, had translated the works of Ivan Turgenev.
7. *Conrad to a Friend: 150 Selected Letters from Joseph Conrad to Richard Curle* (1928; New York: Russell & Russell, 1968) p. 184. The letter is dated 25 March 1924. The final sentence which Epstein quotes is not contained in Curle's edition of the letters.

On 26 March 1924, Conrad wrote to Elbridge Adams that 'Epstein has been here for the last week doing my bust: just head and shoulders. It is really a magnificent piece of work. He will be done modelling this week and there will be five bronze copies cast. Muirhead Bone has arranged this. I was reluctant to sit, but I must say that now I am glad the thing has come off. It is nice to be passed to posterity in this monumental and impressive rendering' (G. Jean-Aubry, *Joseph Conrad: Life and Letters* (New York: Doubleday, Page, 1927) vol. II, p. 341).

8. The National Portrait Gallery later accepted a slightly damaged casting.

Part VII

Conrad in America

Conrad, Sea Writer, Here for First Time*

Joseph Conrad, master writer of sea tales, ex-skipper in sail and steam and Briton by adoption, arrived yesterday by the Anchor liner *Tuscania*[1] by a route unfamiliar to him in his many years of seagoing – that from Glasgow to Sandy Hook, where the Atlantic sea lane ends for European voyagers. All the way across from the Clyde he stood watch on the bridge with another literary skipper, Captain David Bone[2] of the *Tuscania*, and swapped sentiments on nautical and other themes, including the probable boarding at Quarantine of a score of reporters ambitious to analyse the Conradian psychology.

Although Captain Bone had prepared his distinguished shipmate for the ordeal of being interviewed Captain Conrad was not altogether at ease when the attack came. It was noted that he was modest almost to shyness, but it was palpably the modesty of conscious strength, a little disturbed by the unexpected number of the analysts.

Captain Conrad – that is what Captain Bone called him – despite his unassuming manner, looks like the intellectual he professes not to be. He is not a big man as you measure a towering iceberg by sextant, being a bit stocky, but anybody with an eye for supermen would turn around and look at him again on passing him in a Broadway throng.

Naturally one of the topics of the transatlantic chat on the bridge was the skyline of Manhattan, and Captain Conrad confided to Captain Bone as he discerned it mistily coming into Quarantine that it did not seem real, but a mere figment, something like a revival, in magnificent scale, of Arabian Nights' minarets and towers. When he got a better glimpse of the architectural summits he was moved to murmur simply, 'Beautiful, beautiful!' Later as the liner passed the Battery Captain Bone pointed out to Captain Conrad the biggest of the cloud piercers, naming them, and made a jovial remark about Broadway as the wonderful deepwater channel up which the two skippers would sail sometime.

One reason Captain Conrad took so deep an interest in his trip and its ending is that it is his first to the mainland of North America. He had discovered America in 1875, as Columbus did, by a voyage to the West Indies.[3]

* *New York Herald*, 2 May 1923, p. 24.

It was remarked that the two things distinctively English about the great story teller were his monocle and the leisurely enunciation of his adopted language. He submitted to a rapid-fire of all sorts of questions reclining in a settee in Captain Bone's cabin. There the reporters had a chance to note that Captain Conrad's eyes were a dark brown that seemed to glow black when he permitted himself to enthuse. His carefully trimmed beard is grey, his moustache streaked with white and his eyebrows black and bushy. His hair is dark except at the temples, where it is mixed with grey. He has the ruddy and seamed face of an out-of-doors man.

At Quarantine Captain Conrad declined to look, except in a cursory way, at several liners anchored there somewhat smaller than the *Tuscania*, the biggest ship he has ever been aboard, but confined his attention to a trim little three-masted schooner, which he said had more fascination for him than steam-propelled craft, although he had been once master of a British cargo steamship.[4] He seems to be partial to fore-and-afters, and the dainty three-master as she glided under the liner's starboard bow was worthwhile as a picture.

Captain Conrad was manifestly pleased when he was addressed by his nautical title and remarked that he had his master's ticket stowed away in the family strong-box with other prized documents. He surprised some of his younger admirers by admitting that he was a Victorian; that most of his reading was of nineteenth-century writers; that he had read Poe originally in French translation, had read some of J. Fenimore Cooper's novels.[5] He regretted that he had not read the books of John Burroughs, the 'man who chased nightingales'.[6] He was fond of Emerson[7] and Walt Whitman.[8]

In dodging a question involving a criticism of Walt Whitman Captain Conrad said: 'My mind is not critical. I have not the general culture for criticism. My life has not been literary. Twenty years at sea does not form the literary mind. I was a seaman and for a long time never thought of anything else. Even today I do not like writing. It is a frightful grind.'

As to the favourite story of his own creation, Captain Conrad said he had some favourites some days and others others. 'Books,' he continued, 'are like children, for they are children of the mind. It is difficult to explain differences in one's affection. I have two boys, but love them both, yet not always in the same way.'

In answer to a question intimating that he had a 'dual personality', Captain Conrad went the questioner one better by saying that he suspected that he had had three personalities, first as a boy in Poland, then, at seventeen, when he broke away from his native land and became a British seaman, and finally, after twenty years' sea service, when he drifted back to shore. 'Even after I married,' he went on, 'I planned to go to sea again. Various little schemes came up, but at last I had to go back to writing. It was not until after I had written the *Nigger* that I realised that my vocation was to be writing.'

Captain Conrad is here for a month and will return to Scotland with his shipmate Captain Bone on the *Tuscania*'s next eastward trip.[9] He will be the guest of Frank N. Doubleday of Doubleday, Page & Co., who accompanied him from Quarantine. Unlike the usual literary Briton he will not lecture.

NOTES

1. Conrad arrived in America for the first time on 1 May 1923, staying initially at the home of his publisher, Frank N. Doubleday, on Long Island. Conrad was better known to the American public than he was at home and he was bemused to find himself such a celebrity on his arrival. Three days afterwards he wrote to his wife: 'I will not attempt to describe to you my landing, because it is indescribable. To be aimed at by forty cameras held by forty men that look as if they came out of the slums is a nerve-shattering experience.'
2. For details of David Bone, see p. 167.
3. Conrad arrived in St Pierre, Martinique in February 1875, as a passenger in the *Mont Blanc*.
4. Conrad made four trips between Singapore and Borneo in 1887 as first mate in the British cargo steamer, the *Vidar*.
5. James Fenimore Cooper (1789–1851), author of *The Leather-Stocking Tales*, which comprise *The Pioneers* (1823), *The Last of the Mohicans* (1826), *The Prairie* (1827), *The Pathfinder* (1840) and *The Deerslayer* (1841). Conrad discusses his reading of Cooper in 'Tales of the Sea', in *Notes on Life and Letters* (London: J. M. Dent, 1949) pp. 53–7.
6. John Burroughs (1837–1921), American naturalist, essayist, critic and poet, best known as a nature writer.
7. Ralph Waldo Emerson (1803–82), American poet and philosopher.
8. Walt Whitman (1819–92), American poet.
9. He sailed from New York on 2 June 1923 in the *Majestic*, arriving in Southampton a week later.

Arriving with Joseph Conrad*

ROBERT LITTELL

She is a big ship, the *Tuscania*, as she rises above the Staten Island skyline. Too big to be a ship. A sea-going hotel, all iron and bell boys and landlike immobility. Except for the smell, one might just as well climb into the third storey of an office building as go aboard her.

Joseph Conrad is on deck. He has never been in America before. He is a celebrity, a big man, a distinguished visitor – which is more important in the eyes of many of us than being a great artist, so we newspaper reporters go down the bay to meet him, some of us because he is a great artist, others because every celebrity who passes the Statue of Liberty must be made to talk.

In little sea-smelling corners near the Captain's citadel we wait to devour the celebrity. We are getting ready to ask him what he thinks of prohibition, if he first went to sea in Poland, if he likes Al Smith.[1] Fortunately Christopher Morley[2] is with us, and puts us in a more listening mood. 'We'll just go a few at a time into the cabin and let him talk.'

Over the rail can be seen the leaden, glistening harbour, criss-crossed with shrill whistles in every key, with quick-melting little puffs of steam, as if all the vessels were selling peanuts.

Here he comes now, surrounded by both those who would protect and those who would attack him. The figure of a visitor, not a seaman: black derby, white scarf, black overcoat. Proper costume for a floating hotel – the largest ship he has ever been on. An acknowledgement of the presence of land, the invasion of the sea by the land.

No one's protection is any good against photographers. They steal him from us, back him to a wall, shoot him with large, small and medium cameras, take stills and movies, take him from East and West, with his hat and without it.

It is the only completely human, experienced, readable face in the small crowd on the deck. It is a face of a myriad fine lines, quickly passing mobilities, shadowy expressions. At first it looks stern, aristocratic, self-sufficient, but under the stare of the cameramen what seemed stern

* *New Republic*, vol. XXXIV (16 May 1923) p. 319.

becomes tragic, what seemed aristocratic, noble, and the self-sufficiency gives way entirely to a look, in the eyes, of generously helpless fortitude. It is cruel, that camera cannonade, but without it would we have seen flicker, across those seeing, brooding eyes, the shadows of past days?

Finally the boys whose business it is to make a dentist's chair of every liner's bridge let Mr Conrad go, and he is ours. With the horrible example of the photographers before us we treat him with uncommon decency. We ask him not too much about Walt Whitman, about American literature. With the nicest smile in the world he tells us how little he knows: 'My mind isn't critical. I haven't got enough general culture for criticism. A sea life doesn't fit one for that.'

It is a strong low voice, modest and simple, with the natural double richness of a foreign mellowness and strangeness of pronunciation and a better command of English than have any of us. After a few awkward pauses when we by not asking him too much are trying to tell him how much we like him, he begins to talk, for moments, almost as if we weren't there.

'I really don't like writing,' he says; 'it is a frightful grind.' We try to get him to talk about literature, about his novels. What he really wants to talk about is the sea, which has been all his life, about the 'magic monotony of existence between sky and water', about ships on which he has sailed.

'I have a great feeling for the little *Otago*.'[3] That was his first command, and Captain Conrad – he remembers how proud he felt when the agent called him 'Captain' – sailed her from Singapore to Australia.

'They had such good names, those ships. The *Duke of Sutherland* was the most prosaic one. *Skimmer of the Sea*, *Otago*, *Adowa*, *Tremolino*.'[4] He says that last name over thoughtfully, tenderly, forgetting all the people who have come to ask him questions, because that name calls up so much of the past. '*Tremolino*'.

The Past. 'It is frightfully misty now', he says. 'But one doesn't forget twenty-seven years. All that gets merged into one solitary impression.'

We stand on the bridge with him, curiously respectful, considering our trade. We let him sit in a corner, where he is just able to see, over the rail, the mass of lower New York. We ask for few autographs. We don't tell him much about the Statue of Liberty.

And Mr Conrad moves up the bay, as if from the past into some strange future. A slate-blue haze blurs the skyscrapers rather than softens them. Mr Conrad's eyes, those narrowed, seeing eyes, besieged by a thousand wrinkles from looking at the sea, find the prodigious crack in the skyline which is Broadway, and rest on it.

A ferry passes, all painted over with the romantic sea-faring words

'Bureau of Plant and Structures'. Captain Bone of the *Tuscania* knows the poetry of the sea: 'Three times round went our gallant Plant and Structures', he quotes.

'Life on the sea is altogether different now', says Mr Conrad. He does not enlarge upon this. But we see him looking wonderingly at the pilot, who is standing in ordinary street clothes by the telegraph much as if he were looking out through the plate glass of a shoe store.

Not a sail is to be seen in the harbour. Steam, iron, landlubbers have invaded the ocean. A seaman's life is no longer something mysterious and unlearnable.

The windows of the Woolworth tower become singly visible.

Oh for a wilderness of naked, shipless water . . . .

NOTES

1. Alfred Smith (1873–1944), Governor of New York at the time of Conrad's visit.

2. Christopher Morley (1890–1957), journalist on the *New York Evening Post.*

3. Conrad's first command in 1888. See p. 211 for further details.

4. *Duke of Sutherland* (1878–9): Conrad sailed as an ordinary seaman on this wool clipper from Gravesend to Sydney.

Skimmer of the Sea (1878): Conrad made three trips between Lowestoft and Newcastle as an ordinary seaman on this coal schooner.

Adowa (1893–4): Conrad's last ship, a steamer, in which he made a return voyage as second mate from London to Rouen. He began Chapter Ten of *Almayer's Folly* in Rouen harbour.

Tremolino (1877): in *The Mirror of the Sea*, Conrad explains how he and three other adventurers smuggled guns in the *Tremolino* for the supporters of Don Carlos, the Pretender to the Spanish throne, from Marseilles to Spain. The ship had to be run on to the rocks and wrecked to escape the coastguard. However, there is no evidence to support this claim.

Joseph Conrad – Master Mariner and Novelist*

JAMES WALTER SMITH

Joseph Conrad is honest in his dislike of publicity. He is a shy man, seeking no advertisement, and preferring to be judged by his books alone. He grows restless under questioning, especially when asked about his literary methods, his characters and plots. 'Technique', 'philosophy', and other words so frequently on the penpoints of scribbling critics are to him, apparently, anathema. They are not in his vocabulary – at least, he eschews them unless forced by questioners to use them. He chafes visibly at any invasion of his literary privacy. And he has sufficient human irascibility to make you feel not a little uncomfortable when you step beyond the bounds of tact in an interview.

All this was proved on Monday afternoon last when Mr Conrad consented to be interviewed by a score of literary reporters, of both sexes, at the delightful home of Mr Frank N. Doubleday, his publisher, at Oyster Bay, Long Island. Obviously, the whole affair was at first rather distasteful to Mr Conrad, and there were moments when, because of a tactless question, it seemed as if his patience would give way, and that he might flee in desperation from the ordeal. But, thanks to the sympathy of some of the visitors and the charming manner in which the difficulties were surmounted by Mr Conrad's host and hostess, everything passed off all right. Mr Conrad ran the gauntlet safely. Generally, he met the test with great amiability. He proved, in all he said to the numberless questions put to him, clumsily or otherwise, that he was a great human being, a man of infinite experience of life, an earnest seeker of the truth, and withal kindly and companionable. Not one of us came away without a greater admiration than before for the man who is unquestionably the greatest living writer of English prose, and a singular feeling of gratitude to him personally for having risen from a sickbed to greet us.

When we arrived at Mr Doubleday's wonderful home, we found the author of *Lord Jim* standing on a rug in the great reception hall, leaning somewhat heavily upon a cane in his right hand. He was a little bowed, showing that the years – or perhaps it was merely his sufferings – were

* *Boston Evening Telegraph*, 12 May 1923, p. 2.

weighing on him. When I first saw Mr Conrad, nearly thirty years ago, his hair and beard were jet black. But now they are grey almost to whiteness. But the sparkle of his eyes and the liveliness of his face generally are still very marked. He still speaks with a slight accent, but his mastery of the spoken English language is superb, and his intellectual alertness extraordinary. One would not think for an instant that he had ever been at sea. One would place him, with his Van Dyke beard, his monocle and his captivating personality, in the chair of a diplomat, or perhaps more worthy in a fauteuil of the French Academy.

When the first difficult moments were over, Mr Conrad sat down in the circle of interviewers, and glanced over some sheets containing questions which had been sent in beforehand by some of the visitors. It became clear at once that he was inclined more freely to answer queries about old friends and old times than about his books. The first question which he answered was one put by the *Transcript* concerning his early experiences in London and his friendship with Stephen Crane, author of *The Red Badge of Courage.*[1] Frankly, it was in the hope that the mention of Crane's name would lead to some valuable reminiscences of others who knew Mr Conrad in the interesting period following the publication of *Almayer's Folly* that the question was advanced. Mr Conrad responded instantly with apparent delight.

'Ah! Stephen Crane,' he replied, as if delighting in his recollections, 'I was one of the first to know him when he came to London, and I had written something about *The Red Badge.*[2] You know of course that Crane knew nothing about actual warfare, and got his first experience of real fighting during the Greek war. When he returned, he said to me, "*The Red Badge* was right." And it was right!

'Crane was a wonderful and charming fellow. He didn't appear to know much about life or literature. I remember walking in London with him one night for hours when he suddenly asked me about Balzac.[3] "Tell me about him," he said. So I proposed that we first get something to eat, which we did, and I had to wire to my wife that I should not be home that night. It was just after we were married' – with a chuckle – 'and then we talked Balzac until the morning.'

'I've written an eight-page preface for a "Life" of Crane that one of your young writers is going to publish.[4] He came to see me about it in England. You'll find a great deal of new stuff in it, because I loved to put it down. Crane was just a dear fellow. He gave me my first dog, or at least gave it to my little boy. "Every boy ought to have a dog," he said. The dog lived until about six or seven years ago, and died of old age. It was my boy's companion. Stevie used to come and see us very often. He used to ask our advice. Sometimes he talked quite freely. At other times he would say nothing for an hour or more. My wife and I were very fond of him, and we liked his wife.'

'I saw him when he was dying – when he didn't know he was dying. He was at the seaside, lying in bed and looking out of the window at the passing ships. "Life is beautiful," he said. Afterwards –'

Mr Conrad spoke with deep feeling, and doubtless would have told much that was interesting about Crane's life at Brede. But one of the reporters handed Mr Conrad a written question regarding his treatment of character in his novels. It was a long and tortuous question, which, when read aloud, caused Mr Conrad much uneasiness, and elicited something more than a gentle rebuke. The question was largely based upon the author's method in *Lord Jim* of letting other characters tell what was in an individual character's mind rather than telling directly what that individual thought. 'I say what my characters think,' remarked Mr Conrad. 'Every author has a right to say what his people think.' Then, when the case of Lord Jim was cited, Mr Conrad replied, 'I can't remember everything that is in my books. Some readers know them better than I do. If you are talking about what is called the novel of analysis, I know nothing about it.'

This was not the only question that upset the great writer. It must be admitted that some of the afternoon's enjoyment was spoiled for him and others by the pertinacity with which queries were popped on him regarding his methods of work and his handling of character. One young lady mentioned two characters, and gave them wrong names, whereupon Mr Conrad, fixing his monocle on her, said, 'it is plain, my dear young lady, that you don't know my people. I suggest that you read my books.' But this reproof was given after the writer had begun to tire of the implications that he possessed a philosophy. A number of the questions had used the hated word. Promptly Mr Conrad ridiculed the idea. 'I have no philosophy', he said. 'They have invented it for me.'

It may be interesting if I mention here a few questions regarding the Conrad 'philosophy', which Mr Conrad absolutely refused to answer, and one or two regarding his literary methods which appeared to be distasteful to him. 'Your philosophy of life' – thus ran one of the questions – 'as indicated in *Lord Jim*, *Nostromo* and *Victory*, for example, appears to be to last with every ounce he has until borne down. Is that a fair guess?' Another as follows: 'Would you advise the young man, eager to write fiction, to seek the strange places of the earth? Did you find your philosophy there, or did you carry it there with you?' And another: 'In placing the scenes and incidents in your novels, is each incident and scene definitely associated in your mind with some actual place or occurrence, or is the mental connection largely an unconscious one?'

It was a painful effort – all this – to pin Mr Conrad to a formula, and an honest effort, I dare say, because a number of brainy critics of

Mr Conrad's books have honestly felt that a Conradian philosophy really existed. But, when the author was approached from several angles he invariably replied, 'I don't know', or 'You are asking me things about which I know nothing.' When he was asked about his 'style' he answered: 'It's something I never bother about: it is sufficient to get ahead with the story without bothering about such matters.'

On one occasion – in that wonderful preface to *The Nigger of the 'Narcissus'*, which was 'suppressed' when the book was first issued in England, Mr Conrad wrote the following words, unforgettable by anyone who truly loves his books and asks no more than to love them; 'My task which I am trying to achieve is, by the power of the written word to make you hear, to make you feel – it is, before all, to make you *see*. That – and no more, and it is everything.'[5] If there is any Conradian philosophy it is in those words and one is not surprised that Mr Conrad shows restlessness when more is asked.

The well-known Marlow, who, if my memory be right, was called by Henry James 'this impossible, this monstrous master-mariner',[6] naturally came up during the interview, somewhat, I believe, to Mr Conrad's displeasure. It must have seemed to him another attempt to get him to discuss his methods. Whether or not, it succeeded partially, and elicited the best thing about *Lord Jim* which I ever heard. 'I got into *Lord Jim*,' said Mr Conrad, 'and I just had to get out. I had to invent Marlow to carry on the story.[7] It seems the best way. The critics say that Marlow talks the way a man writes. They are right. That's what he does. But when I did it that way, I didn't create a new form of writing – there is no new form of writing novels. I have too much to think of when I am writing to invent new forms. I try to do something to satisfy myself. I have sufficient thinking to do on carrying on the story without bothering about the method. Technique, as you call it, doesn't disturb me. I never preoccupy myself with either methods or technique.'

Someone asked Mr Conrad if some of his work wasn't ironical, and mentioned *The Secret Agent*. 'Was it ironical, and if so, was it truth?' Mr Conrad flashed back, 'Yes, it's ironical. It seemed to me that irony was the only thing to use with those fellows. But to say it isn't truth – well, I have two boys, and they treat me, their father, at times in a very ironical manner. But do you call it untruthful? And' – he laughed, 'don't you believe they love me, for all that?'

One question touched Mr Conrad very closely, and brought upon the questioner a sharp look that nearly ended the whole discussion. The reporter asked if Kurtz, one of the characters in *Heart of Darkness*, was a real person. 'I saw him die', said Mr Conrad.[8] Readers who remember the man who gave up civilisation and drank deep of degradation in the tropics will know how Mr Conrad shot forth those four stinging words.

He was asked if marine conditions had altered – had the sailing ship disappeared before steam, and so on. 'The conditions haven't changed so much. It is the men who have changed. It's not that they are less romantic, it's simply because they are of a different type. The man on a steam vessel suffers less strain on the nerves. His work is easier.' Mr Conrad then told a pathetic story of how, when once 'running the easting down',[9] he had spent two terrible hours in the rigging of his ship, trying to break the ice in the sails, with the aid of a little Australian youth of sixteen, who, amidst the flapping canvas, was terrorised, and crying out wildly with pain and weariness. 'The sailing ship made men,' said Mr Conrad. 'Sailors today are little more than factory hands.'

There was a young woman reporter in the party who had been instructed by her editor to find out Mr Conrad's ideas upon cooking and appropriately brought with her Mrs Conrad's new cookery-book, for which Mr Conrad had written a preface.[10] The appearance of the little volume caused momentary amusement, but the girl went bravely at her task and asked her questions. Did Mr Conrad like the recipes? And what did sailors eat? And would he say the book was good? This last query took Mr Conrad's fancy, seemingly, for he replied, 'Well, I don't propose to advertise your book, but I can say that sailors like good food, especially when they can't get it. By the way, have you ever heard of a palm-oil chop?' 'No,' meekly answered the maiden, whereupon Mr Conrad described a remarkable West African dish, saying 'When you're able to eat it, you are a naturalised citizen of those parts. And now,' he continued, 'I can tell you that I have just received a letter from my wife saying that, on the strength of her cook-book, she has been asked by the editor of a London weekly paper to conduct his cookery columns.'

More questions followed. 'It was the late Sidney Pawling of the Heinemann firm who accepted *The Nigger of the 'Narcissus'*, and what is more he induced Henley to publish it in the *New Review*.[11] It was my *Nigger* that killed the *Review* you know' – (with a laugh). 'Oh, no,' countered one of the group. 'Oh, yes,' retorted the writer, 'It's a fact, and that reminds me that I got acquainted with Henley after *Almayer* was published, and he asked me to let him consider the story for serial use in the *Review*. The opening chapters were sent to him, and then I got a letter from Henley asking me for the rest. "If it's up to the sample, I'll publish it," he wrote.' Then Mr Conrad turned around quizzingly. 'How's that – "up to sample" – for an American commercialism. And from an English editor!'

Mr Conrad added that when Henley read the preface to *The Nigger*, he was so delighted with it, and so amazed that he had published it as an epilogue to the serial. The preface to *The Nigger* is now a Conrad classic, and the history of it should henceforth make the name of Henley more memorable than before to every admirer of Mr Conrad's work. For those were the days when Conrad needed encouragement. He has all he wants of that now – perhaps too much for his own satisfaction as a modest artist.

The 'movies' – of course. Was Mr Conrad interested in them? What did he think of them as a vehicle of expression? What was his attitude toward them? Would they – this was the actual form of one of the questions – ever equal in effect the novel and spoken drama as a medium of popular fiction? Mr Conrad amiably expressed his opinion that the 'cinema' was marvellous. 'Miraculous' was the word. But the 'movies' would never take the place of the novel. 'Before the cinematograph was invented,' he remarked, 'ficition-writers tried to make moving-pictures. This was the first essential of a good story – that it move. The trouble with moving-pictures is that they don't show, except in a superficial way, what the characters are thinking. Barring certain experiments which I have seen, the cinema pictures are lacking in both colour and speech. Yes, I have written a scenario. I was asked by an American firm to submit one, and I struggled with it for a month.[12] It was a terrible month. And then I sent it to them. But they sent it back.'

One question which Mr Conrad didn't answer ran thus: 'Do you plot out your novels in scenario form, or outline them on paper before writing?' (Can you see Mr Conrad doing a preliminary scenario of *Lord Jim*?) But he did reply to a question – everlasting put to him – regarding his method of work. 'Do you write with your hand?' asked one of the ladies. 'Alas, no', answered Mr Conrad, looking swiftly at his hand, which was partly covered by a knitted glove or wrister, 'Not now. I used to. But now I dictate to a lady secretary who sits at the typewriter and takes down what I say – with long intervals between!' The reply was characteristic of the man who has always confessed that writing is hard work. Yes, the hardest kind of work to anyone sincere in his artistry.

He told us with great glee that occasionally he couldn't make out what he had himself written. It was a passage in *Nostromo*, he said, which after the book had been laboriously written, caught his attention in type. 'I read it over a second time,' he said, 'and still it didn't mean anything. I asked myself, "What did I try to say?" And then I put it to a friend who said, "No, I can't quite make it out." It was at the beginning of a chapter.' 'Which chapter,' asked a curious lady reporter. 'I don't know,' replied the author. 'It isn't there now. I struck it out.'

Mr Conrad was showing a little fatigue. Since he arrived in New York he has been confined most of his time to his bed with gout, and it was his feeling of duty to the press and his new friends here that prompted him, while in physical pain, to go through the ordeal of meeting his questioners. 'You know,' he said, 'all this is a new experience for me. The reporters never came to see me in England. But I'll do my best.' All this, of course, before the torture began. And, considering everything, the master went through the ordeal wonderfully. It was left, however, to Mr Doubleday, just before he sent Mr Conrad back to bed, to 'put the punch' in the afternoon's proceedings. He asked Mr Conrad to tell us about *The Rescue*, prefacing the request with the statement that this book, the first part of which was written and sent to Mr Doubleday, was stopped halfway in the writing, and lay unfinished in the publisher's desk for twenty years.[13] It was then taken up again and finished by the author. 'That's so,' remarked Mr Conrad. 'And now, since you literary experts have been asking me a lot of questions, let me ask you one. Is there any one of you who can tell me where the first part broke off and the second part began?'

It was a real gage of battle. And Mr Conrad won out. His eyes twinkled merrily. 'One critic, who prides himself on knowing something about my work,' he said, 'thought he had found the place. But he was wrong. I think only two people have correctly guessed it.' 'And where is the place?' asked an unsophisticated person. 'Ah,' retorted Mr Conrad, 'that's my secret. Can't I have a secret?'

Finally, he told us something about his forthcoming book. It is called *The Rover*. After serial publication it will be published in book form on 1 December.[14] 'The scenes are laid in the Mediterranean during the period of the Napoleonic wars. Napoleon figures in it, but not to any great extent. Nelson is in it, and I think that he and Lady Emma Hamilton occupy only eight or ten pages. I got the motto of the book from an old Breton sailor. It describes the class of sailors that used to navigate the Indian Ocean in the olden days. I think I'll write it down, but there's one word in it that I always have trouble in spelling.' Whereupon, borrowing a pencil, Joseph Conrad bent down and carefully inscribed the following:

> They were of all nations
> English French Dutch
> Spaniards and even blackamoors
> but they were all brothers.

'Yes,' he remarked, as he looked again at the word 'blackamoors', 'I've got it right.' And he put down the pencil.

NOTES

James Walter Smith (1868–1931), graduate of Harvard, was a journalist and editor. He moved to London in 1894, and stayed for twenty years, working for *Strand Magazine* and acting as chief editor for Cassell & Co. He returned to America in 1915, living mainly in New York.

The interview with Conrad took place on Monday, 7 May 1923, the seventh day of Conrad's first and only visit to the United States. Conrad's publisher, Frank N. Doubleday, and his wife, Florence, welcomed Smith and eighteen other reporters to their Oyster Bay home with its view of Long Island Sound.

1. Stephen Crane (1871–1900), author of *The Red Badge of Courage* (1895), had settled in England in 1897 and met Conrad in October of that year. In 1899, Crane and his wife, Cora, moved to Brede Place, a mediaeval mansion in Sussex, where Conrad was a frequent visitor. Crane's tuberculosis necessitated a move to the Black Forest in May 1900. Resting at Dover to gather strength for the crossing, Crane, who was very weak and in isolation, saw Conrad for the last time, in a visit lasting twenty minutes. Crane died the following month in Germany.

2. No such work by Conrad has been identified.

3. Honoré de Balzac (1799–1850), the French novelist.

4. Conrad had written his preface to Thomas Beer's *Stephen Crane: A Study in American Letters* (New York: Knopf, 1923) in the preceding March.

5. Preface to *The Nigger of the 'Narcissus'* (London: J. M. Dent, 1946) p. x. Sidney Pawling, of Heinemann, refused to publish the Preface in the first edition of the book.

6. This remark, probably anecdotal, is consistent with James's view of Marlow in his essay 'The New Novel' in *Notes on Novelists with some other Notes* (London: J. M. Dent, 1914).

7. Marlow begins his narration in Chapter Five.

8. During his stay in the Congo, Conrad took on board his steamer a young Frenchman, Georges Antoine Klein, suffering from dysentry. Klein died during the journey down river. His name, later changed to Kurtz, may be found in the manuscript of *Heart of Darkness.* Apart from his presence and death aboard the steamer, there is no reason to link his character with that of the demonic Kurtz.

9. 'Running the easting down' refers to the long easterly passage from the Cape of Good Hope to Australia in the Roaring Forties, during which the big square-rigged ships took advantage of the prevailing westerly gales.

10. Jessie Conrad, *A Handbook of Cookery for a Small House* (London: Heinemann), published in February 1923.

11. Sidney S. Pawling (1862–1923), a partner of William Heinemann, the publisher, introduced Conrad to Stephen Crane and acquired *The Nigger of the 'Narcissus'* for his firm in 1896, publishing it in the December of the next year after its serialisation in the *New Review* (Aug.–Dec. 1897), a journal published by Heinemann. Its editor was W. E. Henley (1849–1903), a poet and highly influential editor who was the model for Long John Silver. The *New Review* ceased publication in December 1897.

12. Conrad wrote a film script based on his short story, 'Gaspar Ruiz', in September and October 1920. It was never filmed.

13. Begun in 1896, *The Rescue* was laid aside in 1899 and it was not until autumn 1918 that Conrad resumed and extensively revised the novel, completing the work in 1920.

14. *The Rover* was serialised in the *Pictorial Review* (Sept.–Dec. 1923). The epigraph which Conrad described was not eventually used.

Americans Kind, So Why Lecture?*

Joseph Conrad is in Boston today on his 'tour of friendship' in the United States as the guest of Frank Nelson Doubleday, president of Doubleday, Page & Co., his publishers, and Mrs Doubleday. He arrived by motor yesterday with his hosts, and will depart tomorrow. He is neither lecturing nor gathering material for new books.

'The American people have been kind to me: why should I lecture to them?' he asked.

As for possible stories with an American setting, he explained that he does not 'gather material', but writes in retrospect of what he saw and learned during the first 35 years of his life. This is his first trip to the United States, made at the invitation of Mr Doubleday and in return for the publisher's many visits to the author in England. It is, as he expressed it, 'merely a holiday'.

When a representative of the *Christian Science Monitor* was ushered into Mr Conrad's presence at the Copley Plaza this morning he found the author's face beaming with pleasant recollections of his trip from New York. His eyes twinkled merrily as he said: 'Oh, I have had such a delightful time with your American policemen! Those that I have met have been so courteous and cheerful. Yesterday one said to the chauffeur, "I'm sorry, but you'll have to drive on another block before turning." Fancy a policeman saying "I'm sorry!" He was one of those delightful provincial police in a small city en route here. But ah! your fine metropolitan policemen! I do admire them, in their white gloves. Those gloves were the first things I noticed in Boston.'

Mr Conrad spoke with a decidedly foreign accent, recalling the fact that, though a master of English letters, he spoke no word of the

* *Christian Science Monitor*, 19 May 1923, p. 2.

language until more than seventeen years old, and then shipped twenty years with sailormen of various races. Polish is his native tongue, though he speaks quite as fluently in French.

The conversation drifted to his voyage to New York, and he continued: 'It is a dreadful thing to be a passenger! I have finished with the sea, and I shall never go by sea when I can go by land. For many years it was my business to be at sea, and then I liked it. But to be a passenger, with nothing to do but sit around all day . . . no, no!'

Mr Conrad paid a particular tribute to the beauty of Concord, whose charm had impressed him more than most sights in America. After announcing that he would sail 2 June on his way back to England, he discussed his writings.

As an author, he said, he is slow. Words do not tumble in profusion from his pen, nor, in the modern fashion click off mechanically through the medium of a typewriter. He writes by longhand, and his writing is the result of studied thought.

He said: 'I often write no words for weeks. During that time I may sit daily for hours at a time in my chair, and in the evening retire exhausted with my labours, and yet not one word have I set on paper. But this is not a waste of time, for I am planning, thinking, constructing the characters and plots of my books.

'*Nostromo* I consider my greatest effort. I spent two years in writing it. I had to construct a South American republic in my own thoughts, and yet maintain truthful descriptions throughout of life in such a country. When I write I build no Utopias, for I always keep a firm control of my imagination. I have a book in hand now,[1] for there is always something upon which I must be working.'

When Mr Conrad had left the room for a moment, Mr Doubleday told of his relations with the author and his work. He said: 'Mr Conrad is extremely careful in preparing his manuscripts, that there shall be no nonessentials in the printed text. His latest book, *The Rover*, which will be published in the fall, he cut down twenty per cent after writing it. He said to me one day: "Here are twenty lines that I have read over several times, and I am wondering, 'Now, what is that fellow driving at?' If I don't know, no one else will, so I am going to cut it out."

'Mr Conrad did not take possession of the English language, but the English language took possession of him. If he hadn't written in English, he wouldn't have written at all. He feels no freedom of expression in French, but English gives him the medium he wishes.'

NOTES

Conrad and his party arrived in Boston on 16 May 1923 and stayed for five days at the Copley Plaza Hotel.

1. *Suspense*, begun in 1921 and incomplete at the time of his death.

An Evening with Joseph Conrad*

JOHN SHERIDAN ZELIE

To see Joseph Conrad at all was the last thing I had ever dreamed of. I knew that he was in this country and that interest in his coming was at its height but I knew also how much he disliked and avoided publicity and that few were likely to see him.

But a letter from a friend suddenly announced that Mr Conrad was to be his guest for two nights in Great Barrington and asked me to come for one of those nights. When I arrived after dusk my friend explained that I could not meet his guest for a few moments and the reason for the delay only added to the interest of meeting him at all. For there had come to this house from overseas another visitor, a no-less-interesting person than the British etcher, Muirhead Bone,[1] who was at that moment making still another etching of the novelist in the music-room. Taken all together, the British etcher, the evening hour on the edge of the Berkshire forest and the notable act of one great artist employing his art upon another, it was a combination of circumstances sufficiently interesting.

Then we moved indoors and stood looking into the music-room where the etching was going on. Mr Conrad was sitting, stretched far out in an easy chair, his head sunk down into his shoulders and listening to the music. Though he looked quite like the familiar portraits, my first impression of him was one of surprise that he was so much slighter and less robust than they had given one to suppose.

The moment of seeing anyone like Joseph Conrad for the first time is apt to be a rather confused and cloudy moment. One thinks of too many things at once:

> 'And did you once see Shelley plain?
> And did he stop and speak to you?'[2]

And a certain haziness is no inappropriate atmosphere through which

* *Christian Century*, vol. XLII (19 Feb. 1925) pp. 251–3.

to see this novelist for while he could be master of the clean-cut and the sharply etched, as in that gem-like paragraph with which *An Outcast of the Islands* begins, he could also throw a kind of haze around a subject when he willed, and he often willed to do so. So we stood watching the pleasant scene in which the novelist gave not the slightest impression of feeling that he was being posed or watched but only that of a man very much at rest. He said once for whosoever wills to believe it that 'the greatest of his gifts was a consummate capacity for doing nothing'.[3]

As we moved back from the doorway and into the library my host stopped before one of the shelves to tell of an interesting episode of the day before. Pointing to a shelf of books he said it was a complete set of Conrad's first editions and as we handled them together and read the annotations in them he explained how they came to be there. A Conrad enthusiast had learned that Mr Conrad was to be a guest at this house and had politely and through an intermediary broached the question of getting his precious set of first editions before the author with the purpose of having him put his signature in each of them. Puzzled and not knowing what to say, the master of the house had at last reluctantly consented to having them sent on but without any encouragement as to his opening the matter at all and leaving it to chance whether there might arise any way of presenting it. At length he thought of a delicate way of introducing the subject. The novelist, too, was puzzled but finally said that he would be idle the next day and might as well do it. And very handsomely he did it, once he had begun, and the enthusiast was just as handsomely grateful. But best of all was what happened before he signed a single one of them, when he turned to his friend and said, 'But you yourself have a set of my first editions somewhere and if I am going to do this I am going to sign all of yours first.' And this he did and there they stood, the two sets, enough to make any collector's mouth water. I confess, though I have never had anything to do with first editions myself, that I rather like the persistence of this enthusiast with his heart set on this prize, and getting it, and I like still better the thought of the friend who had not set his heart on it, getting it too.

Once more we were looking in upon the etching and I was wondering what Mr Conrad would be like for I had always thought of him as about the most detached person in the world and had imagined him as a bit ironic, certainly austere, and none too ready to meet strangers. The etching was blithely over at last and the group from the music-room came into the library. What Mr Conrad said first after his hearty greeting which would set anybody immediately at ease, I cannot remember, for the artist had brought his plate with him and we were all five looking at this latest portrait together.

I was struck with the foreignness of Conrad's appearance. Others have thought he looked much more like an Englishman than they had expected. But his very foreignness of appearance only intensified my wonder, always great, at the degree to which this man of Poland and the Ukraine, who had never spoken a word of English until he was twenty-one, and had never intended to write it at all, had become so integrated into English life and letters. And he had too a strangeness of accent which now and then made you miss some remark. He had said to the friend he was visiting that it was one of the disappointments of his life that he had never been able to speak in his adopted tongue (or rather the tongue which had adopted him), just as the English do. But for all that he seemed an Englishman to the very centre of him.

Joseph Conrad might be like anyone else for warmth and cordiality and naturalness, as indeed he was, but it was next to impossible not to feel in his presence a great cloud of other personalities such as his very name suggests. It was not easy to separate him from the thousands of people all over the world who have him for a part of their life and still less was it possible not to be thinking all the time of the personalities whom he had himself created.

But what I wanted to ask Mr Conrad most was not what he thought of America but what he thought of Kent. Remarking that I could never quite get used to thinking of him as a resident of England's drowsiest county, he warmed to the subject and said, 'Yes, but it is so and I have now been there just the same length of time that I was at sea.' During the previous year I had been in both of his homes, Kent and the Ukraine, and was curious also to know about his feelings toward that earlier home but he spoke of that as if it were cloudy and remote and sad, while of his present home he spoke with vigour and cheer. Recalling days when I had tramped the Kentish roads with the hop-pickers, he spoke brightly of the partial revival of the hop-picking and the chance that it might flourish again. Then he would branch off into praises of what was now unmistakably his own country and speak of the flexible and amiable way in which Britons govern themselves in neighbourhoods like his and of how little they know about interference. As an instance he told of some uprising and disturbance in that quarter, which elsewhere in the world might have grown to all kinds of mischief, but there in Kent it was dealt with so quietly and almost whimsically engineered by British good sense that the cloud passed over and instead of bursting just dwindled away. He laughed as he recalled the genial way in which it was all disposed of. In his praise of that successful looseness in most things British, was there just a hint of relief from remembrances such as those of his boyhood when he and his mother departed from the Ukraine, a scene described by him with such severity of description in his pages of autobiography?[4]

His identification with his adopted country seemed as complete as could well be and something predestined. One loves that little item in which he records how from the tossing small boat which was putting a pilot on board the first British ship he ever saw, he put out his hand just to touch its side and feel the throb of its engines, long before he had ever stood on a British deck.[5]

He talked warmly about his neighbourhood and though he seemed not to take much part in public affairs, yet his heart and feelings were responsive to them in the spot he had chosen at Bishopsbourne, within sound of Canterbury's bells. I think he said that they had urged him to become a magistrate but that he did not quite wish to do that. He said that he had never spoken in public but once and told laughingly of that one necessary exception, how he felt about it and just what happened. It was on some great occasion in London in connection with the Lifeboat Service.[6] He had been asked to speak and could not well decline. His double connection with the sea and letters was commandeered for that occasion and the thing must be done. But since he must speak he said he resolved that he would speak only five minutes, that he would commit every word of his speech to writing and then to memory and that he would rehearse it at home. While he was practising the last of these resolves one of the servants of the household announced solemnly to Mrs Conrad that 'Mr Conrad was in the drawing room preaching'. When the time came for the delivery of the address he said he slipped into a place at the back of the platform and at last heard Admiral Beatty,[7] who was presiding, announce that the next speaker would be Mr Conrad, 'and without even looking around to see if I were there'. It was all told just as a boy would tell of a narrow escape, with a shrug and a laugh.

An evening could hardly be easier or more natural than this evening with Joseph Conrad and his three friends. He had been assured of privacy and that assurance is not broken by the publication of these reminiscences, for some weeks before his death they passed through his kindly hands at Bishopsbourne and came back with such changes as he desired made and with his permission to publish. The original form of the article with his notes and remarks lies before me as I write. While we talked and moved about, the artist was all the time busy with his sketch-book, catching other glimpses of the guest and chatting the while on all sorts of odd subjects. If Mr Conrad, in his nervous way, turned so that the sketcher could no longer see his face, all one had to do to help him out was just to change one's own position so that Mr Conrad would have to change his position too. The artist interjected all manner of cheerful remarks and, apropos of nothing in particular, quoted Dr Johnson as saying, 'If a man is making money, for heaven's sake let him alone. How could he be more innocently engaged?'[8] Then the sketch-book would be handed around with its last records of Mr Conrad, only a few minutes old, and with them some illustrated letters from the artist's boy who was sketching at Honfleur.[9]

Joseph Conrad's visit to America had come twenty-eight years after the last likelihood of it had seemingly vanished forever and there was a touch of surprise that he should find himself here at all. He had visited Princeton and Yale and Harvard and Williams, he had declined degrees on several occasions because he had declined them at home,[10] he had met but few people but many of these he recalled by name and very heartily. Twice only he had made anything like a public appearance, once when he had spoken to a company of several hundred people in a great house in New York and again when he spoke to the staff at the publishing house in Garden City: 'I must do that you know, they are all friends of my books.' He always spoke with zest of the people who liked his books, and with cheerfulness and friendliness of those who did not.

Joseph Conrad was certainly not vexed with 'viewiness' on all subjects in heaven and earth and a less dogmatic person one could hardly find. He seemed to carry the lightest possible burden of theories about art or his own art but was very certain about what he himself must do and the only chance he had of doing it. He was not profuse in dislikes; he expressed his liking for Keats and his lack of enthusiasm for Shelley but did not explain it; once or twice he indicated very simply at just what point he thought some writer had fallen short of doing all he might have done. His praise of James Fenimore Cooper, so often expressed by him, dropped into the conversation once more with heartiness. Impossible as it was that Joseph Conrad should be unconscious of his place in the world of letters, his whole air through this free and natural evening was the same air one feels in all the little that he has written about himself, a sort of surprise that he should be occupying such a place at all. 'My previous state of existence was not a good equipment for a literary life. Perhaps I should not have used the word literary. That word presupposes an intimacy of acquaintance with letters, a turn of mind and a manner of feeling to which I dare lay no claim. I only love letters; but the love of letters does not make a literary man, any more than the love of the sea makes a seaman.' 'In the career of the most unliterary of writers, in the sense that literary ambition had never entered the world of his imagination, the coming into existence of the first book is quite an inexplicable event.'[11]

There was one subject on which Mr Conrad became open and confidential in a moment and that was the difficulties which accompany the act of writing. When I asked him if he looked forward to getting home, he said, 'Yes, but I don't look forward to writing.' It was one thing, he said, to sit and dream all sorts of things but, oh, such another thing to decide which you will take, what you will do with it and bring it to book. Asked if he did not make notes, he replied, 'No, I never made a note in my life.' When I made bold to suggest that writing was with him what Sainte Beuve said it was to him, 'his sore burden and his great joy', he said that 'it was neither burden nor joy in a positive sense'.

As we sat around the fireplace the talk ran in all directions, turning now and again naturally to Conrad's own works. He was perfectly willing to talk about them and would have been, as one of his friends said, perfectly content never to say a word. He frankly expressed the pleasure he felt over one of his descriptions which experts on the region described said could never have been written save by one who had seen it, yet he had never seen it. Before our gathering that evening he had asked his host, 'Why do people call me a writer of sea-stories? They do not call Mr Hardy "a writer of land-stories"'.

I have read initimate articles on Joseph Conard, written from the standpoint of every possible advantage in the way of privilege to ask whatever questions one would, but it is rather surprising to notice how accurately all such confidences as he has made come back to what he had already told us of himself in that seemingly veiled autobiography, *A Personal Record*. The friend at whose home we had gathered said that once when he was Conrad's guest in Kent he had asked him which one of his books he liked best and expressed a good deal of pleasure and surprise when he spoke of the *Personal Record* as a favourite.

The long evening came to its close, leaving you as he took your hand in both of his to say good-night, quite ready to agree to what James Huneker said of him, in writing about the first men of letters in the world of our time. 'J.C. is certainly the most lovable of them.'[12]

NOTES

Dr John Sheridan Zelie (1866–1942), clergyman, was born in Princeton, Mass. and graduated from Yale in 1890. He later served as an Army chaplain in France, 1918–19. At the time of his meeting with Conrad on 22–3 May 1923, Zelie was a clergyman at Troy, New York. The meeting occurred at the country home of Elbridge Adams in Great Barrington, Mass.

1. For information on Muirhead Bone, see p. 167.
2. From Robert Browning's 'Memorabilia'.
3. A reference to Joseph Conrad, *A Personal Record* (London: J. M. Dent, 1946) p. 90.
4. See ibid., pp. 64–7.
5. See ibid., p. 137.
6. On 17 April 1923, four days before sailing to America, Conrad made a

speech at the annual meeting of the Lifeboat Institution, held at the Aeolian Hall, London. Conrad's first speech in public had been in 1919.

7. Admiral of the Fleet David Beatty (1871–1936); at this date he was First Sea Lord.

8. 'There are few ways in which a man can be more innocently employed than in getting money', quoted in James Boswell's *Life of Samuel Johnson* (1775).

9. Stephen Bone (1904–58), painter and art critic.

10. Conrad declined honorary degrees from the Universities of Durham, Edinburgh, Cambridge, Liverpool and Yale.

11. Conrad, *A Personal Record*, pp. 108, 90.

12. See p. 23.

Conrad, in Light and Shadow, Talks of Crane and Hardy and the Paleness of Words*

LOUIS WEITZENKORN

In the role of a duenna guarding a Spanish virgin, Frank Doubleday personally conducted an 'interview' for me Wednesday with Joseph Conrad. I write still in the shadowy edge of indignation over what will probably be the first and last time that I shall ever have talked with the man I think the greatest writer upon the face of the earth. Conrad is a writer of sea tales. Let us say, for the sake of metaphor, he is himself one of his own ships. On this morning when I saw him his sails were set, a spanking breeze was blowing, there was a hungry creak to his timbers but Frank Doubleday held fast and Conrad never got further from port than quarantine.

Conrad had just finished talking with some shipping man when I came into the Doubleday apartment at No. 52 West 58th Street. I heard the few parting formalities as the anxious publisher took my hat and whispered dramatically:

'You know – he's not feeling so well –'

* *World* (New York), 3 June 1923, Second News Section, pp. 15, 35.

'Yes, I know. I'm not going to board him like a ship news reporter. I just want to talk to him. I haven't one planned question to ask.'

And then I met Joseph Conrad. In the neutral north light of the room I saw a man older than I had hoped to see. There was a great width to his shoulders, the broadness of a once-powerful frame, but the hunching stoop made Conrad seem short. I looked into his face – a face creased and worn, the sunken cheeks bearded – oh, he looked as Robert E. Lee must have looked as Pickett's troopers fell back bleeding at Gettysburg.[1] He looked at me expecting the reportorial flubdub – the 'What do you think of America?' stuff.

Instead we just shook hands and said nothing – nothing at all, and Doubleday came to my assistance.

'Joseph found the reporters here an unusually intelligent lot,' he said.

Conrad's face lit up and a Niagara of phrases rushed from him. His accent is pronounced, and unless one listens carefully his key words are easily missed. A word like 'very' would be 'vairy'!

'I found they knew me,' he said. 'They were very considerate. I was fatigued, but it was interesting. Especially the photographers. They were – were –'

'Tough.' I volunteered.

Conrad slapped his leg.

'Tough. That's it. But they were unusual. They posed me. Turn this way and turn that.' He laughed gaily at the recollection.

I spoke of Stephen Crane, for whom Conrad has a deep admiration.

'Joseph knew Crane in London,' said Doubleday.[2]

'It was strange,' Conrad said. 'Stephen was the first one who ever called me Joseph. You know my Christian name is Conrad. People think it funny that my wife calls me Conrad – but that is my name. When Crane called me Joseph I used to think there was another man standing behind me. I did not know he was talking to me. Ah, it was a pity he died so young. His *The Red Badge of Courage* was a notable book. When he came to London he was well known and something of a sensation. I knew him, of course, and we visited each other. There would always be a great crowd around him and I was absolutely unknown then.

'One literary critic said: "Why do you have that man around?"' Conrad laughed again, a short, full laugh. 'He meant me. I used to sit in a corner and wait until Stephen got free of them.'

'You are joking, Joseph,' said Doubleday.

'Absolutely not,' insisted Conrad.

At this point Conrad slumped down in his chair. His head sunk upon his collar and he closed his eyes. For a minute the world was obliterated for him. I saw his Marlow stopping to recollect a thought – an incident in the life of Lord Jim.

When he returned we spoke of Thomas Hardy. Conrad agreed that Hardy was the last of the Elizabethans. Then he qualified it. 'They are all Elizabethans, the English. Hardy is Victorian, also.'

'One of the strange things about your work,' I said, 'is the actual personal love you evoke through your books. I don't know of anyone else who does. People who don't even know what you look like. Shaw is too mocking. It is the same thing that Eugene Debs inspires.'[3]

Conrad was intensely interested. 'Who – Debs. He writes, too?'

'No,' interposed Doubleday. 'Not exactly – pamphlets, you know. Joseph still suffers from a fever he got in Africa,' said the publisher apropos of nothing.

This led to *Heart of Darkness*, to me the greatest of the Conrad stories. I said I thought it contained his finest line, that famous description in futility – the French gunboat shelling natives ashore: 'In the empty immensity of earth, sky, and water, there she was, incomprehensible, firing into a continent.'[4]

I quoted it. He chuckled.

'That,' he said, 'sounds to me just like Conrad.' His buoyancy swelled. He talked of Dona Rita in *The Arrow of Gold*. I asked him how he had put his finger upon that extraordinary bit of psychology – Dona Rita's physical cowardice.

At that he slumped down again, the head sunken, the eyes hidden by his lids. There was a long silence – the very silence of his books. Suddenly he said:

'It was not an accident.'

He grew voluble again, talked of his extraordinary difficulty in writing.

'I never penned a line, except in letters to my uncle, until I was thirty-six.[5] It is very hard for me to write. I go for a week and get a line done – then something strikes me.'

'You are an excellent letter writer, Joseph,' said Doubleday.

Conrad waved his hand depreciatingly.

'I am not, really. And I do not like to write letters. It uses me up.'

Doubleday insisted upon Conrad's genius for letter writing and won the point. Conrad remained silent.

He asked me my age. I told him thirty.

'You have plenty of time,' he said. He spoke of the difficulty of self-revelation, of one being full of words, of talking, talking within, incessantly – and unable to project them as carriage of thought.

'It is impossible to reveal oneself,' he said. 'The words lose their meaning – pale.' Again came that silence of his reveries. It was the third time in half an hour. Doubleday awoke him from it with a cigarette. We began talking of the sea and I told him of Joshua Wanhope, one of the pioneers in the new American navy after the Civil War.[6]

'He was a most voluble man. Talked incessantly – and said nothing. He left newspaper work when the World War broke out – took examinations and got a first mate's berth. He was torpedoed on his first trip.'

'He must be an older man than I,' said Conrad. 'How old is he? Will he come ashore again?'

I said I didn't think he would and Doubleday said:

'Sea captains never talk very much, do they, Joseph?'

'Yes – well – I've found them talkative. It depends.'

'I've crossed the ocean sixty times,' Doubleday went on, 'and I never found it so. Sixty times. I was never able to make friends with a ship's captain. They don't talk much.'

This left another silence upon our hands and the bell rang. Doubleday ushered in a young man and introduced him to Conrad:

'This is Young Boswell, Joseph,'[7] Doubleday turned to me *sotto voce*: 'He has an appointment with Joseph,' he said. It was a broadsword hint but I stuck.

'I'll not say a word,' I promised. I didn't think he'd throw me out and he didn't. I turned to the Boswellian interviewer and saw a youth, looking like a Yale undergraduate pondering the Junior prom. Suddenly Young Boswell took a sheaf of paper from an inside pocket. Conrad straightened up stiffly.

'I've got a few questions I'd like to ask,' said Young Boswell. 'You know what I do. I'm the modern Boswell and write short biographies for my paper –'

Conrad broke in.

'It is very nice – but – but I can't be a Johnson to your Boswell. It is artificial. You play a game.' He shrugged. 'I can't play it. But I shall answer your questions.' He smiled.

Young Boswell drew up his legs in the position of a man about to drop a tea cup from his knees. He spread out his questions.

'You visited some of our colleges,' he began. 'Did you like them?'

'He only saw the outside,' said Doubleday.

'I saw many faces – interesting American faces,' Conrad replied for himself. 'You know, I get my hints from a passing face. I saw Lord Jim that way.'[8]

Young Boswell wrote steadily for a minute. Then:

'Did you like the appearance of the college buildings at Yale? I'm fond of New Haven myself. I want to go back there often.'

Conrad complimented the buildings at Yale.[9] Boswell, reminded of youth, spoke of Conrad's book of that name.

'The spirit of youth,' said Boswell. 'That's it. But how did you get it?' He poised his pencil.

Conrad did not answer at once. Doubleday stood up, walked down the room and back. He drew out his watch and spoke – in the air – of a luncheon appointment. Conrad was hunched again in his chair. The hollows of his cheeks seemed deeper. Under his closed eyelids one could fancy the eyes drawn up as when a man strains for a coloured mental picture. The hiss of the Boswellian pencil went softly on. Doubleday again looked at his watch.

'Youth.' The word came very low from the man huddled in the chair. The Boswell legs came up until the feet rested upon their points. Doubleday was looking at his watch. 'I wrote *Youth* when I was forty,' said Conrad.

'We have a luncheon engagement,' said Doubleday.

'But the spirit of youth.' said Boswell.

'One can remember it'. Conrad closed his eyes and the scrape of the Boswell pencil resumed its course.

NOTES

Louis Weitzenkorn (1894–1943), American journalist, editor and playwright. He fought in France during the First World War. He was married five times and died in a fire at the age of forty-eight. He interviewed Conrad on 30 May 1923, in the New York apartment of Conrad's publisher, Frank N. Doubleday.

1. Robert E. Lee, commander of the Confederate army in the Civil War, occupied Gettysburg, Pennsylvania. Major-General George Edward Pickett led his 4500 Confederate muskets in a courageous attempt to break through the Union lines, but was forced back after losing three-quarters of his men.
2. See p. 188.
3. Eugene Debs (1855–1926), a crusading American socialist leader.
4. Joseph Conrad, in *Youth, Heart of Darkness, The End of the Tether: Three Stories* (London: J. M. Dent, 1946) pp. 61–2.
5. Conrad began writing *Almayer's Folly* at the age of thirty-one.
6. Joshua Wanhope was a socialist editor and author of pamphlets. No official record of his pioneering naval work appears to exist.
7. 'Young Boswell' was Harold Stark, graduate of Yale, who published during 1922–3 in the New York *Tribune* a series of interviews with some 175 writers, artists and musicians. His article on Conrad, 'Young Boswell interviews Joseph Conrad', appeared in the *Tribune* on 31 May 1923.
8. In his 'Author's Note' to *Lord Jim*, Conrad says of the 'model' for Jim that 'one sunny morning in the commonplace surroundings of an Eastern roadstead, I saw his form pass by – appealing – significant – under a cloud – perfectly silent'.
9. Conrad visited New Haven on 15–16 May 1923.

Part VIII

Pen Portraits

Conrad in Cracow*

GEORGE PALMER PUTNAM

'That is where Korzeniowski lived.' Konstantin Buszczyński,[1] then Consul-General of Poland to the United States, pointed out a drab building, none too interesting in outward appearance. We were driving through the streets of Cracow, in reborn Poland, last November, my host exhibiting the highlights of his extraordinarily fascinating native city.

'Indeed!' I breathed. I supposed he referred to one of the old Polish kings, or perhaps a lesser patriot-martyr, with whose memories Poland is proudly replete.

His interest, at least, was more lively than my own. At a word the driver pulled the pair of fine black mares to a halt beside the narrow sidewalk.

'There,' said he, pointing to upper windows of the building at No. 9 Ulica Szpitalna, which is by way of saying Hospital Street,[2] 'is where we had great fun as youngsters; Józef and I used to throw toy torpedoes down on the black caftans of passing Jews, enjoying ourselves hugely when they exploded. . . . A pogrom, I suppose,' he laughed. Poles today don't relish that word, or the way it has been misused over here.

'And in there, in a corner of the courtyard,' he continued, pointing through the archway, 'that strange boy told us – his play-mates – the most extraordinary stories. They were always of the sea and ships and far-away countries. Somehow, the scent of salt water was in the very blood of Conrad.'

And at that a great light broke upon me. Joseph Conrad! Of course; Teodor Józef Konrad Korzeniowski and the best-loved creator of *Lord Jim*, *The Nigger of the 'Narcissus'*, and the rest of them, one and the same being!

I did know that Joseph Conrad was not his real name – not all of it, anyway. Afterward I remembered, too, that I had known he was a Pole. But at the time all that was quite outside of my mind.

So I was at the boyhood home of Joseph Conrad, with a boyhood chum of his! At once we left the *fiacre* and entered that historic courtyard. And there, as we strolled about, even climbing the outside stairway to the balcony on the third floor, whence a door opened into the old

* *Outlook* (New York), vol. CXXIV (3 March 1920) pp. 382–3.

apartment once occupied by Conrad, Buszczyński reminisced.

'My host's father, Stefan, and Conrad's father, Apollo Korzeniowski, were intimate friends. Conrad's mother died in Siberia, and his father followed her shortly after he had been returned to his home from Siberian exile, his health ruined and his spirit all but broken.

'He was suspected of complicity in the anti-Russian uprising of 1863,' Buszczyński told me. 'Only suspected, though. If anything had been proved, he would have been shot.'

On the grave of the elder Conrad this inscription was placed by his friend Stefan Buszczyński:

I will rise, Lord, when you call me;
But let me rest, for I am very weary.

At the time of his father's death, 1870, Conrad was about thirteen years old. My informer's memory placed his birth in the year 1859, but in Richard Curle's biography, doubtless more accurate, the date is given as 1857.[3]

'What tales that boy told us!' my companion went on. 'Over on those steps we often sat, a group of us, while Conrad spun yarns, as you Yankees say. They were weird and fantastic almost beyond belief, but in the way he told them they seemed to us actual happenings. The power of weaving tales – tales that literally seemed to live before one's eyes – was born in him. And always they were about the sea. Curious, that, for outside of Asia there probably is not a single other city so far from salt water as Cracow, and Conrad had never seen it.'

The youthful story-teller was a flat failure in his study, with the notable exception of geography. In that he excelled, and small wonder, as he loved it. Even with a private tutor he could not keep up with his classes. He was sickly, too, and very nervous, and given at times to epileptic seizures. And always he talked of the sea, and yearned for it, declaring that only as a sailor could he be well and happy. Which prediction, it happens, worked out exactly. I'm told that during his twenty seafaring years the Polish mariner was practically an embodiment of perfect health.

An uncle, then in Russia, supplied the funds for Conrad's upbringing. Finally the boy's condition grew so serious that Stefan Buszczyński wrote to him urging that his charge be permitted to have his way.

'While that letter made its slow way toward Central Russia,' Stefan's son told me, 'Conrad disappeared. He had done what many a lad has done before and since, run away to sea. A long run, too. Finally the tutor, who was sent in pursuit, located him at Trieste on the Adriatic just as he returned from his first cruise, a short one on a small steamer to Venice and back. But even that brief experience had worked wonders.

Apparently the psychological effect of winning his wish had conquered the physical disabilities. The epilepsy had gone never to return'.[4]

A few months later, after another enforced try at landlubber life in Cracow, Conrad was sent to sea; this time in style and with the approval of his uncle. His 'official' maritime career commenced at Marseilles when he was seventeen years old.[5]

Three years after that, for the first time he set foot in England.[6] And then, too, for the first time he learned to speak English, and later to write the language. It is common knowledge now that he does the latter rather well. Indeed, there is no exaggeration in saying that the prose English of this Polish sailor, who spoke English first when he was twenty and wrote his first book when he was nearly forty, is unsurpassed – which is a literary phenomenon in itself unmatched.

Conrad went to sea in 1875. Thirty-nine years later, in 1914, Buszczyński and his boyhood friend met again in Cracow for the first time since that parting. It was just before the Great War broke over Europe, Conrad having brought his wife and children to see his boyhood home. And what a happy reunion it must have been for the two Poles, both practically raised by the same father!

'It was in June 1875,[7] that I last saw your father,' said Conrad to Buszczyński at that time, his words exactly remembered by the friend to whom he spoke them. 'In my mind now I can see him as clearly as in life and hear his words as he bade me God-speed and pressed my hand: "Conrad, you have your wish. You shall be a sailor. But wherever ships carry you, remember always you are a Pole and that you shall come back to Poland." . . . I never forgot.'

NOTES

1. Konstanty Buszczyński (1856–1921) was the boyhood friend of Conrad in Cracow from 1869 to 1873. He was to establish a renowned seed firm in Cracow. His father, Stefan (1821–92), was a friend and biographer of Conrad's father, and active in the 1863 insurrection.
2. The address of Conrad's maternal grandmother where he lived from late 1870 until May 1873.
3. Conrad was born on 3 December 1857 and was eleven years of age when his father died in May 1869. For details of Richard Curle, see p. 229.
4. This anecdote is entirely apocryphal.
5. Conrad left Cracow for Marseilles on 13 October 1874.
6. Conrad first set foot on English soil at Lowestoft on 10 June 1878. See p. 32 for further details.
7. Conrad never met Stefan Buszczyński again after leaving Poland in October 1874.

'The phonetics of English is indeed a dismal thing'*

R. L. MÉGROZ

Once we were safely ensconced in our chairs in that deserted lounge, Conrad charmingly invalidated his own objections to giving an admirer a personal interview. Remembering his essay 'Poland Revisited' in *Notes on Life and Letters*,[1] I asked him first what he had got out of his schooldays in Cracow. In the *Notes* he tells how, walking the streets of the old city with his son at night, 'it seemed to me that if I remained longer there in that narrow street I should become the helpless prey of the Shadows I had called up. They were crowding upon me, enigmatic and insistent, in their clinging air of the grave that tasted of dust and of the bitter vanity of old hopes.'[2]

Here is one side of old memory, the personal but imaginative aspect belonging to the theme he is treating. His casual remarks to me, indicating the unstrained, matter-of-fact but equally intimate recollection of youth, remind one how incomplete as autobiography any of Conrad's written – and therefore carefully selected – reminiscences must be. When he spoke of Cracow, it was just the place which held his old school, 'St Anne's, where I was a scholar. . . .[3] The school was "on the classical side", you know, along old-fashioned lines. . . . I was good at mathematics, fairly good at history, and my composition could always pull me up in the class. But I was no good at grammar. Oh, what a grind I had when (later) I tried to get hold of English grammar! As I had always been a reading boy I remained a reader after going to sea, and reading is the best way to pick up any language. But I still absolutely refused to learn grammar, and I picked up my first English by hearing it spoken on colliers along the East Coast.[4] After all, grammar is so arbitrary, why bother about it? And my boys have inherited that inability, distaste and horror of grammar.'

'I should like to hear what made you start writing.'

'Simply because I needed an occupation for my leisure. It was not the need of self-expression. After three or four years in the Indian Ocean I gave myself leave, allowed myself to come to London for my

* From *Joseph Conrad's Mind and Method: A Study of Personality in Art* (London: Faber & Faber, 1931) pp. 28–31, 31–4.

Merchant Marine certificates.[5] There was a famous coaching school, "Boult's", on Tower Hill; it is now removed to Barking. That was the only English school I was ever in.'

Conrad paused, lit a cigarette, offered me one, and asked: 'How old are you?'

'Thirty.'

'A fine age, a splendid age! Isn't it?'

'Well, one feels rather old at thirty – no longer in the twenties!'

'Yes; that is a strange thing; one does feel exactly like that. But you'll get over it! I managed to get my first command before I was thirty.[6] That pleased me immensely, I remember, although I wanted only three or four months to complete my thirtieth year. I was made captain of an Australian merchantman, and sailed her in the Indian Ocean. I was a merchant seaman for about twenty years, and when I came to London, I remember particulary how surprised I was at finding Italian restaurants, which were just spreading then.'

* * *

Conrad's reminiscences were getting rather far from the motives which made him write, but they were too interesting to interrupt when he continued: 'I had just returned for the last time from sea when Mr Gladstone had won a sensational victory at the polls.[7] Like all seamen, I went to call on my agent, who was in Fenchurch Street. He was a Liberal. There he was in his office, his hat pushed back, spectacles on his forehead, hurriedly eating a chop, in the style of the City man of those days. I myself wore my marine clothes – black-peaked cap and blue jersey and so on. I expected the usual warm welcome back from the sea. But suddenly as I stood there he banged his fist on the table, and with a great shout cried: "Clean sweep!" I gaped, of course. He added: "There will never be another Conservative Government in England."'

'Extraordinary!' Conrad–Marlow went on with a gasping chuckle, 'but he absolutely believed it! Of course it was a stunning victory for Gladstone, but only a year later the Government was tottering. Parties then did seem to mean something. Mr Gladstone's prestige was wonderful; it stood for something real. But to-day' – and Marlow shrugged his shoulder at the contemplation of the Coalition Government's recent campaign 'what does all this noise mean?'[8]

'But I am watching things with intense interest,' he resumed, as one who loves humanity. 'I am basing all my hopes for Europe on England. . . .'

I said something about being curious as to how he really did master the English language; I could not imagine that conversations with the crews of colliery barges on the East Coast had taught him the subtleties of the language.

'After hearing it spoken and when I could talk enough, I read,' he replied. 'I have still a thick, green-covered volume of Shakespeare I bought with my first earnings. It had beastly print, but it had everything in it, including the sonnets. I had read the whole of Shakespeare by 1880 and I re-read him in the following years. While I was at sea there was another book I used to read a lot, and it pulled my English together. That was Mill's *Political Economy*.[9] It was most interesting, but also it was an excellent soporific – Mill charms your mind into sleep.

'But perhaps I could say I learnt English by reading the newspapers. I learnt a great deal from the old *Standard* when it was under Mudford.[10] He was a remarkable journalist, a cultured man; and in those days they paid great attention to style. "Telegraphese" and "punch" were unknown to English journalism.

'The origin of the very word "punch" is instructive, I think,' Conrad said suddenly as if struck by his idea. 'It came from America, from "cowpuncher". Probably "punching" the cow referred to the blow with the branding-iron!

'Now look at that word "punch" – all the meanings it has. It is a technical noun and it is several other common things. Also there is the "punch" immortalised by Dickens in *Pickwick*.[11] Can you wonder that I experienced enormous difficulty in learning the English language? Look at the words pronounced alike and meaning different things – words ending in "ough" for instance. The phonetics of English is indeed a dismal thing for foreigners'.

'What do you think of the idea of a universal language to remove a barrier between the nations?'

'I do not think that will be ever possible. I am certainly inclined to be afraid of any such experiment. There are so many shades of meanings in every language. Besides, I do not think that language is the biggest barrier between nations. And language must possess an individual genius. Those old cave-man ancestors were quite right. They simply used language to express themselves, whether the people in the next cave could understand or not. I am often quite shocked at the disrespect we show to our primitive ancestors. They may have possessed genius equal to ours, though perhaps [smiling] they did generally use it in a different manner, from force of circumstances. No, a universal language does not sound possible. Every people should be proud of their own language'.

The transfer from the mind of Marlow[12] to that of Conrad may be observed beginning after the return to the subject of a universal language. Then it was completed: 'They have treated me much better in France than they have treated my poor friend M. Anatole France in England.[13] The English translations of his books are dreadful, dreadful. But I am very pleased to know that the new generation in France are, according to the publishers, reading my books in English. That is surely a great victory for English!'

NOTES

Rodolphe Louis Mégroz (1891–1968), journalist and lecturer, interviewed Conrad in the lounge of the Curzon Hotel, London, on 2 November 1922. Conrad was there for the opening of his play, 'The Secret Agent', at the Ambassadors Theatre that evening. The play, which Conrad had dramatised from his novel, closed after nine days.

1. 'Poland Revisited', an account of Conrad's trip to Poland in 1914, was published the following year and reprinted in *Notes on Life and Letters* (London: J. M. Dent, 1949) pp. 141–73.
2. Ibid., pp. 169–70. Conrad and his father moved to Cracow in February 1869, just before the latter's death in May. Conrad lived there with his maternal grandmother for the next four years.
3. It is doubtful whether Conrad attended any school in Cracow; there are certainly no records of his attendance at St Anne's Gymnasium. He probably received private lessons from a regular tutor.
4. On 10 June 1878 Conrad arrived at Lowestoft and set foot on English soil for the first time. In the next three months, he made three round trips between Lowestoft and Newcastle in the *Skimmer of the Sea*, a coastal coal schooner.
5. In November 1886 Conrad obtained his master's certificate at the second attempt.
6. A few weeks after his thirtieth birthday, on 24 January 1888, Conrad took command of the *Otago*, sailing from Bangkok to Australia and Mauritius. The *Otago*, an iron barque, was registered in Port Adelaide.
7. W. E. Gladstone formed a Liberal Government on 11 August 1892, after a General Election. He resigned in 1894, after the Liberal division over Home Rule for Ireland. Conrad left his last ship in January 1894.
8. A General Election was to be held on 17 November 1922.
9. John Stuart Mill, *Principles of Political Economy* (1848).
10. W. H. Mudford, (1839–1916) began as editor of the *Standard* in the early 1870s and resigned in 1900.
11. The 'capital cold punch' in Charles Dickens's *Pickwick Papers* is decidedly of the alcoholic variety.
12. Conrad's narrator in 'Youth' (1898), *Heart of Darkness* (1899), *Lord Jim* (1900) and *Chance* (1912).
13. French novelist (1844–1924). Conrad was a great admirer of his work.

Conrad the Personality*

Since Mr Joseph Conrad wrote *The Nigger of the 'Narcissus'* there has been no question of his being a personality in modern literature, and personalities in modern literature are not too numerous. His point of view, his knowledge, his mode of expression are emphatically his own.

I have a theory that it is almost impossible to entirely understand a man's work without knowing something of the man. The personality of the artist is often the explanatory note of his art. This is, of course, the apology of the journalist who is responsible for interviews and personal sketches, and there is much to be said for it.

Unfortunately, perhaps, the man whose work is most worth understanding is generally most loth to supply this personal annotation. Genius is often shy, and to this rule Mr Joseph Conrad is not an exception.

I once 'interviewed' Mr Conrad and I vividly remember the terror with which he regarded me when he met me at the station. Happily I was soon able to convince him I had no curiosity for trivial impertinences, and it was my fortune, while chatting to him in an old-world farmhouse garden through a long summer afternoon, to catch something of his unique individuality.

Joseph Conrad is a Pole and a sailor – in itself a strange combination. Born far inland, he caught the sea fascination in some mystic way in his youth and was never contented till he lived upon it. Essentially a stylist in English, it is only to him a borrowed language, though his love for it may perhaps be not a little due to the fact that he learnt it from East Coast fishermen with whom he worked for a while.[2]

I can think of no other instance of a foreigner learning to write English as Mr Conrad writes it, while certainly few native writers have anything approaching his veneration for its beauties and its possibilities. He takes infinite pains to express thoughts and ideas in what to him is the most perfect manner. In a real sense he is an artist in words.

Here then are the facts of the personality that surely illustrate the work – a Pole, one of the strange unconquerable race that Seton Merriman called the 'Frenchmen of the North',[3] a sailor with a poet's insight and imagination, and a foreigner with a knowledge of more than one other language, deliberately choosing English for the expression of his imaginings.

* 'Personalities: Joseph Conrad', *Academy*, vol. LX (20 Feb. 1904) p. 198.

In appearance Mr Conrad suggests the seaman. His figure is stalwart and short, his dark beard well trimmed, and his walk nautical. Meet him near the docks and one would write him down 'ship's captain' without hesitation.

But his eyes, curiously distinctive and striking, mark him out from his kind. Ship captain he may be, but his eyes proclaim him an artist.

It is some time since my talk with Mr Conrad, but he is not a man to be easily forgotten, for, apart from his personal charm, he has all the qualities to include him within Schopenhauer's famous definition of genius: 'The mind of genius is among other minds what the carbuncle is among precious stones, it sends forth light of its own, while the others reflect only that which they have received'.

One remark of Mr Conrad's is worth quoting as illustrating his attitude to criticism: 'Praise and blame to my mind are of singularly small import, yet one cares for the recognition of a certain ampleness of purpose'.

NOTES

This anonymous interview is an indication of Conrad's increasing reputation in the early years of the century.

1. Published as a serial in the *New Review*, Aug.–Dec. 1897.
2. See note to p. 208.
3. Henry Seton Merriman, pseudonym of Hugh Stowell Scott (1862–1903), novelist.

Some Recollections of Joseph Conrad*

ERNEST DAWSON

I used to visit W. E. Henley,[1] then living at Worthing. We talked one day of *Lord Jim* and *Youth*. Henley, who had never met Conrad in the flesh, remarked that Conrad was 'about due'; he had the idea that any writer of promise (and Conrad was obviously that, and more) ought

* From 'Some Recollections of Joseph Conrad', *Fortnightly Review*, vol. CXXIV (1 Aug. 1928) pp. 203–12.

to pay him the compliment of a visit. 'Yes,' said Henley, 'Conrad is a Swell: he is a *damned* swell; you know, I sometimes think Conrad is the *damnedest* swell we've got. Would you like to meet him?'

My answer was given with an alacrity comparable to that with which, as a schoolboy, I replied to a benevolent uncle who asked if I would like to go to the play, and the matter was then and there arranged. Conrad was known to inhabit a farmhouse a few miles from Sandgate. At Sandgate lived Mr H. G. Wells, who was of the band of 'Henley's Men'. In the manner of an affectionate Pontiff, Henley wrote to Wells, and bade him invite me for a week-end and 'have Conrad on tap'.

In due course Wells (whom I had never seen) sent me a friendly note of invitation, and received me with much kindness at his queer but comfortable and convenient house. On the Sunday, after luncheon, Conrad arrived in a dogcart. The day was rough, and he wore a peaked cap of maritime cut, which, with his jacket and trousers of stout blue cloth, gave him somewhat of the aspect of a pilot. Apart from details of costume, you knew him quickly for a sailor; as quickly for a *sahib*. He stood an inch or two below middle height, but never looked small; his square, high breadth of shoulders and short neck gave an impression of compact power. His face was sallowish, the skin weathered and puckered round the full dark eyes by habitual staring into the night or over the brightness of the sunlit sea. The hair and clipped, pointed beard were wiry and almost black. He wore an eyeglass, which he seldom used; when he did screw it into his eye the effect was slightly incongruous. I never saw him use any other aid to vision, though in reading he held his book nearer his eyes than is usual with persons of normal eyesight. In some portraits of him, notably in the admirable 'Ulysses' etching by Muirhead Bone,[2] you get that effect of a steady watching look, the gaze of sailors and shepherds.

He smoked almost incessantly and always cigarettes; at that time he rolled them for himself. He used a handsome old amber smoking-tube which had belonged to a distinguished and adventurous uncle, probably 'Mr Nicholas B.' (that great-hearted veteran) of *A Personal Record*.

Conrad and I forgathered, that afternoon, upon some geographical turn of the conversation, over maps; it happened we were both map-lovers. But he and my host had much to say to each other, and my part was mainly a listening one. Conrad's personality impressed and fascinated me. I watched him drive away into the squally evening, handling the dogcart like a man steering a dinghy, and I wanted him for a friend.

* * *

His knowledge of English, literary and colloquial, need not here be praised. But those of his readers who heard him speak were continually surprised because he could not utter two words in English without betraying that it was not his mother tongue. And there were certain words which he, so to speak, declined to learn. One very odd example was the word *vowel*; he transposed the 'v' and 'w' sounds, so that it became *wowvel*; I have been told that he would even write it so. He pronounced *used* as two syllables, something like *usit*.

In conversing, he often dropped into French for a sentence or two. Oftener still, he used a phrase of French apparently without knowing it. Quite commonly he would address one as *my dear*, as a Frenchman says *mon cher*.

The very wealth of his knowledge of our language, with its slang and familiar idioms, made these quaint lapses sound doubly whimsical; his talk thus gained a singular individuality, and it might be said that he spoke English with an un-English grace. His taste was unerring; he must have had many of his early lessons in the vernacular from the fo'c'sle, yet one never heard him use a 'vulgar' expression.

* * *

He had read much of English history and memoirs, and of the best fiction in the language, but, I think, not much poetry. Classics apart, the power of enjoying the poetry of any language other than one's own is probably very rare.

His attitude towards what he did not care for, in literature, was often curiously inimical, or, at best, slighting. I once quoted some lines of *Andrea del Sarto*, and, as one does, added 'Isn't that how it goes?' To which he answered indifferently: 'I don't remember: to be more truthful, I don't know; I do not know my Browning'. Another time he was criticising a story deliberately written in the *New Arabian Nights* vein, and said: 'Ah, yes, I daresay it is very good of its kind; I don't know my Stevenson at all well, but . . . *ought to do much better than that*!' Which seemed to me almost blasphemy.

NOTES

Major Ernest Dawson (1884–1960). H. G. Wells introduced him to Conrad in 1901 or 1902. He spent much of his life in Burma. His brother, A. J. Dawson, novelist and traveller, also became a friend of Conrad. They remained in contact with Conrad until his death and attended his funeral.

1. For details of Henley, see p. 188.
2. See p. 167.

Memories of an Edwardian*

EDGAR JEPSON

Only once did I see Conrad at the Square Club,[1] and then he looked to be very much on his guard and doubtful of his wisdom in letting himself be brought to it. It was at Dymchurch that I first met him, one hot summer, when he came from his home in the hills above the marsh, bringing his family, to spend the day with Perceval Gibbon.[2] It seemed to me that he found his family an oppression that kept him irritable; he looked like a man who might easily suffer from a persecution mania. Mr Epstein's[3] bust of him is several notes above the Conrad I met.

I spent most of the afternoon with him and Perceval Gibbon on Dymchurch wall, and they talked and talked of the number and colour of the funnels of steamers that came round Dungeness point and passed us, and of the number and colour of the rings round the funnels, for the number and colour of the steamers' funnels and the rings round them told them what lines they belonged to, and one line recalled another, and it went on and on, and it seemed to me that, when those steamers were not carrying unimportant people to unimportant places, they were carrying things of no value to places of no importance, and always when Conrad and Gibbon had finished with the steamer in front of us, and I thought it was all over, round the point another steamer would come, and on and on they went. They might have been cricketers talking of averages, and it was a summer afternoon. I thought that Conrad would have been a happier man if he had never left the sea.

NOTES

Edgar Jepson (1863–1938), a minor bellelettrist of the period, is immortalised in Ezra Pound's *Pisan Cantos*, where he features in a roll-call of Edwardian luminaries as 'Jepson lover of jade'. He published his first book at the age of

* From *Memories of an Edwardian and Neo-Georgian* (London: Richards, 1937) pp. 142–3.

thirty-two, and proceeded to write fifty more. He was the grandfather of the novelist, Fay Weldon.

1. Square Club: founded by G. K. Chesterton about 1908 in honour of Henry Fielding; its members included Ford Madox Ford, most of the *English Review* set, De La Mare, Galsworthy and Edward Thomas.

2. This particular visit to Perceval Gibbon's holiday home in Dymchurch probably occurred in June 1911. Dymchurch is a small village on the Kent coast between Hythe and New Romney. The Conrads went down to Dymchurch in their Cadillac, driven by Borys, who was thirteen years of age at the time.

For details of Perceval Gibbon, see p. 148.

3. Jacob Epstein: see p. 172.

'I was uneasy with Conrad'*

EDWARD THOMAS

I am too stupid to tell about Conrad, except that he looks something like Sir Richard Burton[1] in the head, black hair, & moustache & beard & a jutting out face, & pale thin lips extraordinarily mobile among the black hair, flashing eyes and astonishing eyebrows, and a way of throwing his head right back to laugh which he often does at things which tickle him – such as Hueffer's 'harsh and oppressive' treatment of the National Liberal Club porter.[2] But I was uneasy with Conrad – though he is very friendly to me – and kept saying things I neither meant nor wished it to be supposed I meant. Alas! if only I could live in solitude complete.

NOTES

Edward Thomas (1878–1917), poet and critic, was the son of a Welsh railway clerk. He graduated from Oxford in 1900, and then earned his living by reviewing, criticism and studies of country life. He met Conrad at the Tuesday literary luncheons in the Mont-Blanc restaurant, Gerrard Street, and in 1910 Conrad enlisted his help as a ghost-writer, if necessary, for some reviews he was tackling for the *Daily Mail*. In August 1910 there occurred the visit which Thomas describes in his letter to Gordon Bottomley, dated 26 August 1910.

* From *Letters from Edward Thomas to Gordon Bottomley*, ed. R. G. Thomas (London: Oxford University Press, 1968) p. 207.

Thomas had cycled over from his home in Kent to spent a couple of days with the Conrads while awaiting the birth of his third child.

Thomas enlisted in 1915, and visited Conrad for the last time on 10 December 1916. He was killed four months later, on 9 April 1917, at Arras, France.

1. Sir Richard Burton (1821–90), English explorer who discovered Lake Tanganyika. He also produced the first unabridged translation of *The Thousand Nights and a Night*.

2. For details of Ford Madox Ford (Hueffer), see p. 106.

Conrad and Lawrence of Arabia*

T. E. LAWRENCE

I shall look forward to the promised photograph of the MUG. Likeness – yes, it's desirable in a named ship; but I hope you have kept scale and broad treatment, too. A figurehead should grow clearly out of the vessel's lines. How fortunate that Conrad had that streamlined face . . . or hair on his face, anyhow. What I shall always remember is his lame walk, with the stick to help him, and that sudden upturning of the lined face, with its eager eyes under their membrane of eyelid. They drooped over the eye-socket and the sun shone red through them, as we walked up and down the garden. Put the cameraman in a boat under the forefoot, and have a fish's-eye view of the head, please!

NOTE

Thomas Edward Lawrence (1888–1935), 'Lawrence of Arabia', met Conrad at the home of Hugh Walpole in July 1920. In 1919–21, Lawrence was a research fellow at All Souls College, Oxford, and was engaged in re-writing his *Seven Pillars of Wisdom*, published posthumously in 1935. In 1922 he enlisted in the ranks of the RAF under the name of J. H. Ross in order to escape publicity.

In his letter (dated 26 January 1935) to Bruce Rogers, the American designer, Lawrence is discussing the figurehead of the *Conrad*, a sailing frigate owned by Rogers's friend, Alan Villiers.

* From *The Letters of T. E. Lawrence*, ed. David Garnett (London: Cape, 1938) p. 843.

'The radar-like sensitivity of Conrad'*

WILLIAM PLOMER

If tape recordings had been as easy then as they are now, I would have tried to persuade [Hugh Walpole] to record some of the stories he had to tell. They were sometimes scandalous, but none the duller for that; and he told them with a lively humour and a kind of worldly scepticism that are not, I think, conspicuous in his books. I remember particularly an extraordinary account of a visit paid to Conrad by Robert Hichens,[1] accompanied by an intimate friend who was male, large in body, a cook by vocation, and Russian by nationality. The radar-like sensitivity of Conrad to the intrusion into his domestic sphere of a Russian became even more agitated by what seemed to him the social solecism of causing it and by his instantaneous suspicion of what seemed to him an equivocal relationship; and the combustion set up in the great man by the duties of a host, the prejudices of a Pole, and the antipathy of a heterosexual almost caused him to explode. Mrs Conrad, a faithful pourer of oil upon waters more often troubled than not, found on this occasion that all her years of practice were of very little help. It is sad to think what golden harvests of scandal are lost because the reapers do not, for various reasons, record them. And it is pleasant to think that Hugh Walpole was once kissed in public by Conrad,[2] who recorded in writing his feeling that thanks were due to a 'Higher Power'[3] for the friendship of which that was a token. The man who won that tribute is not to be written off as a nonentity or an ass.

NOTES

For details of Hugh Walpole, see p. 138.

1. Robert Smythe Hichens (1864–1950), journalist and novelist.
2. In February 1922, at a meeting in London, Walpole consoled Conrad on the recent death of his friend and agent, J. B. Pinker, and received Conrad's token of gratitude in return.
3. Conrad expresses this sentiment in his letter to Walpole on Boxing Day

* From *At Home* (London: Cape, 1958) pp. 93–4.

1920; see Gérard Jean-Aubry, *Joseph Conrad: Life and Letters* (New York: Doubleday, Page, 1927) vol. II, p. 252.

Where Conrad Held Court*

FRED ARNOLD

Myself when young did eagerly frequent the Fleur-de-Lys in Canterbury, so perhaps I may suggest yet another reason why this attractive old inn should be saved.

I have not seen mentioned the fact that the Fleur-de-Lys was Joseph Conrad's favourite and, I believe, only port of call in Canterbury while he lived nearby.

In his declining years, both before and after his visit to the United States in 1923, each evening when it pleased him, at about nine o'clock, Conrad would enter the Fleur-de-Lys. Turning in right-handed round the partition which separated the tiny saloon bar from the manager's office, he would take up the seat tacitly reserved for him to the right of the window.

There he would chat for an hour in his forceful and staccato fashion with certain acquaintances or with the innkeeper of those days, Marcelle Sheppard, taking aboard the while a healthy master mariner's ration of his favourite gin. He almost invariably wore his old but well-brushed bowler hat but, if memory serves, very occasionally affected a rough homespun homburg with small blue 'flash' feather.

Canterbury should see that the Fleur-de-Lys is saved for its historic associations. Conrad is now one of them. And at least part of the old hotel's architecture is fourteenth-century, though little of that date is left.

Could not a small plaque be placed over the seat where this great and very human old sea-dog sat and voiced his robust opinions?

May I add that the force of character emanating from Conrad himself, and the never-failing courtesy and kindliness of his latterly much-crippled but always most charming wife, are two of my outstanding and treasured memories.

* Letter to the Editor, *Daily Telegraph*, 8 June 1958, p. 6.

'They all made me feel so *dowdy*'*

ST-JOHN PERSE

'Conrad would never judge a friend morally or intellectually,' Perse continues. 'Friendship was sacred for him. He did *not* love the sea, of course – he lived forty-two miles inland, you know – but man-against-the-sea, and ships, and he never understood me when I talked about the sea itself. I think he must have disliked my poems, though the only literature that I am certain he positively hated was Dostoevsky. Conrad once told me about a dinner he had had somewhere in the country with Shaw, Wells, Bennett. When these *savants cyniques* of the literary industry talked about writing as "action", poor Conrad, horrified, left the table pretending he had to catch an earlier train. He told me later, in *épouvantable* French,[1] except for one English word I will never forget, "Writing, for me, is an act of faith. They all made me feel so *dowdy*."'

NOTES

St-John Perse (1887–1975) was the pseudonym of the poet Marie-René Alexis Saint-Léger Léger. Born on a small coral island which his family owned near Guadelope, he had a diplomatic career in France and at one time lived in America. His first poem was published in 1909, and his reputation rests on a long poem, *Anabase* (1924), which T. S. Eliot translated in 1930. He won the Nobel prize for literature in 1960.

St-John Perse, bearing an introduction from Conrad's friend Agnes Tobin, came to visit Conrad at Capel House in the summer of 1912 and stayed for a few days. Half a century later, he recalled the visit in conversation with Robert Craft, during which he also remarked that Conrad was '"the most perfect aristocrat and the truest friend I have ever known"'.

1. St-John Perse's description of Conrad's French as 'dreadful' is a rare, perhaps unique, criticism of his command of the spoken language.

* Igor Stravinsky and Robert Craft, *Dialogues and a Diary* (London: Faber & Faber, 1968) p. 250.

The Joseph Conrad I Knew*

MACDONALD HASTINGS

I remember regarding Joseph Conrad when I met him first with a surprise which he detected at once. 'Unlike my books?' he asked, with a smile that was as much at my expense as his. 'On the contrary,' I hastened to explain, 'just like your books, and not in the least like a retired captain of sailing-ships.'

He put his head on one side, a birdlike gesture that was common with him, and thought this over – or did not. When he talked to me he showed enthusiasm only when I said anything challenging. His eyes would light up, and he would argue eagerly, at the same time giving the impression that he was trying to satisfy himself that I was right. Never was there a more flattering talker. He raised all those with whom he came in contact. It was as if one had been blessed.

I do not suppose he bared his soul to anyone save in his books. Like another famous novelist I know, he charmed you into telling your thoughts, but did not fail to reward you at the end with a comment which revealed close listening. Never was there indeed a more courteous man, and I think he was conscious of this quality and proud of it. Indeed, I suspect that he took no trouble to get rid of his foreign accent, because it marked him apart from a race which certainly does not observe the cognate bodily attitude as exquisitely as do the Poles. He was conscious of his exotic position, and though without vanity had a shrewd knowledge of his eminence in the world of letters.

Once he spoke to me of a book then published which summarised the careers of, I think, six leading men of letters.[1] He was one of them, and nodded his head over the fact. I tried to tease him about the books, saying that there was no particular credit in being ranked with one of the six. Instantly he took up the cudgels for the novelist I was belittling. 'He counts. Certainly he counts. He may not be read many years hence, but he has left a definite mark on his time.' True enough, I suppose, but one felt he was defending the chooser of the 'Big Six' rather than the novelist.

After I had read the first act of my dramatisation of *Victory* to the company engaged to perform it he expressed warm approval. 'Rhythm,' he said; 'that is it, rhythm. Lena, the *grande amoureuse*, should be so.'

* *Ladies Half-Way* (London: Harrap, 1927) pp. 264–7.

And he made waves in the air with his hand. I pointed out to him that the management had not yet secured an actor to play Schomberg, the beastly German hotel proprietor. 'You can play Schomberg,' he retorted. 'You read him as he is.' Disrespectfully I retorted: 'I shall play Schomberg if you will agree to play Pedro.' Now Pedro, as readers of the book will know, is a hairy, apelike creature, barely human. Conrad fixed me with a reproving eye. The company had laughed at my suggestion, and I think the great man felt his dignity had been hurt.

There has, by the way, been a great deal of nonsense written about this dramatisation of *Victory*, some people going out of their way to state that Conrad disowned it. In point of fact he approved of it most warmly, and begged me not only to dramatise other of his novels, but to collaborate with him in an entirely new work. It is true that by agreement there was no collaboration, but the reason was that I was then in the army, and the daily intercourse necessary for collaboration was out of the question. Still, this did not hinder Conrad from scheming and suggesting in letters a great deal of the building of the play, and writing many pages of vivid dialogue.

At our first meeting I said: 'There are not two forms for a work of art. This thing is only worth doing for the money there may be in it. If you are rich, it would be absurd for you to agree.' He retorted that for twenty years he had been 'performing on a tight-rope – without a net', was still at it, and would like to see some prospect of getting down at last. He had not the least compunction about the most drastic alteration of his story for stage purposes. He it was, my dear critics, who suggested the happy ending – Lena in Heyst's arms, instead of the holocaust. So, when you blamed me for that, you were more royalist than the king.

He was very proud of his little one-act play, *One Day More*.[2] Personally I thought it hopeless from a theatrical standpoint, and largely because of this divergence of view I had most reluctantly to decline collaboration with him on a new play. The little work has a definite technique, but it has no stagecraft. Yet Conrad believed it perfect, and never could understand criticism of it. The truth of the matter is that his mental attitude, prompted by his temperament, did not allow him to appreciate what is theatrically significant. I asked him if he had ever seen the play acted. 'Yes,' he replied, 'and it was a painful experience, I assure you.' He blamed the actors, be it observed, but no actors could make *One Day More* actable.

I used to press him to go to the theatre frequently, as the only way to acquire the ability to visualise scenes. He would shake his head and say: 'I admit that I cannot even imagine a scenic effect, but I cannot learn anything from watching.' Talking of casting plays, I pointed out how valuable it was to know the abilities of all the actors and actresses available. 'You must not ask me to watch actresses, Hastings,' he would reply. 'I was fed once with chocolates by Madame Modjeska,[3] but that was in the Middle Ages.' I did persuade him, however, to see H. B. Irving's *Hamlet*. When I sought his views, he praised warmly the actor who played Horatio, whose name I do not remember, and the actor who played Polonius, Mr Holman Clark.

NOTES

Basil Macdonald Hastings (1881–1928), a dramatist, had his first play produced in 1912. During the war, he enlisted in the army and was later commissioned into the Royal Air Force. Hastings approached Conrad about dramatising his novel, *Victory*, in early 1916 and produced an adaptation in the following April. Conrad had reservations about it, but came to regard it as a sure commercial success and showed great interest in the casting. (Conrad also planned to collaborate with Hastings on an original play, set in Italy with English characters, about a forged painting by an Old Master.) In a letter of 25 January 1917, Conrad wrote to Hastings that 'you can have no conception of my ignorance in theatrical art. I can't even imagine a scenic effect but reading your adaptation, I, even I, felt something what I imagine to be the scenic emotion, come through to me – got home.' Production of 'Victory' was delayed by the conditions of war and the illness of a principal actor, but the three-act play eventually opened on 26 March 1919 at the Globe Theatre, London (Conrad was not present) and it enjoyed considerable success, running for eighty-three performances until 7 June 1919.

1. Possibly Helen Thomas Follett and Wilson Follett, *Some Modern Novelists: Appreciations and Estimates* (New York: Holt, 1918), which discusses Conrad, Galsworthy, Bennett, Wells, Edith Wharton and Eden Phillpotts as six 'Novelists of Today'.

2. Conrad dramatised his short story, 'To-morrow', into a one-act play, *One Day More*, in 1904 and it was produced the following year. See p. 120 for further details.

3. Helena Modrzejewska (Modjeska), 1840–1909, was a famous actress in Cracow theatres until her retirement in May 1872. Her husband, Karol Bodzenta Chłapowski, was a friend of Conrad's father.

Part IX
Conrad's Death

Conrad's Last Day*

RICHARD CURLE

About eight o'clock his two sons, his eldest son's wife and his little grandson of six months arrived by motor from London. They had not been specially summoned – nobody realised the danger – but had come down by arrangement to spend the Bank Holiday at home. Conrad insisted on his daughter-in-law and his grandson being brought to his bedside at once: there must be no delay. It was, indeed, as though he knew that it was his last chance of seeing them.

His breathing had become very bad, and a doctor was summoned from Canterbury, which is only about four and a half miles from Oswalds, as against Ashford's sixteen. But this doctor, too, having regard to the excellence of the pulse, was not alarmed, though he ordered cylinders of oxygen to be sent out from Canterbury Hospital to relieve the breathing. It had again been better while he was there.

Perhaps it was unfortunate that the Conrads' usual Canterbury doctor was away in the country, and that the one who saw him then was a stranger who knew nothing about his history or physique. And yet I do not really believe it would have made the least difference. The sands were running out. But if Conrad obtained no benefit from his advice, he did derive pleasure from his visit. He was a Scotsman, and Conrad had a particular liking for Scotsmen. He referred to him after his departure in friendly terms: even at such a time he had an eye for characteristics.

It was impossible, in face of the repeated assurances of these two skilled medical men (who must have been misled by symptoms that on previous occasions had meant little), to believe that there was anything desperately wrong. Even his dreadful fighting for breath, agonising to witness, was assumed by all of us to have its origin in violent asthmatic indigestion; and when he panted out in one of his gasping fits that he could not get better, we, having seen him so often in illness and despondency, did not take the words at their full worth. But throughout his life he had been a man of few illusions, and I think perhaps he was under no illusion then. Heaven knows: possibly the

* From *The Last Twelve Years of Joseph Conrad* (London: Sampson Low, Marston, 1928) pp. 229–34.

struggle wrung this cry from him, as prophetic words are sometimes wrung from those in distress.

But his thoughtfulness for others, which was always so apparent, did not desert him. When, later in the evening, his younger son and I were in his room, he begged us to leave so that we should not have the pain of watching him suffer. 'Go away, dear boys, I can't bear you to see me like this.'

There was nothing more I could do, though, ineed, I had done nothing. I sat in Mrs Conrad's room with her sons and daughter-in-law till quite late: we tried to talk cheerfully, but I am sure that each one of us felt the sense of something imminent and unthinkable in the air. It was not so much the foreboding of an actual crisis, as a feeling of vague gloom which it was impossible to shake off.

The night passed much as the day had done. Conrad got out of bed and insisted on sitting up in his chair, dozing off for a few minutes at a time. At six in the morning he seemed to be in less difficulty and told his eldest son that he must see about getting a male nurse, as Foote, his faithful manservant, was worn out after many hours of constant attendance. He was full of consideration and gratitude and said how finely Foote had behaved.

Later, I spoke to Foote, who told me that the night had not been a very good one, but that Mr Conrad now appeared easier. (He had just previously called out jokingly to his wife, to relieve her anxiety, 'I'm better this morning. I can always get a rise out of you!') It was as though a load had been taken off my heart. Not long after his eldest son rushed in to fetch me. Everything was over.

At the actual moment of death nobody was in the room. Foote had gone out with a message and Conrad was resting. There was no particular anxiety, for only half-an-hour before his pulse had been taken by Mrs Vinten,[4] who was a trained nurse, and found to be normal. His wife, lying powerless next door, heard a cry, 'Here . . .' as if a second word had been stifled, and a fall. People ran in: he had slipped, dead, on to the floor from his chair. It was just on eight-thirty.

As I entered he was lying on his back beside the bed, where he had been laid when all efforts at resuscitation had failed. Mrs Vinten and Foote were kneeling one on either side of him. At the opening of the door Mrs Vinten turned round and looked up at me: the shake of her head told me everything. He looked incredibly noble and splendid. All the ravage and pain had ebbed from his features, and absolute aloofness and calm were written there. Yes, and a kind of haughty indifference which brought out startlingly the classic grandeur of his face.

To me it was as if I had never seen him till then. So absorbed! – he did not want any of us any more. I gazed at him, not for long but intently, and then I went away. I felt quite frozen.

He was at rest after suffering and I have thought of some words out of *The Mirror of the Sea* which appear to me beautifully appropriate to the passing of his great spirit:

> Nobody can say with what thoughts, with what regrets, with what words on their lips they died. But there is something fine in the sudden passing away of these hearts from the extremity of struggle and stress and tremendous uproar – from the vast, unrestful rage of the surface to the profound peace of the depths, sleeping untroubled since the beginning of ages.[2]

I could not bear to look on him again in death, who for so many years had shown me all the tenderness of a father, whose infinite understanding and unbroken friendship had meant so much to my happiness, but I am assured that gradually the marks of age and weariness faded from his face and that his hair looked strangely black. It was as though youth had returned to him at last to stay with him for ever and comfort him even in the grave. And that is fitting – is it not? – for his works are inspired with the genius of immortal youth and his personality never grew old, never hardened, never ceased to be young in compassion and generosity.

I wandered out on to the drive. The soft morning, already warm in the full tide of summer, spoke only of teeming and joyous life. Everything was still and quiet, as it is on a Sunday in the country, and the thought of death seemed utterly incongruous. Dr Fox, of Ashford, and Dr Reid, of Canterbury, had been telephoned for, and their cars, standing empty before the door, gave a curiously festive effect to the solitude as though some social gathering were in progress within the house. As I stood there I saw several strangers enter the drive gates. They, too, suggested the arrival of guests for a party. I went forward to intercept them. They were Americans and they had come, they said, to look over the house with a view to renting it. How little they suspected that upstairs the man, who was probably more beloved and regarded in America than any other contemporary author, was lying dead!

NOTES

Richard Curle (1883–1969), journalist, critic and author. After writing an appreciation of Conrad's works, Curle met him in November 1912 and, although Curle was many years Conrad's junior, the two men became close friends. His *Joseph Conrad: A Study* (London: Kegan Paul, 1914) was the first book-length criticism of Conrad's fiction, and written with his approval. *The*

Arrow of Gold (London: T. Fisher Unwin, 1919) was dedicated to him.

Curle came to stay for the weekend with the Conrads on Friday, 1 August 1924. He found Conrad in sociable mood, healthy, buoyant and planning new work. On the Saturday, they drove to examine a house about eight miles away which Conrad was thinking of leasing (the Conrads were planning to leave Oswalds, Bishopsbourne, at the end of September), but before they reached it, Conrad was seized by a pain in his chest. This was almost certainly a heart attack, but his doctor, summoned from Ashford, ascribed it to acute indigestion. Later that evening, as Curle records at the beginning of this extract, Conrad's two sons arrived, Borys being accompanied by his wife and baby son Philip, born the previous January.

Conrad died on the morning of 3 August 1924, at the age of sixty-six.

1. A member of Conrad's domestic staff. Her brother was the chauffeur.
3. *The Mirror of the Sea*, p. 61.

*Inveni Portum**

R. B. CUNNINGHAME GRAHAM

A light warm rain fell upon the old-world streets. The houses, with their casement windows, timbered upper storeys and overhanging eaves, still kept the air as of an older world. The gateways, with their battlements and low archways through which the mediaeval traffic once had flowed, with men-at-arms and archers, strings of pack horses, monks, nuns and pilgrims come to worship at the shrine of Becket, were now mere monuments.

Time had but mellowed without defacing them, although the damp had made the stone peel off in flakes, giving it a look of scales. Long stretches of the city wall still stood, covered with a growth of wallflowers and of valerian, loved of cats. Houses and yet more houses crowded in upon the cathedral, usurping what by rights should have been a grassy close, guarded by elm trees or by limes, with nests for rooks, who with their cawing supplemented the murmuring masses in the adjacent choir, for surely rooks in a cathedral close must ever praise the Lord for their quiet sheltered lives. Grouped round its dominating church the city huddled as if it sought protection against progress and modernity. Bell Harry in his beauty seemed a giant lighthouse pointing Heavenwards. It was indeed a haven where a man who had had his fill of this world's din might well retire to and find rest, for the incoming

* *Saturday Review*, vol. CXXXVIII (16 Aug. 1924) pp. 162–3.

cricketers were evidently but birds of passage, and when they all departed once more the town would sink back to repose. Although the streets were decorated with flags and floral arches and filled with sunburned athletes, and the companions of their pads and bats with cohorts of the clergy come up from their parsonages, greeting effusively Old Brown of Brasenose or Smith of Wadham, whom they met annually at this, the week of weeks – for cricket is a sport that clergymen can attend without offence – nothing could take away the air of mediaeval quiet that broods upon the town. The peaceful landscape with the slow Medway winding through its fields of lush, green grass, full of contemplative cows, its apple orchards, its rubble churches, with their truncated spires and air of immortality, is restful to the eye. The town itself, resting from its long strife with time, brings quiet to the soul.

On every side are relics of the past – gates, barbicans and walls, the grassy mound of the Dane John, about whose origin so many legends cluster, the square, squat tower, all that remains to show where once the church of Mary of Magdala stood, the crypt where exiled Huguenots performed their maimed rites, the helm and gauntlets of the Black Prince of Wales and Gascony, about his tomb in the cathedral, speak of the past, the resting past, for in the present, as in the days when past was present, there can be no peace. The quiet old city seemed indeed a fitting place in which to harbour one who long had battled with tempestuous seas, had heard the tropic rollers kissing the coral reefs and felt the sting of spindrift coating his beard with salt. So to the chapel of the older faith he held, not only as a faith, but as a bulwark against Oriental barbarism, we bore his coffin, buried under flowers, laid it before the altar railings, and his friends, Catholic and Protestant alike, with those who hold that God will not damn whom He created with the potentialities of damnation in their bodies and their souls for the mere fun of damning, all listen to the 'blessed muttering of the Mass' devoutly, on their knees. Within that little fane, with its images of saints, enough for faith, for faith works miracles, even upon the optic nerve, perhaps, but not enough for art, all became Catholics for the nonce. When all is said and done, of all the faiths it is the most consolatory, and tears stood in the eyes of many of the heterogeneous congregation. What, after all, is better for the soul than prayer to an unseen God, in an uncomprehended tongue? When the priest got to *Ite missa est* no one appeared to have found the service wearisome, for somehow it seemed to join us to the friend whom we should see no more, a little longer.

Then, through the streets all hung with flowers, as if to honour him whom we were taking to his anchorage, we took our way out to the cemetery. We passed through ancient archways, skirted the crumbling walls, caught glimpses of the cathedral towers, up winding streets, marvelled at the number of the churches, and marked the advertisement of something or another carried out in the vile bodies of three poor Christians, decked with huge, grinning cardboard heads, as in a pantomime.

I think there was little that we did not see, from the collected band of cricketers, who, standing at the chief hotel, saluted as we passed, as reverently as if the funeral had been that of one of their own mystery, to dogs, that nearly sacrificed themselves beneath the wheels, a skewbald horse that drew a gipsies' caravan, and bullocks going to the slaughter-house, for when the soul is stirred the external eye looks upon the world more keenly than when we sit at home smoking a good cigar. Those sorts of drives in funeral carriages appear to last for ever, in fact one almost wishes that they would, for it is well that now and then a man should see *memento mori* written up plainly before his eyes for him to read and inwardly digest. As we rolled slowly on into the open country the engine of the motor hearse slowed down to the jog-trot of the old-time funeral horse, so heavily the hand of custom bears upon the reins of everything. I fell into what in the North we call a 'dwawm', that state in which the mind is active and as if freed from its subjection to the flesh. Time put the clock back for some five-and-twenty years or so, and I saw him who now lay in his coffin underneath the flowers, his battle over and his place assured in the great fellowship that Chaucer captains, struggling to make his way. What were his trials, what his disillusions, and what he suffered at the hands of fools, only himself could tell, and he was never one who wore his heart upon his sleeve for critics and for daws to peck at. For leagues we journeyed, as it appeared to me, passing men tedding haycocks in the field, Boy Scouts in brakes, and now and then a Kentish farmer in an old-fashioned dogcart.

All the dead man had written and had done welled up in my mind. *Nostromo*, with its immortal picture of the old follower of Garibaldi,[1] its keen analysis of character, and the local colour that he divined rather than knew by actual experience, its subtle humour and the completeness of it all, forming an epic, as it were, of South America, written by one who saw it to the core, by intuition, amazed me just as it did when I first read it, *Consule Planco*, in the years that have slipped past. Then came *The Nigger of the 'Narcissus'*, into which he put the very soul of the old sailing ships, and that of those who sailed and suffered in them, as he himself once sailed and suffered and emerged tempered and chastened by the sea. *Youth* and *Heart of Darkness*, and then the tale of 'Laughing Anne', so deep and moving in its presentment of a lost woman's soul, all flitted through my mind. Lastly, *The Mirror of the Sea*, with its old Danish skipper who intoned the dirge of ships, past, present and to come, haunted my memory.[2] So dreaming with my eyes wide open, all the long years of friendship rolled back again, and my lost friend appeared, as I remembered him – was it a hundred years ago, or was it yesterday? For death annihilates perspective, blots out all sense of time, and leaves the memory of those that we have lost blurred in the outline, but more present to the mind than when Time, seeming but an invention of the poets with his unmeaning hour-glass, his unnecessary scythe, still rolled on, as it seemed eternally, just as a man when dozing on his horse during a tedious night march, or jogging on behind a troop of cattle in the sun, thinks that his whole existence has consisted but of an ache between the shoulders and a dull throbbing at the knees. Waking or sleeping, or in a mixture of the two, but with my senses wide awake enough, I seemed to see my friend.

His nose was aquiline, his eyes most luminous and full. It seemed his very soul looked out of them, piercing the thoughts of those whom he addressed; his beard trimmed to a point was flecked with grey a little and his moustache was full. His face of the dull yellow hue that much exposure to the tropic sun in youth so often causes, was lined and furrowed by the weather. His hair, dark and wiry, age had respected, except that it had grown a little thin upon the temples, leaving his forehead bare. His cheek bones, high and jutting out a little, revealed his Eastern European origin, just as his strong, square figure and his walk showed him a sailor who never seems to find the solid earth a quite familiar footing after a sloping deck. His feet were small and delicately shaped and his fine, nervous hands, never at rest a minute in his life, attracted you at once. They supplemented his incisive speech by indefinable slight movements, not gestures in the Latin sense, for they were never raised into the air nor used for emphasis. They seemed to help him to express the meaning of his words without his own volition in a most admirable way. Something there was about him, both of the Court and of the quarterdeck, an air of courtesy and of high breeding, and yet with something of command. His mind, as often is the case with men of genius – and first and foremost what most struck one was his genius – seemed a strange compact of the conflicting qualities, compounded in an extraordinary degree, of a deep subtlety and analytic power and great simplicity.

As he discoursed upon the things that interested him, recalled his personal experiences, or poured his scorn and his contempt upon unworthy motives and writers who to attain their facile triumphs had pandered to bad taste, an inward fire seemed to be smouldering ready to break out just as the fire that so long smouldered in the hold of the doomed ship in which he made his first voyage to the East suddenly burst out into flames. His tricks of speech and manner, the way he grasped both of your hands in his, his sudden breaking into French, especially when he was moved by anything, as when I asked him to attend some meeting or another, and he replied, '*Non, il y aura des Russes*', grinding his teeth with rage.[3] England, the land of his adoption, he loved fervently; and could not tolerate that anything with which he had been once familiar should be tampered with, as often happens when a man adopts a second fatherland, for to change that which first attracted him seems a flat blasphemy.

As the car drew up at the cemetery gate with a harsh, grating noise upon the gravel, I wakened from my dream. The rain had cleared and the sun poured down upon us, as in procession, headed by the acolytes and priests, we bore the coffin to the grave. A semi-circle of Scotch firs formed, as it were, a little harbour for him. The breeze blew freshly south-west by south a little westerly – a good wind, as I thought, to steer up Channel by, and one that he who would no longer feel it on his cheek, looking aloft to see if all the sails were drawing properly, must have been glad to carry when he struck soundings, passing the Wolf Rock or the Smalls after foul weather in the Bay.

Handsomely, as he who lay in it might well have said, they lowered the coffin down. The priest had left his Latin and said a prayer or two in English, and I was glad of it, for English surely was the speech the Master Mariner most loved, and honoured in the loving with new graces of his own.

The voyage was over and the great spirit rested from its toil, safe in the English earth that he had dreamed of as a child in far Ukrainia. A gleam of sun lit up the red-brick houses of the town. It fell upon the tower of the cathedral, turning it into a great glowing beacon pointing to the sky. The trees moved gently in the breeze, and in the fields the ripening corn was undulating softly, just as the waves waft in on an atoll in the Pacific, with a light swishing sound. All was well chosen for his resting-place, and so we left him with his sails all duly furled, rope flemished down, and with the anchor holding truly in the kind Kentish earth, until the judgment day. The gulls will bring him tidings as they fly past above his grave, with their wild voices, if he should weary for the sea and the salt smell of it.

NOTES

Robert Bontine Cunninghame Graham (1852–1936), Scottish aristocrat, Liberal MP (1886–92), traveller, writer and socialist radical. At his death he was leader of the Scottish Nationalist Party. It was Cunninghame Graham's sympathy with the criticism of colonialism in Conrad's 'An Outpost of Progress' that led him to write to its author and they first met in November 1897. The resulting friendship was extremely valuable to Conrad, and his surviving letters to Graham show him at his most intellectually stimulating and receptive. Of all his friends, Conrad probably found Graham the closest in temperament, and he is reported to have said to Arthur Symons, 'Could you conceive for a moment that I could go on existing if Cunninghame Graham were to die?'

Conrad's funeral on 7 August 1924 was preceded by a Mass in St Thomas Roman Catholic Church, Canterbury. It was not a great occasion, being attended only by his family and fewer than fifty other people. He is buried in Canterbury cemetery. The city, as Graham records, was decorated for its annual Cricket Week. The value of Conrad's estate was £20 045.

The name on Conrad's grave, testifying to his wife's uncertain grasp of Polish, is Joseph Teador Conrad Korzeniowski. The lines on his tombstone are those which Conrad had chosen as the epigraph for *The Rover*:

> Sleep after toyle, port after stormie seas,
> Ease after warre, death after life, does greatly please.

They are from Spenser's *The Faerie Queene* (I.IX.40), and are spoken by Despayre, who is urging the Red Cross Knight to commit suicide.

Cunninghame Graham's article was originally published with the title '*Inveni Partum*' (I have found the door). Later reprintings have usually entitled it '*Inveni Portum*' (I have found the haven) which, on the internal evidence of the article, is almost certainly correct.

1. Giorgio Viola.

2. See Joseph Conrad, *The Mirror of the Sea* (London: J. M. Dent, 1946) chapter 36.

3. 'No, there will be Russians.' Graham had invited Conrad to a meeting of the Social Democratic Federation in Piccadilly on 8 March 1899. Conrad did in fact attend. See C. T. Watts (ed.), *Joseph Conrad's Letters to R. B. Cunninghame Graham* (Cambridge: Cambridge University Press, 1969) p. 116.

Index